What They Are Saying about Parenting Children with Health Issues

"Thank you for your book. As a Helicopter Parent, it is hard for me to not take over and ensure that Tyler is going to be fine. Your book helps me see that in teaching HIM responsibility, I am giving him a greater gift than glucose levels. Although the ultimate responsibility will be Tyler's, I know that I can now give him the tools to make it. If he chooses, he can live a happy, healthy life with diabetes."

—*Stephanie, mom of nine-year-old Tyler with diabetes*

"This book captures the many thoughts, concerns, challenges and questions I have heard from families living with cystic fibrosis and you answered all to a T. It is much better than anything I have seen for parenting a special child. We need this!"

—*Beverley Donelson, Co-founder of CF Pharmacy, Inc.,*
and grandmother to an adult with CF

"Love and Logic is a great solution for all of us moms who find they yell a lot. By putting the responsibility back on my child, our home has become more peaceful and orderly. Using these parenting techniques with my child who has a chronic illness has also allowed me freedom from guilt, repeating myself, and worrying because my child is able to understand the natural consequences of his actions as it relates to his illness. I would definitely recommend this book to any family...with or without chronic illness."

—*Patty Acedo-Holmquist, mom of child with cystic fibrosis*

"*Parenting Children with Health Issues* equips families facing critical healthcare issues with strategies for weathering the crises that are a part of chronic illness. It empowers us all with a philosophy of parenting that helps us think rationally during emotionally challenging times. It encourages us to make decisions that allow others to own their responsibilities and it offers practical tools to communicate clearly. This book helps us understand that parenting is not a quick sprint. We are distance runners, pacing for the marathon with coaches who are there for us. I cannot think of anything more valuable!"

—*Carroll Jenkins, Executive Director, Cystic Fibrosis Research, Inc (CFRI), stepmom of an adult with CF*

"This compassionate and heartwarming guide should occupy the bookshelves of every parent with a chronically ill child. It delivers not only practical lessons in living with chronic illness but also shows that encouragement, love, and understanding are key to addressing the challenges chronic illness imposes on children and their parents."   —*Tim O'Hagan, editor and author of 11 books,* including the Reader's Digest Guide to Alternative Medicine *and* Discovering the Wonders of Our World

"Parenting, in general, requires great courage and parenting children with serious health issues is nothing short of heroism. Dr. Cline and Lisa Greene give such parents the necessary tools and backbone they need to empower their children to cope with difficult circumstances rather than further disable them. Thank you for this easy-to-read yet powerfully instructional book."

—*Mitzi Gadd, R.N., M.S.,* *Pediatric Nurse and Marriage & Family Therapist*

"A few books fall into the Great Work category. This is one of them. This book is a beacon of insight and guidance for parents in the most challenging of parenting circumstances. It is with great enthusiasm that I recommend this book to my colleagues and all parents of children with chronic medical conditions."

—*Frazier H. King, M.D., Board Certified Family Practitioner*

Parenting Children
Children
with
Health Issues

Parenting
Children
with
Health Issues
Foster W. Cline, MD
and Lisa C. Greene

**Essential Tools, Tips, and Tactics
for Raising Kids with Chronic Illness,
Medical Conditions & Special Healthcare Needs**

Love and Logic®
INSTITUTE, Inc.

Parenting Children with Health Issues: Essential Tools, Tips and Tactics for Raising Kids with Chronic Illness, Medical Conditions and Special Healthcare Needs
By Foster W. Cline, MD, and Lisa C. Greene

Published by The Love and Logic Press, The Love and Logic Institute, 2207 Jackson St., Suite 102 Golden, Colorado 80401-2300   www.loveandlogic.com

The information published in this book and any other derivative material is the opinion of the publishers only and is not meant to supplant or replace professional medical or mental healthcare, advice, or treatment in any way. Persons should always seek the advice of a physician or professional healthcare worker and consider more than one professional opinion when making decisions and choices about personal healthcare or treatment. The publishers are not responsible for any situation or outcome as a result of the personal use of the information published in this book or any other derivative material.

Cover and interior design by Pneuma Books, LLC. www.pneumabooks.com
Cover photograph courtesy of Jupiter Images
Photograph on page 303 by Christopher of Kirkland

Library of Congress Cataloging-in-Publication Data

Cline, Foster.
  Parenting children with health issues : essential tools, tips, and tactics for raising kids with chronic illness, medical conditions & special healthcare needs / Foster W. Cline and Lisa C. Greene.
     p. cm.
  Includes bibliographical references and index.
  ISBN-13: 978-1-930429-89-5 (pbk. : alk. paper)
  ISBN-10: 1-930429-89-4 (pbk. : alk. paper)
   1. Chronically ill children—Care—Popular works. 2. Children with disabilities—Care—Popular works. 3. Child development deviations—Popular works. I. Greene, Lisa C. II. Title.
  RJ380.C62 2007
  618.92—dc22
                          2007008598

Printed in the United States of America

12 11 10 09 08 07   6 5 4 3 2 1

People are like stained-glass windows.
They sparkle and shine when the sun is out,
but when the darkness sets in,
their true beauty is revealed only if
there is a light from within.
—Elisabeth Kübler-Ross (1926-2004)

Acknowledgments

Thank You!

With our deepest gratitude, we thank all who have made this book possible by contributing their time, talent, and encouragement. Writing a book takes an amazing amount of effort and the unfailing support of our families and friends helped make the process not only possible but enjoyable. *We could never have done this without you.*

- ♥ Our immediate family members tolerated long work hours: Hermie Drill Cline and Carl, Jacob, and Kasey Greene

- ♥ Extended family and friends generously contributed their hands, hearts, and minds including Andrew Cline and Lisa's moms Betty Greene and Geri Espinosa

- ♥ Brian and Nina Taylor at Pneuma Books, LLC, who are professional, talented, and a pleasure to work with

- The whole crew at The Love and Logic Institute, Inc.

- Dr. Dennis Nielson, Dr. Nancy Lewis, and the University of San Francisco Pediatric Pulmonary Center

- Linda Noah and staff at Valley Christian Center of Dublin, CA

- Carroll Jenkins and staff at CFRI

- Pastor Ron Pinkston and staff at Eastbay Fellowship of Danville, CA

- Ron and Jeannine Bailey, Kathleen and Sharon Burke, Shaun Collins, and Tori Johnson

- All of those who have shared their lives and stories which you will find within these pages.

Jacob & Kasey Greene

 special tribute goes to Jacob and Kasey Greene. Their struggles, perseverance, and optimism have been an ongoing inspiration. They, and all of the children they represent, are our heroes.

Contents

Foreword

Tracy Trotter, MD FAAP
Pediatric and Adolescent Medicine

As I read this book, it sounded like a compilation of my last 30 years of caring for children with special healthcare needs. Dr. Foster Cline and Lisa Greene have captured the advice and recommendations I have been presenting to those children's parents regarding behavior and discipline, only in a far clearer and organized fashion. It literally felt as though the authors had been sitting in the corner of my exam rooms for all the 180,000 office visits (my wife's calculation). The fact that both Dr. Cline and Lisa Greene have had children with chronic, life-shortening illnesses comes through loud and clear in their authenticity, compassion, and honesty. You will enjoy their superb use of cases, scenarios, and examples. Parents of children with special healthcare needs will see themselves and their children many times as they read this book. It quickly becomes apparent that effective parenting of children with chronic illness and medical conditions is truly a matter of life and death.

For nearly thirty years, the Love and Logic program has been helping parents and educators raise children who are respectful, responsible, and a joy to be around. *Love*, as defined in the Oxford

Dictionary, is "caring for someone more than you care for yourself" and *logic* has the characteristics of being "clear, consistent, rational, and reasonable." This book explores and polishes those definitions which are so important in everyday parenting and so essential in parenting children with chronic medical conditions. In this work readers will find the very best of traditional parenting with a large helping of common sense, compassion, and awareness of the special problems inherent in families dealing with chronic medical conditions.

As with nearly every pediatrician, my patients have taught me as much as I have taught them. One of the most powerful messages delivered to me came from a young couple I met during my first year in my office in California. I attended the delivery of their first child, a beautiful baby girl named Christine. As I examined Christine in the delivery room, I found, sadly, she had a severe case of spina bifida, a neural tube defect that occurs in the first month of pregnancy when the spinal column doesn't close completely. The young mother, Dawn, was a physical therapist at our local children's hospital and knew immediately that this meant multiple surgeries, including the placement of a shunt for associated hydrocephalus, a lifetime in a wheelchair as a complete paraplegic, and the myriad medical problems that go hand-in-hand with this diagnosis. I was devastated by the finding and had more than a little anxiety as I approached Dawn's room to update her and her husband on Christine's progress, as she was already about to have the first of many surgical procedures. Dawn's first question, delivered more as a statement, was, "What's next? Let's get going." I was immediately buoyed by their steadfast feeling that this problem would not prevent their daughter from attaining any goal. I have now been blessed to share the past 20 years watching Christine grow into a delightful young lady with a can-do attitude. She is resilient, confident, and fiercely independent. She has become a superb student, a national wheelchair basketball player, and a responsible adult who lives life to the fullest. Christine's parents seemed to know instinctively that teaching her to become responsible for caring for herself would ultimately be their greatest gift. Their house had no pity, but it did have empathy and enormous amounts of love and encouragement. Unfortunately, not every parent of such a child instinctively knows how to teach responsibility. I have many other stories of parents who have unintentionally made the way for their special child even more difficult by using ineffective parenting skills. The past 20 years as Christine's pediatrician have been a wonderful journey and I wouldn't have missed it for anything. I am grateful for a resource that organizes, clarifies, and gives examples of the parenting skills that helped Christine grow into a beautiful, productive young lady who is responsible, respectful, and a joy to be around.

Parenting children with special healthcare needs magnifies the results of effective and ineffective parental/caregiver responses. Raising a child with a chronic illness involves an often-confusing state of mixed uncertainty, apprehension, and heightened responsibility. I have had a special interest in medical genetics and children with special healthcare needs throughout my entire career and, until now, have never come across a book or program that truly meets the needs of these families. One of my mantras for many years has been, "Don't disable a child with disabilities!" As this book points out so clearly, these children, even more so than children who are not obviously medically impacted, need to be confident, competent, respectful, responsible, and, ultimately, independent.

—*Tracy L. Trotter, MD, FAAP*
Pediatric & Adolescent Medicine

Introduction

About Parenting Children with Health Issues

Learning is not attained by chance;
it must be sought for with ardor and
attended to with diligence.
—Abigail Adams (1744-1818)

About This Book

Welcome to Love and Logic's *Parenting Children with Health Issues*. This book is part of a comprehensive program that includes video, audio, and web-based support for families and medical providers. It was specifically created for parents and guardians who are raising children with any chronic illness or medical condition, whether it be an allergy, AIDS, asthma, a birth defect, cancer, chronic obesity, cystic fibrosis, diabetes, an eating disorder, epilepsy, hemophilia, muscular dystrophy, sickle cell anemia, etc. — or even a traumatic injury. If your child's good health depends on routine medical/health care, then this book provides essential information for you. It is also valuable for medical professionals, mental health professionals, and other caregivers who work with these children and their families. This material is not intended to replace professional medical and mental health support. Changes in family dynamics and parenting styles, even for the better, in the midst of life-threatening situations should be supervised by professionals who know the specifics of each situation.

Medical science is advancing so rapidly that many diseases now considered life threatening, life shortening, or terminal will soon become treatable and perhaps simply a maintenance issue. Children who comply with their treatment programs have a much better chance of maintaining their optimum health potential in order to take advantage of revolutionary new treatments which most certainly loom on the horizon for many. This program is designed to give you the parenting skills you need to increase the odds that your children will follow doctor's orders, make good health decisions, and choose to live the fullest, richest life possible.

Love and Logic's *Parenting Children with Health Issues* will help you respond to your children in ways that will encourage them to accept responsibility for their healthcare, while imparting hope and teaching coping skills. Even at an early age, it is critical that children accept the importance of complying with medical regimens, whether they are special diets, insulin shots, daily medication, breathing treatments, or physical therapy. Parenting styles can either help or hinder the life-impacting process of accepting responsibility and accountability.

All parents who face the daunting prospect of raising a child with a chronic medical condition experience similar psychological and behavioral challenges. How parents manage these challenges can make a difference in how *well* and how *long* their children live. Parents must avoid control battles over healthcare issues because these issues can become a manipulative "weapon" used by the child who, naturally, resists painful, unpleasant, or annoying medical procedures, especially in the potentially rebellious teenage years. Some particularly strong-willed children refuse to comply with medical requirements nearly to the point of death. We want our children to choose *life*. The parenting techniques we use can make all the difference.

Every moment with our special children matters. Will these moments be spent in anger, worry, fear, and frustration, or with a calm, confident, and relaxed attitude? The choice is ours. As parents, the only thing we can ultimately control is our ability to be the best parents possible. That is certainly easier said than done. After all, what does the "best possible parent" really look like, and how does one get from "here" to "there"? This program will answer important questions such as:

- ♥ How do I encourage my child to really love life?
- ♥ How do I handle refusal to take medication?
- ♥ How do I encourage my child's concern for her illness without frightening her?
- ♥ How can I best separate the "can'ts" from the "won'ts"?
- ♥ How do I encourage responsibility without harping, nagging, or lecturing?
- ♥ How do I communicate with my child about his/her illness in ways he/she will understand?

As we examine these and other difficult issues that arise when parenting a child with medical challenges, we use a wide variety of examples from different medical conditions. Many of our examples focus on cystic fibrosis, which is a genetic disease that primarily causes the mucous in the lungs to become thick and sticky. This results in lung infections, scar tissue, and eventual lung failure. The median life expectancy is currently 37 years and rising. See www.cff.org for more information.

CF is used as a paradigm for all ongoing childhood medical issues because it is an illness with a broad range of medical care requirements. Parents and their children are required to implement a variety of strategies for managing their particular symptoms. These include daily breathing treatments, the management of dietary requirements, extensive and multiple hospitalizations, coping with invasive medical procedures and tests, taking massive amounts of oral and/or intravenous medications, and possible organ transplants. It is not uncommon for those with CF to also have secondary diseases, such as diabetes. Since, at the time of this writing, CF is a very serious disease with life-shortening implications, this illness can more than adequately cover the spectrum of medical conditions from the most severe to the least critical.

The goal of this program is to inform, teach, support, and inspire you as your family copes with the challenging issues of parenting very special children who live each day with medical conditions. Be a great parent... when every moment matters.

About the Authors
Foster W. Cline, MD

Foster W. Cline, M.D., co-founder of the Love and Logic Institute, is an internationally known child and adult psychiatrist who has worked with parents and children for over thirty-five years. Throughout his distinguished career, Dr. Cline has specialized in attachment and bonding in children, the gifted and talented child, parenting and child management, classroom behavior management, and families with children who have serious medical issues.

Dr. Cline graduated cum laude from the University of Colorado and earned his MD degree from the University of Colorado Medical School in Denver. He spent his medical internship in the Gorgas

Hospital, a federal hospital in the Panama Canal Zone. He completed his adult and child psychiatric residencies at the University of Washington in Seattle.

His love of children and passion for changing lives give him a unique sense of clarity as he turns difficult and often confusing child development concepts into straight talk and answers for adults. He has served as a consultant to school systems, pupil personnel teams, and hospitals around the world.

As a gifted public speaker, Dr. Cline is in high demand. In a three year period, he presented workshops and seminars to professionals in eleven countries and twenty-three states. He has taught extensively for the University of Northern Colorado, Colorado State University, and other institutions of higher learning. The North American Council on Adoptable Children presented him with an award for Outstanding Contributions to Children.

Dr. Cline and his wife, Hermie, have raised three birth children, adopted one child from residential treatment at the age of eight, and fostered three children; they enjoy many grandchildren.

A Personal Note from Foster

Here I sit here at the computer, writing to you good parents, watching the snow fall gently, and taking a swig of chocolate milk.

In the back of my mind I'm aware that my pancreas is going to have to pump out a bit more insulin, but I think my system can handle these chocolate carbs, despite my diabetes. Still, I'll prick my finger in about an hour and check my blood glucose level on the meter inherited from my daughter. Dealing with chronic illness means being increasingly aware of one's own body. It takes a little extra effort and a little more responsibility. I can handle that, and I want to make sure my blood sugar reading never creeps up near the level that sucked the life out of dear daughter Melinda.

It's one thing to write about caring for children with chronic illnesses and it's another thing to live it. It's one thing to know that death greedily waits to snatch some of our children, and it's another to have experienced the end of the wait.

Alone late on a Saturday night and with thinking that was probably fuzzy from the deadly levels of sugar that coursed though her body, Mel fell to the bathroom floor, where she was found by others who were concerned when she didn't show up Monday for work. Amidst the grief, a more agonizing pain would like to claw its way into the sorrow: self-incrimination. "What more could we have done?" We remember the happy phone calls during that last week, and our often-asked question, "How's your diabetes doing, Mel?" And we remember her laughing reply, "Don't worry about it, Dad. It's all under control."

Then came the phone call. "Melinda was found dead in her apartment this morning." Shock, pain, and grief. However, except for stabs of healthy self-examination, the torment of grief was not augmented by the angst of guilt. We had been Love and Logic parents. And when times get tough and life deals our children difficult hands, that knowledge — that we were Love and Logic parents — helps carry the day.

After adopting Melinda at age eight, we had raised a daughter who, most of the time, truly turned out to be responsible, respectful, and fun to be around. Not that the road was easy or without moments of frustration. Not that there weren't bumps. You see, Melinda had disrupted other adoptive homes before we adopted her. She had spent a well-earned three-year stint in residential treatment. But we look back and laugh at the bumps, and, in retrospect, enjoy the anthills of issues that loomed like mountains at the time. Like other parents who have lost children — parents we have interviewed in this work — we remember the good times. We rejoice in the life that was shared with us. But what helped us immensely was the knowledge that we did things right. I hope this knowledge will help you, too.

Amidst the joy of life, our beloved children will experience both the rumblings and occasional magma of life's inevitable volcanoes. They will be burned as we have. But let them always have an optimistic, self-assured, can-do attitude, which is the hallmark of children who model their lives on loving, effective parents. The use of Love and Logic will never guarantee an inevitably happy outcome but it will always provide you with the comforting knowledge that you showed your love by using predictably effective tools and techniques in an unpredictable world.

I wish you all the relaxing Love and Logic knowledge that will facilitate your children's smooth transition to adulthood; that they will never take the rebellious path to spite you; that they will never live a life of blame and accusation because of an entitled upbringing; and that they will never lack the ability to cope because you continually rescued them.

Lisa C. Greene

As the mother of two children with cystic fibrosis, Lisa Greene initiated the concept of this program after recognizing her own dire need for it. She has been using Love and Logic's parenting curriculum for many years with her children and, as an independent Love and Logic facilitator, teaches the program to hundreds of parents each year.

Lisa graduated from Central Washington University in 1994 with a BS degree in Business Administration. Since 2004, she has been working with Dr. Cline to create this multimedia program for parenting kids with special healthcare needs. Lisa enjoys being a mother, wife, parent coach, and Love and Logic facilitator. She lives with her husband and two children in Northern California.

A Personal Note from Lisa

I've always dreamed of writing a book but never did I dream that this would be the one. And even though this book isn't exactly the thrilling whodunnit of my dreams, it contains my heart and soul in a way that no other book ever will. It doesn't matter that the subject of our book won't lead it to the best-seller lists. What does matter is the opportunity to provide crucial and life-changing information for the many families who, like us, struggle with parenting children with serious medical issues. My deepest thanks go to Foster, Jim, Charles, and the Love and Logic Institute for making this program happen and for giving us all a place to go for answers and hope.

Having two beautiful children with a chronic, life-shortening illness has given me a perspective on life that I don't think I would have otherwise grasped: Life is so precious, and every moment counts. Each new day we get to share with our children is a gift.

Since the birth of our son Jacob and his immediate diagnosis with cystic fibrosis, I have also come to realize that, as a parent, the only thing I have control over is to be a great parent. This realization has been anything but easy.

The early days of Jacob's diagnosis were a blur of disbelief, anger, and grief. Through the pain and tears, I decided it was my job to keep him healthy. I also wanted to be the best Mommy there ever was to this precious little boy and to make the days he has be the best days possible. The problem was, I really didn't know how to do it. Oh, but I thought I did! When things were going okay, I had it handled. It was only when things weren't going "as planned" that I realized I needed help with my parenting skills.

One day, as I "recovered" from another close encounter with Jacob over taking his medication, which had ended in a doozey of a temper tantrum (his!), I reflected deeply on our challenges. I wanted so much more for our kids. I wanted the time we did have together to be spent loving each other and having fun, instead of filled with fighting and arguing over medical treatments. My heart said, "Just love them," and my head said, "Just be a great parent." But how? The difficulties seemed so huge. Where could I go for answers?

Enter Love and Logic. My husband and I took one of their parenting classes and haven't looked back since. I sent a letter to Jim Fay and Dr. Foster Cline asking them to create a Love and Logic Program for parenting kids with medical conditions to help us with the special issues that are a part of life for so many of us. One evening, Dr. Cline called and said they wanted to do the program. It was like talking to Santa Claus! Foster was clearly eager and qualified to help our family and other families like us. So here we are.

As I mentioned, I have finally come to realize that the only thing I really have any control over is my parenting skills. I have no control over how well my kids will learn in school, who they will choose as friends, which sports they will excel in, or the talents they will develop. And, I have no control over how healthy they will be or how long they will live.

The irony is that no parent does. I was reminded again of this recently during the funeral of a 23-year-old neighbor who died unexpectedly of cancer. I listened and wept at the testimony of his life that had been so meaningful to so many. Donald Harris was a successful young man of excellent character who made a difference in lives. Sparkling within the many different facets of his life, I saw the reflections of the great parents who loved him. Once again, I vowed to be a great parent.

As I've worked with Foster on this book over the last two years, I've found it to be an experience filled with both joy and sorrow. It has forced me to look at some issues that I had neatly avoided but needed to face. And although the information we share within these pages may not always be comfortable to read, it is necessary, life-changing, and, possibly, life saving. I have learned how to implement Love and Logic's powerful parenting tools at a much deeper level and, just like you, I am still a work in progress. This book will end but our stories won't. Love and Logic will continue to give the training and support we need to successfully navigate around the obstacles we face as we strive to be great parents in difficult parenting circumstances.

If it's possible for me to learn and use these tools, then it's possible for every one of you, too, even on those tough days when we don't exactly feel like great parents. The fact that you are reading these words indicates your desire to walk the path of learning, growing, questioning, and changing. That's what it's all about. We become aware of good parenting techniques; we toss away those that aren't good, and take the necessary steps toward showing our love effectively. We are all on this journey together, showing our children a love that is logical and ensuring that all our logic is laced with love. This will enable and empower us to be great parents to our very special children when every moment matters.

About Love and Logic ®

Jim Fay, an educator, and Foster W. Cline, MD, a child psychiatrist, founded the Love and Logic Institute, Inc. in 1977. For thirty years Love and Logic has been teaching parents and educators around the world how to raise kids who are respectful, responsible, and a joy to be around.

Love and Logic is a philosophy of raising and teaching children which enables adults to be happier, empowered, and more skilled in their interactions with children. This in turn leads to emotionally healthy children who have self-control, a high self-image, and the ability to cope with life's frustrations with a positive attitude. The concepts behind the Love and Logic philosophy address basic human needs. These needs encompass inclusion, structure, control, and affection, and exist in all groups and cultures. Love and Logic places a heavy emphasis on respect and dignity for children, while teaching adults how to set limits and maintain appropriate control. Love and Logic is a way of working with children that preserves loving adult/child relationships, teaches children to be responsible, and prepares young people to live in the real world, with its many choices and consequences.

Years of extensive research support Love and Logic's strategies for working with children. The Love and Logic approach captures powerful, time-tested psychological techniques, and incorporates them into easy-to-use parenting tools which produce immediate results because they are simple, practical, and easy to learn.

Every year, Love and Logic changes the lives of hundreds of thousands of families and educators worldwide, who attend classes and use the multi-media products. School systems across the nation have adopted Love and Logic's curriculum for educators. Both Jim and Foster have written several books, including the recently revised *Parenting with Love and Logic* and *Parenting Teens with Love and Logic*, which are among the nation's best-selling parenting books. Jim Fay's video, "How to Discipline Your Kids without Losing Their Love and Respect" is shown on PBS stations across the country, and Love and Logic was recently featured on Good Morning America.

Part 1

Love and Logic
Basic Training

The Foundation: Parenting with Love and Logic

An ounce of prevention is worth a pound of cure.
—Henry de Bracton, De Legibus (in 1240)

The information in this book incorporates the Love and Logic parent-training curriculum, which emphasizes that love allows children to grow through their mistakes, and logic allows them to learn from the consequences of their choices. Wouldn't it be great if your children could learn, early on, that every choice they make might affect the quality of their lives? One goal of Love and Logic is to train parents how to teach their children life lessons in a loving way through the mistakes they make as early as possible while the price tag is still low. However, when dealing with illnesses, the price tag for mistakes and poor decisions can be high, even when children are young. Therefore, in this program, the price tag may be less dependent on the child's age and more dependent on the medical choices the child is allowed to make for him- or herself. Love and Logic encourages children to make their own decisions (and mistakes) in non-life-threatening situations, thus increasing the odds that they will become better decision makers when the consequences *really* matter; such as taking an insulin shot while at a party with their friends, even though they don't feel like doing it. Parenting with Love and Logic teaches children *self-control.*

When children make mistakes or misbehave, many parents fail to respond in ways that help their children see the "folly of their ways." In other words, they don't hold their children accountable for their poor decisions. Some parents respond by lecturing, warning, or yelling at their children. These responses are generally ineffective in the long run. Others don't want their children to think they're mean so they don't take action when mistakes or misbehavior occur. This results in parents who essentially excuse incorrect behavior and find it easier to hold others, including themselves, accountable for their children's irresponsibility. This is a particularly common response when parents deal with their children's medical issues. The perfect example is a parent who says, "Why do *I* always have to be responsible for remembering your medication?!" while continuing to remember the medication. On the other hand, if the parent didn't remind the child, both might see the parent as neglectful for "not taking good care of" the child. The child blames, and the parent feels guilty! We will give you the tools to avoid these all too common parenting traps.

Parents of all children want their offspring to be well prepared for life. Successful parents know most mistakes are really learning opportunities. However, when the stakes are increased with the presence of medical issues, there is more opportunity for the child to make really serious mistakes. Parents often react to these mistakes with rescue and/or stronger demands, which, in turn, can cause ever-increasing power struggles. We will teach parents how to stop this nonproductive and potentially life-threatening cycle.

Love and Logic emphasizes locking in our "empathy, love, and understanding" *prior* to the children experiencing negative consequences of their actions. This leads children to see their parents as the "good guys," and their own poor decisions as the "bad guy." When empathy is used correctly on a regular basis, kids develop an internal voice that says, "I wonder how much pain my next decision will cause me?" This is extremely important when dealing with medical problems, and this book will teach you how to use empathy in this special way.

When a child forgets an important self-administered medical treatment, one parent might understandably become angry. Another parent may show sorrow and register sadness. The first says, "It makes me so angry when you don't take care of yourself!" The child of such a parent realizes (consciously or not) that he or she is in control of the parent's emotions — a very powerful position few children can resist. The second parent asks, "Honey, if I were in your shoes, I'd be pretty worried about my health. Are you very concerned about that? You are making decisions that could definitely affect how long you will live." The parent who responds in this way maintains self-control, and the child has no power over the parent's emotions. All the responsibility is lovingly laid on the child. Parents have trouble with this second response because they must accept their own inability to force another person to make a particular healthcare decision. This may be a bitter pill for parents to swallow but it's a necessary one. Which parent do you think will have better results? Love and Logic teaches that although parents may be understandably frightened about using the second method, it almost always works better, especially when started early in the child's life.

In the following chapters you will be introduced to *shared control*, another useful concept in your arsenal of effective parenting. If parents don't share control with their child, then the child will be forced to attempt to take *all* control, often in ways that are neither healthy nor appropriate. Teenage rebellion is a perfect example. A simple way to share control with children is to offer lots of choices rather than just telling them what to do. Sharing control with lots of choices is especially important when your child must comply with medical procedures. You will learn the proper ways to use choices and be amazed at how well they work, especially with younger children. But even when given choices, some children will argue about them, especially those concerning treatments or taking medication. Rather than engaging in a see-saw exchange that goes nowhere, Love and Logic teaches parents a simple method to neutralize arguments and avoid escalating power struggles. This book will teach you this useful technique and others to facilitate productive discussions with your child about difficult and emotionally charged medical issues.

Love and Logic teaches that parents who continually rescue their children from the consequences of their own mistakes (including medical mistakes), fix their problems, or nag them are *Helicopter Parents*. Another type of parent demands compliance, is directive, and tells children how to solve their problems. These are *Drill Sergeant Parents*. Both types of parents steal away their children's opportunities to learn, grow, and make good decisions. Both Helicopter Parents and Drill Sergeants make it more difficult for their children to become independent and responsible in self-care matters. No matter what our children's medical situation may be, parents cannot always be there to advise them about important life-and-death decisions. In the long run, somehow, children must learn to make life-and-death decisions for themselves. *Consultant Parents* make this important learning process possible.

Medical issues are so important it is understandable parents feel like *reminding, ranting, raving,* or *rescuing.* These Four Rs will never work as well as the Es of Love and Logic: *Example, Experience, Empathy, Expectations,* and *Encouragement.* Parenting with Love and

Logic prepares children for living as healthy a life as possible in the real world. Allowing non-life-threatening consequences to occur, and not rescuing the child, takes guts and gumption. Limiting a child's responsibility may appear easier and quicker than limiting our own parental responses. However, Love and Logic's limits generally deal more with how a parent responds than with what children can or cannot do. A Love and Logic Parent is less likely to say, "Hurry up and change your bandages now!" This parent will be more likely to say, "I'll be happy to take you to your game when you have finished changing your bandages." With Love and Logic, children learn how to live with the consequences of their actions, they avoid blaming others for their problems, and they make wise care decisions. Most importantly, parents respond in a way that increases the odds that both their healthy *and* chronically ill children will live responsible, productive, and joyful lives.

First Things First: Self-Care

Let's start right out by dealing with the most difficult issue of all: self-care of caregivers. Why? Because parents provide the model and set the example that the rest of the family will follow. If the parents are handling things well, the odds are much better that the children will cope well, too. Conversely, if the parents aren't coping, then it's likely the kids will have trouble managing their issues. As the old saying goes, "If mama ain't happy, then nobody's happy!" Of course, this applies to dads, too. Great parents are good models on how to take care of themselves and each other as parents, spouses, and individuals. Let's look at some important ways parents of kids with chronic illnesses[1] can take good care of themselves.

When a child has a chronic illness or other special medical needs, inordinate demands are placed on parental time, energy, finances, and emotions. It is understandable that in the midst of exhorting their children to take good care of their health, the parents themselves are worn to a frazzle, often not taking adequate time to rest and rejuvenate themselves.

Eating properly, exercising, and getting plenty of sleep is important. Children learn how to take care of their bodies by following their parents' example. Reading this material, putting the tools into place and discussing the concepts presented in this program with loved ones will help you to rejuvenate yourself and help you feel more relaxed and effective during critical parenting moments.

Parents of ill children need time alone and away to "regroup" from the chronic stress of care. However, the more severe the child's illness, the more physically and psychologically difficult it is to simply drop problems and participate in an activity that renews the individual and/or enhances the couple's relationship. Coping with a child's day-to-day health problems complicates respites and getaways for the following reasons:

- ♥ The more difficult the child's health problem is, the longer the "wind-down" must be before the getaway is truly restful.
- ♥ At the same time, the more difficult the child's issue, the harder it is to leave them for longer periods.

Parents may find themselves stuck between a rock and a hard place that can eventually undermine a marriage, causing even further stress to the family. Having an awareness of the importance of getaway time for caretakers dealing with a chronic illness is a necessary first step. Without awareness and intentional planning for vacations, retreats, or getaways, a couple can end up going for months or even years without this essential renewing time.

Sometimes finding adequate financial resources for respite care is not easy. And even when funding is available, it is often difficult to find a reliable person capable of caring for the child. There is no easy answer to this dilemma, but we suggest you be purposeful in cultivating close relationships with friends and family; teach them about your child's medical needs, and let them help. People are often more willing to help than one might expect. By allowing others to help, we help them grow, understand the issues, and give their own lives even more meaning. As parents, we don't have to "do it all." It is okay and healthy to ask for help, as difficult as it can be at times for some of us. John Donne said, "No man is an island, entire of itself," especially when one has a child with significant health issues. Community support can truly enhance the quality of everyone's lives.

Some parents have found it effective to play touch tag with particular physical or emotional problems. "Honey, this week you have the coping patrol. I'll take it next week." Just having a break from being "the responsible one" can help substantially. And, of course, as children take more and more responsibility for their own healthcare, that helps too.

Family vacations can be great fun and a good way to get away from the daily grind, but, unfortunately, the child's medical needs don't take a vacation! Individual and couple downtime is still essential. Maybe Dad can take time off from work so Mom can go on a vacation with her friends, and then she can handle the kids during a week of the hunting season to give Dad some downtime.

Summer camp and support groups are often available with a little searching. Parent organizations have resource lists available. The Internet is packed with parent-help forums that provide useful summer ideas. It is essential for parents to learn if their children behave or function at a higher level for others or in a non-home environment, such as a summer camp. If a child functions more independently or more respectfully when away from the parents, it is diagnostic of overdependence and/or manipulation. Then parents must correct life at home by encouraging the child to accept more responsibility and/or respond with age-appropriate behavior. Parental expectations (or a lack of them) may need to be re-examined.

We have found that, almost inevitably, strong faith helps ease the burden for most parents. It is good to know we are not bearing all these burdens alone, and it is liberating to have a faith that encourages "turning things over to God." When a family has a strong sense of faith, they generally have more hope and an increased sense of security and solace. Often there are fewer control battles and more thoughtful introspection on personal values.

In summary, parents will increase the odds of raising happy, responsible, health-conscious children when using Love and Logic's tools, techniques, and attitudes. Before delving into the nitty-gritty of these tools, techniques, and attitudes, we encourage wise parents to take good care of themselves by:

- ♥ Enriching their relationship by taking vacations together away from the children, as well as taking individual breaks from the stress that full-time care of a chronically ill child can impose.
- ♥ Ensuring they have a bi-monthly or weekly date-night.
- ♥ Ensuring that available respite care and support systems are in place.
- ♥ Refusing to tolerate children's disrespect.
- ♥ Modeling their ability to handle frustration and difficult times.
- ♥ Making good nutrition, exercise, and sufficient sleep a priority.

When medical problems are present, huge pressure can be brought to bear on coping skills. Maintaining a cheerful attitude and responsive demeanor seems almost impossible at times. Apart from the time and energy required to address special healthcare needs, parents and children may receive disquieting and difficult information they would understandably rather not hear. Children will learn disquieting or vexing information about their medical condition from many outside sources. Such information is available online at many websites and in library books and may be thoughtlessly passed on by school peers. On the DVD version of this program, which includes interviews with children and their parents,[2] one child with CF notes that a dismissive "friend" asked her, "Why do you cough so much?" then added, "You're going to die." Children coping with a chronic illness are going to get information that is nasty, incorrect, and upsetting. Children may come home crying when they can't participate in activities others handle easily. When children hurt, parents hurt. Problems can be aggravated when children see their own hurt amplified by the pain their parents feel, and the hurt becomes greater. Such hurt bounces back and forth like a ping-pong ball. Empathy slides into sympathy, which slips into mutual woe. The child absorbs the woe and angst and then becomes even more distressed.

So what is a parent to do? Rather than register pain, angst, and woe, a wise parent in the above example might say, "I bet you feel upset when kids say nasty things to you in school. Luckily, I think you are one of those kids who can handle it. Let's look at some options for talking to your schoolmates."

We have some good news. No matter what children learn from the Internet and from peers, no matter what they read in library books or hear on television, the cues loving parents give their children almost always have the strongest influence on a child's character. *Regardless of all our technical advances, parents will always be the most important source of information and values for their growing children.* Parents set the example their kids will almost always copy.

How do parents provide the cues? They use the Four Basic Love and Logic Principles that apply in all situations, whether they are medically related or not. Let's look at an example of how these principles are applied to a child with CF who is trying to decide whether or not to skip ice hockey practice because of his worsening cough. Rather than the parent just saying, "You're not going," Love and Logic teaches that it is critically important to allow kids the opportunity to learn about the real world by making as many decisions as possible in non-life-threatening situations.

The Four Basic Love and Logic Principles
Principle 1
Build the child's self-concept with high expectations of his or her ability to cope while showing empathy first, then curiosity and

interest, by asking what they think about issues that directly affect their lives. Questions cause children to think. Commands generally lead to resistance. As applied to the ice hockey situation, a parent might say:

- ♥ "What a tough situation. I understand you're very disappointed but if anyone can handle this, it's you. What are your thoughts about this?"
- ♥ "How important do you really feel it is to get control of that cough?"
- ♥ "Do you have some thoughts about when you might talk with your coach about the reasons for missing practice?"

Principle 2

Share the control or decision-making by using one or more of the following options:

- ♥ Share your thoughts and observations instead of telling the child what to do:
  - "One way other children might handle this is..."
  - "Personally, I don't think I'd go to practice today with such a bad cough. I'd be afraid I'd get even sicker and end up in the hospital, but I guess you're not me, so you need to decide what is right for you."
- ♥ Giving choices with alternatives that are acceptable to the parent:
  - "Would you prefer to go and just watch from the bleachers, or stay home and relax?"
  - "What would you rather do today: play your hockey video game or watch your hockey DVD?"
- ♥ Instead of telling children what they have to do, tell them what we are willing to do.
  - Ineffective: "You're not going to practice with that cough! You'll end up in the hospital next week."
  - Effective: "I am happy to support your playing ice hockey, as long as the decisions you make are good for your body."

Principle 3
Offer empathy first, then consequences:
- ♥ "Honey, I know it might be upsetting to miss practice, but it will probably be easier than spending time in the hospital."
- ♥ "It's a bummer to miss practice, but if you decide to play when you're getting sick then perhaps you'll need to contribute to the hospital costs if you end up there."

Principle 4
Share the thinking and problem solving:
- ♥ "Even if you aren't playing, there may be something else you can do during practice that would help the team. Would you like to hear how other kids might have handled it?"
- ♥ "Would you like to come up with another way you can show your support to the guys and the coach?"

The next chapter will discuss these four basic principles in detail.

Chapter 1 Key Concepts

1. For children with healthcare issues, the price tag for mistakes and poor decisions can be high, even when children are young, so it's important to learn parenting techniques that will increase the odds that your children will make wise decisions, especially concerning their healthcare. Love and Logic teaches our children self-control.

2. All children, including those with chronic illnesses and medical conditions, must be held accountable for poor decisions and irresponsibility. Successful parents accept that mistakes are really learning opportunities and therefore allow children to live with the consequences of their actions. When kids have significant medical conditions, this is much more difficult

because of the medical issues themselves, the intensity of the situation, and the possibility of really serious mistakes. Power struggles occur when parents use excessive rescue strategies and insist on their own solutions because of their fear. Instead of allowing consequences to occur, many parents become angry, frustrated, or show great angst, which is understandable. Generally, these responses are ineffective. Empathy, love, and understanding help when given to children before they experience the negative consequences of their actions.

3. Shared control encourages parents to offer choices, and children feel empowered and involved in their treatment.

4. Helicopter Parents rescue, fix, and nag. Drill Sergeant Parents demand compliance and are directive. Consultant Parents help children solve problems. The goal is to be a Consultant Parent.

5. Medical issues are so important it is understandable parents feel like reminding, ranting, raving, or rescuing. These four Rs will never work as well as the Es of Love and Logic: *Example*, *Experience*, *Empathy*, *Expectations*, and *Encouragement*. Parenting with Love and Logic prepares a child for living as healthy a life as possible in the real world.

6. Caregivers may have real difficulty ensuring that their own self-care is a priority. Taking the time and finding respite from the children may be very difficult, but taking good care of yourself as a parent is essential because example plays such an important role in parenting,

7. Four basic Love and Logic Principles apply in all situations, whether or not they are medically related: build the child's self-concept, share the control or decision making, provide

empathy before delivering consequences, and share the thinking and problem solving.

Chapter 2

The Basic Principles: Just What the Doctor Ordered

Few things can help an individual more than to place responsibility on him, and to let him know that you trust him.
—Booker T. Washington (1856-1915)

Now that you have the "big picture view" of Love and Logic, let's begin with some in-depth training concerning the Four Basic Principles: build self-concept, share control, provide empathy before delivering consequences, and share the thinking and problem solving.

Principle 1:
Build Your Child's Self-Concept
Perhaps it's best to begin the study of self-concept

by looking at things that have nothing at all to do with developing a high self-concept.

- ♥ Wealth has nothing to do with self-concept because rich kids can have a very poor self-concept and poor kids can feel great about themselves.
- ♥ When parents talk to their children "sweetly," that is certainly "nice." All of us feel better when someone is nice to us. We are not against "nice-ness." The problem is that some parents think that simply being nice to their children will somehow result in a child with a high self-concept. Don't all of us know of sweet and caring parents who raised very nasty children who have a very poor self-image? Being nice is good, but it doesn't raise a child with a high self-concept.
- ♥ Sometimes parents give their children material goods, hoping that it will make them feel better, and you know what? It might make them feel better for the moment but it doesn't build their self-concept.

So then, what *does* build a child's self-concept? A child's self-concept is built little by little over the years by parents who:

- ♥ Offer empathy, understanding, and unconditional love.
- ♥ Show high, but reasonable, expectations of the child's ability to cope with life's problems.
- ♥ Show curiosity and interest by asking children their thoughts about issues that directly affect their lives.
- ♥ Allow children to solve their own problems.

The truth is this: self-concept is built on *pride*. If folks have pride, it means they have *done* something they are proud of. *Self-concept is inextricably connected with doing things right.* Every time our children make a decision that improves their health or improves the quality of life for others, their self-concept skyrockets. For instance:

"John, you're late getting home from school. What happened?"

"Oh, Robert was in the handicapped bathroom, and stuff had fallen off the back of his wheelchair. He was having trouble turning around and getting out, so I helped him. Then his battery was about to run out, so I pushed him out to the van and stayed with him while he waited..."

Self-concept increases every time a parent looks at their child and says, "Gee thanks" for something they've done. It is lowered every time a parent says, "Can't you ever...?" Parents are powerful people. We see it every time a little kid smiles about an accomplishment and says, "My dad told me I could do it!"

Principle 2: Share the Control

Children who have special medical needs almost always feel a loss of control. They think, "Other kids are able to do everything. They don't know what it's like! Other kids don't have to take medication, see the doctor, have reconstructive surgery, or fill their time with visits to the hospital. It's just not fair!!!" Therefore, children with special medical needs must be encouraged to develop a sense of control and a sense of ownership about what happens to them in life because frustrations could rob them of control and seem overwhelming. The frustrations they face are far greater than the everyday hassles many "normal folks" cope with poorly: Have you ever dropped coins into a soda machine — and nothing came out, including the coins? Have you ever misplaced your TV remote control? Have you ever waited in line at the grocery store when the clerk closes up just as it's finally your turn? Has your car ever failed to start when you were already late for an appointment? These simple issues throw some people into a rage.

Now, put yourself in the place of a child with a chronic illness or other medical challenges. What are the everyday frustrations of a healthy adult compared to the problem of putting on a shirt and dressing every morning with only one arm? Or taking your daily blood-pressure check and finding your beta-blockers aren't keeping your soaring hypertension down? Or the frustration that wells up inside when other children can run, and your sixth foot surgery won't allow you to run at all? These feelings can be devastating to a child. What about the frustration and loss of control when the other kids talk about the camp-out while you spent the weekend in the hospital for another cardiac catheterization or phlebotomy?

What makes any situation frustrating? Often it is the feeling of loss of control. We feel it when no matter how hard we kick the soda machine, no soda or money drops out. We feel it when the car won't start, no matter how many times we turn the ignition key. We feel powerless. It's that simple. Control is a basic human emotional need.

A search for life's answers can be seen as a search for control and predictability. Everyone wants to make sense out of life's challenges. *There must be some purpose to this. What did I do to deserve this?* Unconsciously, we reason: "If I can make sense out of the world's bad happenings, if there is a reason for it all, then maybe I have some control over it." For example, one might think: "If having this disease is God's way of testing or punishing me, then maybe if I promise to be really, really good, I'll be healed." The book of Job in the Bible illustrates this clearly. That's why every chronically ill child asks over and over again, "Why did this happen to me?" And when wonderful things happen for other children, they wonder, "Why not me?" Both questions are variations on the thought, "What did I do wrong and how can I fix it?" or "What can I do to have some control over what happens to me?" Human beings need control.

Children use rebellion, negativism, and a refusal to take care of themselves as ways of saying, "I have to have some say here and I will, no matter what I need to do to get it!" Suicide is the ultimate form of control, and can be a way of saying, "At least I get to decide when I die." *The more we try to control our kids with medical needs, when in many ways they already have less control than others, the more likely they are to rebel.* Children saddled with daily treatment regimens and hospital visits need to be included in choices concerning their care.

Louisa

Louisa, a 12-year-old diabetic, had parents who were very controlling around her healthcare. Her entire week was filled with complex schedules her parents insisted on using to oversee her glucose levels and insulin dosages. They gave her few choices, even on non-health-related issues. They told her how to dress and when to go to bed; what to eat and when to get up. Her parents were in constant fear of diabetic complications and made sure Louisa knew it. Louisa used this fear to her advantage as she became progressively rebellious. This, of course, led to a vicious cycle of more parental fear, which then caused Louisa to increase her manipulation.

There were no real discussions about how the insulin schedules might be modified, and no attempt was made to explore Louisa's feelings. One morning, she screamed at her mother that she didn't care if she did die and rushed off to school. Unknown to her mother, she had left her injection at home. Later, at the hospital, her mom and dad sat at her bedside, exhausted from the ordeal of keeping her healthy, and finally had to admit they had no control over her. After a great deal of soul searching, they decided to drop the anger, rancor, and frustration, and tell Louisa simply that they loved her, and that from that day on they would no longer attempt to be in charge of her health.

They kissed her and said that even if she died, they would have wonderful memories of the times they had shared together.

Louisa's mom explained later, "Things were awful for the first few days after she came home from the hospital. She ignored some care issues and kept repeating that she wished she were dead. But she took her insulin. On Wednesday, two days after coming home, she hung around me and actually hissed, 'I bet my blood sugar is through the roof.' And I said, 'Gosh, honey, that's a real bummer for your body. I'd certainly consider taking better care of *my* body if it were me.' That really made her mad. But you know what? Shortly after I said to her, 'Gosh, that's a bummer,' I saw her sitting there with her glucose meter in hand, finger pricked, figuring out what dose she might need. And her self-care has definitely been improving! She just needed to know she had control. When I think of all the years we had wasted wrangling over control, I think, 'Well geez! What took me so long to finally let go of something I never had control of in the first place?!'"

You will soon learn some effective techniques concerning the specifics of sharing control, such as using effective, healthy choices and the use of enforceable statements. You will also learn how to guide your children to solve their own problems. When we share the control correctly, our kids learn self-care and self-control.

Principle 3: Empathy *Before* Consequences

Using empathy is a very important skill and differentiates Love and Logic from the many other parenting resources available. Most of them mention the importance of unconditional love but a cornerstone of Love and Logic is this special way of demonstrating unconditional love: providing empathy before delivering consequences.

Nearly thirty years ago, Dr. Foster Cline and Jim Fay discovered an almost magical formula for disciplining kids without losing their love and respect. From watching thousands of naturally successful parents, they observed the following: *The most successful parents delivered a strong dose of empathy, or sadness for the child, before they described the consequence.*

They also noticed that these parents kept it very simple by choosing just one short sentence and using it every time they were about to deliver a consequence. Some examples are:

- ♥ "This is so sad..."
- ♥ "Oh, man..."
- ♥ "What a bummer..."
- ♥ "Oh no, honey..."
- ♥ "Oh, that's too bad..."
- ♥ "This is hard..."

Foster and Jim also noticed that the most successful parents delivered their empathy with sincerity, not sarcasm. Since the 1970s, scientific research on the human brain has taught us that anger, lectures, warnings, and sarcasm create flight-or-flight reactions. Empathy prevents fight-or-flight.

By delivering a strong dose of empathy before delivering consequences, parents can help their children think and learn from their mistakes, rather than rebel or run. This is critically important when children are making life-impacting medical decisions. We want our kids to be really, really good at thinking! We also want to have great relationships with our children each step of the way, because every moment matters. Empathy maintains lifelong, loving relationships.[3]

Natural Logical Consequences with Empathy

Every child makes mistakes. They make mistakes about medical issues and nonmedical issues. When children make mistakes concerning healthcare issues that affect their lives, it is understandable when parents show anger. The anger is almost always laced with frustration over the question: "How can I *make* this kid take good care of him/herself?" The answer is, as we have emphasized, you *can't*. Parents have a very hard time accepting this fact, but the sooner they do, the better off their children will be. Accepting the universal truth that we can't absolutely control the actions of another human being may determine the longevity of our chronically ill child's life. All of us, including our children, have been born with a God-given right, and need, to exercise our own free will.

When a child makes a bad decision, parents need to do something far more difficult than simply getting mad and "forcing" a child to comply. They have to let naturally occurring consequences happen and show empathy. Since most mistakes have natural consequences, often the best course is for parents to sit back, and with a ready arm around the child's shoulder, show sorrow instead of anger. Love and Logic says, "*Be sad for, not mad at.*"

Jenni

Jenni was a fairly resistant teenager with CF. She complied with her medical regimen half-heartedly and relied upon her mother's nagging, lecturing, and eventual anger to "remind" her to take her pancreatic enzymes and do her breathing treatments. Jenni knew the importance of taking care of her body but with her mother making sure her medications were taken, she figured, "Why should I have to worry too? Mom worries enough for the both of us!"

After attending a Love and Logic conference, which included a chat with Dr. Cline, Mom made a plan. She vowed to let Jenni "be the one in charge" of managing her pancreatic enzymes. The following conversation took place: "Jenni, sweetheart, I have to apologize to you. I have been interfering with your life and your ability to take good care of yourself. I am turning all of the responsibility for your enzymes over to you. I will no longer remind you to take them. I know you can do a great job managing this. I'm here if you need me, and I'm interested in how this works out for you."

Jenni did okay managing her enzymes at first but started to slip a bit and became a little forgetful about making sure they were in her purse. All went relatively well until the night of the prom. During the excitement of preparing for the big night, Jenni forgot to refill her empty enzyme case. Later, at a fancy dinner party with her friends, she went to take her enzymes and had none. Shrugging her shoulders, she figured, "Oh well" and enjoyed a big meal. Later that evening she felt the rumblings of stomach cramps but danced on. Halfway through the dance, however, she could no longer ignore the severe cramping and an overpowering urge to use the bathroom. Even relieving herself did not relieve the pain, so she decided to call Mom to come pick her up and take her home. "Foster," Mom later said in a note, "That ride home was one of the best and worst nights of my life. I felt so bad for her. She was really in a lot of pain and was so disappointed about missing the dance and party afterwards. I bit my tongue so hard all the way home that it hurt the next day! But I managed to simply hug her and say, 'Oh sweetie, what a shame. I'm sorry your stomach hurts so badly.' I wanted to say, 'If only you'd listened to me then this wouldn't have happened' but I didn't. On one hand, I felt very sad for her but on the other hand, my heart said, 'Yesss! What an amazing learning opportunity for her.' It turned out to be a good evening, after all, for both of us. We went home, snuggled by the fire, watched a movie, and she hasn't forgotten her enzymes since."

Imposed Logical Consequences with Empathy

Sometimes, unlike Jenni's situation, a child's poor decision doesn't necessarily affect the child personally. If a child's mistakes decrease the quality of life for others, or if a child's decisions affect the functioning of a family, natural consequences may not occur. For example: if a child is snippy or nasty around the house and the parents do nothing, then there are no natural consequences. If a child has a bad cough and leaves phlegm-soaked tissues scattered across the floor and mom picks them all up, there are no natural consequences. If she picks them up and later has her child mop the kitchen floor, then mom has taken action with an imposed consequence that makes sense; it's logical.

When any child's misbehavior affects others, we may have to "do something." That's especially difficult when the "something" means our special child may be upset or experience discomfort. Whether it is a "recovery time," grounding, or missing a party, our child is bound to be distressed. Now who of us wants to upset our child? None of us! Unfortunately, many parents feel guilty when they "do something" that upsets their child. When the child is ill or challenged one way or another, this can be a reason to feel double guilty! When parents feel guilty, they often become angry because they don't like feeling "forced" into doing something they'd prefer not to. The person who loses coins in a soda machine or tries to start a car with a dead battery feels a similar sense of anger or frustration because of a lack of control. And there is nothing, absolutely nothing, more fun for any child than knowing they can cause an adult to react with helpless, angry frustration. Children love to hear: "Am I going to have to supervise every one of your treatments?!!" Deep down, most children derive great pleasure at the thought of "making" us "have to" do just about anything! Instead of giving a warning or a threat, wise parents simply state, "Honey, I'll be ready to leave at 4:00. I'll be happy to drive you to Boy Scouts when you have done your breathing treatments. See you then." This type of matter-of-fact, *imposed consequence* is similar to that given when a parent says to a disrespectful child, "You're welcome to stay here with us as long as you can be sweet."

Such imposed consequences:
- ♥ Set the model when parents take good care of their own needs and feelings
- ♥ Emphasize the positive
- ♥ Are given without anger and frustration
- ♥ Are enforceable

The guidelines for imposing logical consequences are:
- ♥ They are carried out calmly, in a matter-of-fact manner; never with anger or frustration.
- ♥ The consequences make sense and are related to the "crime."
- ♥ They are never so severe that the parent is racked with guilt.
- ♥ They are not carried out with the *intent* to make the child feel "bad" (although that may be the frosting on the cake).
- ♥ Consequences need not be immediate (even young children have long-term memories!):
  - • "I'm kind of put out right now. I'll get back to you later. Try not to worry about it."
  - • "I think it would be better for us both if I decide later what to do about this."
  - • "Obviously, I need to consult your mom. But we'll be in touch."

When consequences are imposed:

1. Parents must swallow any frustration and anger and *show empathy for the child's feelings* by using an empathetic statement or Love and Logic one-liner.

   Examples of statements that *don't* work:
   - "I know how you feel."
   - "I know just what you mean."
   - "I understand exactly how you feel."
   - "Been there, done that!"

   Examples of empathetic statements that *do* work:
   - "Oh, no. I bet that feels terrible."
   - "Wow. What a bummer."
   - "I can hardly imagine how bad that feels."
   - "Gosh, that must be really sad for you."

2. Parents must be "matter of fact" about the consequence itself but empathetic with the child's feelings.

3. Parents must be consistently willing and able to carry out the same consequence again without guilt.

4. If the imposed consequence is absolutely ineffective, wise parents try something else. One clever definition of insanity is doing the same thing over and over and expecting different results. Using a metaphor: people don't sit in the car on a cold day and turn the key harder believing that it will make the car start! Let's look at an example that demonstrates the imposition of consequences:

Ricky

Ricky was born with cerebral palsy and needed to use a wheelchair at school. He always felt a little different, and sometimes the other children made fun of him. For weeks he had looked forward to a new motorized wheelchair. When he finally received the new chair, he turned the hallways of his parochial school into the

Daytona Speedway. Now he had some real control and power! Those other kids who had given him a hard time had better move out of the way! The sisters at the school were aghast, and they showed it. They monitored Ricky closely and told him to be more careful. They even prayed he would use his wheelchair to simply roll about, not roll over others! But their prayers went unanswered, and the monitoring didn't seem to work. Ricky's mom had an easy answer. She decided to take away the motorized wheelchair and put Ricky back into his old "kid-powered" vehicle.

Take away his wheelchair?!! The sisters thought this was far too mean, and the rest of Ricky's family agreed, but Mom stuck to her guns. For three whole days, Ricky's shiny new wheelchair sat in the garage, and he went to school riding his old chariot. However, after the three days, he was back in school with his new wheelchair and was a changed boy. He was thoughtful, cooperative, and adhered to the speed limit! *The sisters were surprised at the affection and respect Ricky showed his mother, when often they had received so little of it themselves.* What was her secret?

Her secret was simple:
1. She was matter-of-fact about consequences.
2. She led with empathy in recognizing her son's feelings.
3. She set the model by taking good care of herself.
4. And she chose an issue that was enforceable. Insisting that he stop using the motorized wheelchair to threaten others could be difficult to enforce. Taking Ricky's wheelchair away was simple to enforce!

Let's listen to how this great mom handled the situation:

Ricky's Mom

"Ricky honey, I know how fun it must be to run that wheelchair at full speed to test it out, when you've had to push yourself around for so long. And I'm really sure it's fun to run down nasty kids who give you a hard time. But you know what, honey? When I go to work and think about your turning the halls of Blessed Sacrament into the Speedway, I feel like an accessory to a crime, and it takes my mind off all the things my boss expects me to do. I keep thinking about what might be happening down at St. Speedway, so I get distracted and don't do as well. I would like to be really relaxed at work 'cause I've been tense over the past week thinking about you running kids down. So I thought, 'Shoot, Ricky did well without a motorized chair for years at school. He's a great kid. He doesn't need it at all. We can save it for weekends.' It's so great I don't have to worry anymore, because when you're at school, the new wheelchair will hang out in the garage. However, after you get home, we will help you get into it. But don't worry about it. If anyone has built up their biceps wheeling with kid power, it's you! You'll probably do a lot better without a motor."

To say Ricky was upset that night is like saying Mt. Vesuvius burped the day it buried Pompeii. Ricky had every reason to believe he had lost the use of the wheelchair at school for at least the rest of the semester, maybe for the year or maybe even forever! However, on the third night mom said, "You know, I've been so relaxed at work. I think I can handle the idea of you having the new wheelchair at school, and if I don't hear of anyone being run down, I think I'll continue to be relaxed." Ricky responded with glee, "Gee, thanks

Mom!!!" Now Mom had morphed into his benevolent savior. Mom noted, "The rest of the year at school, Ricky drove that chair like my grandmother drives her Pontiac. We're talkin' real slow and real careful!"

Paradoxically, even when the consequences are heavy, parents using empathy draw their children closer, and the children's respect for the parents, and subsequently their own self-respect, grows. *When parents show anger but give no consequences, children feel more distant and respect the parents less and, consequently, their self-respect and self-esteem plummets.*

A final and important note about consequences: When dealing with medical compliance issues, it may be necessary to rely more heavily on imposed logical consequences than upon more severe natural consequences. *Natural consequences should never be used when they can result in danger to life or limb.* Wise parents become very good at using imposed consequences that logically fit the child's bad decision. For example, a child with diabetes would never be allowed to skip vital glucose readings and become hypoglycemic (a natural consequence). However, a parent may decide he or she can't take the risk of driving a child to a ballgame or dance class when "your glucose levels might be off, so until we know, I guess we'll stay home," an imposed logical consequence.

Principle 4: Share the Thinking and Problem Solving

What determines a child's ability to think and solve problems? Why, practice, of course! Practice at making choices, thinking about mistakes that have been made, and considering the reality of cause and effect. Children who are always told how to solve their problems don't get this essential practice in the game of life.

Mutual problem solving, or the ability to effectively guide others to solve their own problems, is a characteristic of a good leader, an adept counselor, and a skillful parent. It's easy to tell another person what to do; it's not so easy to be a consultant. Whether a child brings a problem to you ("Mom, I forgot to take my medicine at school today") or you need to address a behavioral issue with your child ("Susie, I'd like to talk with you about how you've been treating the nurses"), it's important to remember this parenting factoid: *Children generally appreciate their parents' thoughts, observations, and guidance. They often resent demands and orders.* "Advice" is something that "should" be followed. "Thoughts" are offered for consideration; something to think about. Wording and attitude make a world of difference.

Problem solving must always take place in an atmosphere of mutual respect. It is far too easy for parents to slip into the stance of a cross examining attorney when attempting to get to the "root" of the problem.

Use the following guidelines when exploring thoughts or problem behavior. Good communication techniques are universal, so these tools are also useful for adult relationships.

1. Pick a time when the child is in a receptive mood and you know how you are going to present your thoughts and observations. In other words, everyone is in a good mood.

2. Ask the child for permission.
   - "Jack, is this a good time to talk about changing your meds?"
   - "When would be a good time to talk about your medical compliance?"
   - "I've noticed that you've seemed frustrated lately about something. Is now a good time to talk about it or would you prefer to talk after dinner?"

3. Always show curiosity and interest in your child's thoughts before you share your own.
   - First, "I'm curious, what are your thoughts about..." And then, "Now, may I share some thoughts with you?"
   - "First, "Do you have an opinion about ...?" And then, "I've made some observations about the way you care for your diabetes that might be of interest. Would you like to hear them?"

- First, "Do you know why you are acting like you're (frustrated, depressed...)?" And then, "I have some ideas about why you might be feeling depressed. Are you interested in them?"

Helping a child change self-destructive behavior and resolve problems generally requires recognition of, and sharing, feelings. *Angry and resentful feelings drive most of the world's self-destructive behavior. That's a universal truth that applies to both terrorists and our children.* An individual's self-destructive behavior is never changed until feelings are explored in an atmosphere of love. Sometimes, a counselor is needed to help a child explore feelings and resolve problems. The next chapter gives an excellent example of using these general rules when a mother explores her son's frustration with his brother's illness.

When a child brings a specific problem to you or the issue is more fact-based, rather than emotionally charged, Love and Logic's *Five Steps to Guide the Child to Solve the Problem* can be effective:

1. Express curiosity, interest, and empathy: "I bet that hurt!"
2. Send the power message: "What do you think you'll do?"
3. Offer choices: "Would you like to hear what other kids have tried?"
4. Have the child state the consequences.
5. Give the child permission to either solve or not solve the problem.

Let's look at an example of how this formula can be used with some variation. A parent arrives at school after being called by the principal, and the following discussion takes place:

- ♥ What happened?
  - "Gosh, Billy, what was going on?"
- ♥ What were you feeling?
  - "I can see how you would forget your meds with all that going on. You must have been really frustrated."
- ♥ So what did you do?

- "So, then you had a seizure right there on the playground?"
♥ And how did that work out?
- "I can imagine that the kids were all scared!"
♥ So what did you learn from that?
- "Wow, I bet that was embarrassing and scary for you!"
♥ How do you think you will handle it next time?
- "So you're going to keep some extra medicine right in your pocket. Maybe that's a good idea. Let me know how that works out for you."

Children often surprise us by coming up with very good solutions to their own problems but they still need to hear adult thoughts and observations. After all, they are still children and don't yet have the wisdom and discernment of adults. The key is to provide *options, choices, thoughts,* and *ideas* rather than telling them what they "ought to" or "should" do.

♥ "Would you like to know how other kids with diabetes handle their sweet tooth?"
♥ "If I were in your shoes I might check out the store for diabetic food I would like."
♥ "I wonder if they might have sugarless candy down in that little candy store on the mall."

Great problem-solving discussions with children should end with sincere statements of encouragement:

♥ "Hope it goes better next time."
♥ "I expect you can always figure that one out."
♥ "Well, good luck! Let me know how it goes."

Chapter 2 Key Concepts

1. Build the child's self-concept. High self-concept is not built on

wealth, sweet/nice parents, or material things. Self-concept is built on the pride of accomplishing a job well done.

2. Share the control or decision making. It is especially important for children with medical needs to develop a sense of control and ownership about life because the many frustrations that rob them of control can be overwhelming. "Feeling in control" is a basic human emotional need. A child often uses rebellion, negativism, and a refusal to take care of him/herself as a means of gaining control. Effective techniques are based on the specifics of sharing control, as well as using choices and enforceable statements properly.

3. Provide empathy *before* delivering consequences. Empathy is most important. Ultimately, parents cannot force their children to take good care of themselves. Lectures are generally ineffective, so children must learn though consequences, natural or imposed. Love and Logic parents are encouraged to "Be sad for; not mad at" their children. Safety always comes first.

4. If a child's poor decision doesn't affect the child personally but affects others, parents are encouraged to artfully and properly impose consequences. Properly imposing consequences with empathy is illustrated and explored. Empathy draws children closer, increasing respect for their parents, which subsequently increases their own self-respect.

5. Share the thinking and problem solving. Children appreciate thoughts, observations, and guidance but resent demands and orders. The rules for sharing the thinking and problem solving are explored.

Chapter 3

Loving Limits: Preparing Kids for the Real World

You cannot escape the responsibility
of tomorrow by evading it today.
—Abraham Lincoln (1809-1865)

Properly setting appropriate limits is one of the biggest challenges parents have and is even more so when the child has a serious medical situation. Many parents are either too permissive, too strict, or toggle back and forth between the two. The mother of a two-year-old just diagnosed with brain cancer expresses this dilemma to us: "My biggest challenge with her right now is knowing how to discipline her. Should I say no and set off a tantrum? But allowing her free reign is obviously not the answer, either. Because of the cancer, I just don't know how I should parent her. I am afraid to be too strict and afraid to let her get away with too much. What should I do?" This chapter, and the next, will answer these questions. Some parents fear the child will see them as mean if they set firm limits; others fear a loss of parental control or erosion of authority if they are not strict enough. Both ends of the spectrum can create serious problems when the child with medical issues hits the teen years. The key is to be firm and loving at the same time. Chapters 3 and 4 will give you all the parenting tools you need to be a loving and firm *Consultant Parent*, which is the parenting style that naturally results when using Love and Logic tools and techniques.

Developing the Self-Limiting Child

On the radio and television we are bombarded with the advice, "Love your children enough to tell them no." But many parents think that by setting firm limits, they will stifle the child's creativity and inventiveness. This belief is far from the truth:

> "If you want your children to have inner controls and inner freedom, you must first provide them with external controls. A child who is given boundaries, and *choices within those boundaries*, is actually freer to be creative, inventive, active, and insightful. How you expose your kids to the life around them — how you encourage them to use their creativity within limits, by modeling yours — is key to developing their personal identity and freedom. Setting limits does not discourage inventiveness. The world is full of limits within which we must all live. Give your children a gift. Teach them how to be creative within these limits." [4]

This concept of creativity and inventiveness within limits is especially important to children with chronic medical conditions. Teaching our children to accept and cope well with limits in nonmedical areas of life also teaches them to accept and cope well with the limitations of their bodies. When they become accustomed to living within limits, they begin to accept "the way things are" in the real world *and* in *their* world. This is the beginning of accepting their own physical challenges and limitations. Such children can then have the freedom to be creative and inventive to make their lives and their world better, given these limitations. For instance, if a child struggles to take pills in front of schoolmates at lunchtime, the child can brainstorm creative solutions to this challenge, such as taking the pills in the bathroom or hiding them in food, etc. rather than not taking the meds at all. Or, the child may decide to become a resident "kid expert" on medication, teaching his/her buddies what each capsule does and how it works. Within the accepted limit of "I need to take my meds and follow doctor's orders," the child becomes innovative.

So, given that setting limits is critically important for proper emotional and social development, should a parent risk evoking a control battle by saying "no" — especially with a rebellious teenager who has medical issues? In one book, a drug-abusing adolescent, angry with her parents, purportedly says she is angry because, when she was a child, her parents didn't tell her "no" enough. This may make good reading, but in over thirty years of working with children and families, we have never run into even one teenager who complained during therapy, "My parents just don't control me tightly enough. I really wish they'd say 'no' to me more often." Frankly, we believe it seldom happens. Don't get us wrong; as adults, some look back and wish their parents had enforced tighter limits. But whether or not the teen would have complied with tighter limits is an open question. Certainly, blaming parents in retrospect for not being controlling enough allows adult children to ignore responsibility for their own poor choices. Nathan is a typical example of this:

Nathan

By the time he reached age 28, Nathan was suffering many of the effects of childhood diabetes. His eyesight was poor, he was in danger of losing a limb, and his kidney function was endangered. This was the understandable result of poor self-care. Now, looking back on his childhood, Nathan blames his parents. "They should have made me take better care of myself." Of course, the parents remember it differently: "We tried but he wouldn't listen to us."

So then, when can parents safely just say "no" and expect the "no" to "stick"?

As we have discussed, a parent can't *make* a child take care of him/herself, especially a resistant older child. So, how can limits be set on a child's behavior without creating even more frustration and rebellion from "overcontrol?" Before we answer this question, let's explore the rules for successfully setting limits or saying "no" to our child with special medical needs.

♥ **Rule 1**: When children are very young, *that* is the time to say "no" and tell them what to do.

When a small hemophiliac child wants to run up and down cement stairs, the parents must say, one way or another, "No." If a little kid doesn't like the limit, that's basically just too bad! If he/she continues to resist and wants to run, he/she will be carried by loving adults. Small children really have no choice in the most critical matters; and if parents are able to avoid becoming obviously frustrated and angry and remain available and loving, almost all small children soon learn to accept their parents' limits that can be physically enforced when necessary. Parents can always carry children off to the bedroom for a little "recovery time."

💜 **Rule 2**: We can tell other people what to do only when they respect and/or love us enough to do what we ask them to do.

When parents know without a doubt that their child will "obey the no," and the no is absolutely necessary, then, by all means, "just say no." Just remember that too many "no's" will soon erode the child's willingness to obey even the most respected (or feared) parent, particularly around the age of 12! Think about this: even though you respect your boss, if he told you what to do all day long and micromanaged your every move, you'd soon be looking for a new job. Kids don't have that luxury, so they might react to overcontrol in other ways, like sneaking around, depression, or outright rebellion. With healthcare issues, the results can be very serious.

💜 **Rule 3**: We can say "no" and set limits on children's behavior when they are older if, after disobeying, the imposed or natural consequences are strong enough to do the teaching and will lead to future compliance.

However, even here, is saying "no" the best option when the expectation is that the child will probably disobey? In such situations it is almost always more effective for a parent to give thoughtful advice outlining the consequences: "It appears to me you are making a poor choice because..."

Saying no, setting limits, and "making" kids take good care of their bodies is self-defeating in any but the above three situations. Certainly, kids will follow orders when it is strongly or covertly implied that they will be "dead meat" if they don't obey. But, at some point, the implied "you will be dead meat" approach based on the parent's power simply must end. In rare cases, strong parents and very compliant kids can live with that process through high school. For a sweet young adolescent named Anne, the process worked until she spiraled downhill during her first semester of college. She simply hadn't learned how to figure things out on her own. Never having grown up with choices, she was unable to handle the countless choices available in a large state university setting.

Clearly, even in those situations where parents are able to say "no" and set limits, that's not really what most parents want to have to say when they listen to the quiet voice deep in their hearts. Obviously, it is best when a child says "no" to him/herself; and the sooner, the better. Our souls don't wish to discipline children just for discipline's sake. Parental souls long for self-disciplined children. Parents have been known to express this hopeful aspiration: "I just wish he could figure this out for himself, without involving me." Parents can certainly set limits, but wise parents really want a child who thoughtfully limits himself and who exercises self-control. But, how do children learn to be self-limiting? Let's learn about the process as it begins in early childhood.

Robert

Robert is diabetic; therefore a high-carbohydrate diet means death — maybe not immediately, but ultimately. As a toddler and during his early childhood years, Robert's parents have been wise to control his diet. If they say "no" when he wants candy and show oodles of joy, joy, joy when he eats his vegetables and fish during those early years, a wonderful thing happens. Robert "puts his loving, fun parents inside him" as his role model. Because his mother is loving and responsive to him as a toddler, he wants to make her happy. Soon, he becomes happy when she's happy and pleased.

Then, one day in early childhood, he feels happy doing what she wants, even when she isn't around. In kindergarten he sits down and "reads" a book. He has memorized his mother's sweet words and uses her inflections and tone of voice as he reads. Now she is inside of him and Robert has a conscience! Like Jiminy Cricket on Pinocchio's shoulder, Robert's mom sparks her way through Robert's little neurons.

Now, instead of telling Robert to give himself a shot of insulin, it's better for his mom to count on the "ghost" of herself that lives inside of Robert. Now it is best for her to say, "Sweetheart, how are you feeling?" And Robert, listening to the ghost of his mother inside, will hear her say, "Hey, you forgot to take your insulin!" And his mother's inner voice will merge with his thoughts, and he'll think taking his shot is his idea!

Instead of telling the child, "Take your insulin shot!" some parents manage to keep a gentle sense of humor even around some significant health issues:

- ♥ "Rob, do you wonder if your blood would attract ants?"
- ♥ "Jesus loves you so much, I can almost hear him tromping through your heart right now!"
- ♥ "What's all that food sticking to? I thought you were missing a few ribs!"

Don't get us wrong. We are not against telling kids, "no." We are not against giving kids orders. We are not against telling them what they have to do. Sometimes it is necessary. But unless the child is very young, when it is necessary, that's sad for the child. It indicates he or she needs direction from the outside because he or she surely doesn't have it from the inside! Children grow up to become husbands and wives and parents themselves and must learn to take care of their own bodies, make wise choices, and accept consequences. Those are the only things that work for successful adults. Since those concepts need to be learned sometime, we might as well start traveling down that road as early as possible! *If you set as many rules as necessary but as few as possible* when the kids are young, then you are much more likely to enjoy those teen years and beyond!

So, continuing with our original question: How can limits be set on a child's behavior without creating even more frustration and rebellion from "overcontrol"? Keep reading...

Creativity and Fun Help Children Accept Limits

We have repeatedly stressed how parents' attitudes and perceptions rub off on their ill children. A bit of creativity and a spirit of fun can help children learn to accept limits. The following examples illustrate how a creative attitude can change the experiences and mindset of those with a serious medical problem:

- ♥ Two boys with severe cystic fibrosis loved to go sailing in Puget Sound with their dad and mom. Their oxygen tanks were secured on the deck of the boat.

- ♥ Linda looks at her daughter and says, "Living with a child with hemophilia is a constant roller-coaster ride. I've always enjoyed roller-coasters!"

- ♥ When Jacob and Kasey do their chest physical therapy with a mechanical vest that vibrates their torsos as they sit in a chair for a long time, it's family game time, or time for their very favorite video game they play at no other time.

- ♥ Cynthia feels very special when she shows her little sister: "My veins are like pipes, and the blood rushes through them; I make it really easy for those nurses in the hospital. I'm special, because I have so many other people's blood in me. I can't help but be smart."

Debbie Attig recounts a sweet story about how she used creativity, humor, and silliness to get her young daughter with CF to do her breathing treatments:

Natalynn

Natalynn hated doing her nebulizing treatment and fought against it. I had tried everything, including videotapes, drawing, and reading books. Nothing worked. Then, one day I saw a bird hopping around right outside our window. I told Natalynn, "Look at that bird! He sees a funny girl with this thing on her face and he wants to know what it is." So we would move closer to the window, and when he flew away, I said, "I'll bet he is going to go get some more friends to come and see this funny-looking girl in the window!" Sure enough, another bird would come back and if they flew into a tree I'd say, "They are hiding because they think you look so goofy." Then I'd say, "Oh wait, they want to come and get a closer look. Oh look, here come more. They think you look funny!" We would both just giggle, and I would keep the story going about the birds coming to look at her, and she just loved it. She would get so excited to see these birds that she would look forward to her treatments. Natalynn still talks about this today and she is eight years old.

Everyone in life has to climb unexpected mountains that were never wished for nor requested. A lucky few figure out how to enjoy the hike!

Using creativity and fun is only one way to set limits without being demanding or saying "no." The next chapter will teach you other ways to set healthy limits without creating power struggles.

Chapter 3 Key Concepts

1. Setting firm limits does not stifle a child's creativity and inventiveness if the child is taught to be creative within limits. This

concept of creativity and inventiveness within limits is especially important to children with chronic medical conditions.
When they become accustomed to living within limits, they
begin to accept "the way things are" in the real world and in
their world. This is the beginning of accepting their own physical challenges and the opportunities those challenges provide.

2. Telling a child "no" may be a part of limit-setting. When can
   parents safely just say "no"?
   a. When children are young and parents can easily enforce
      the limits they set.
   b. When children respect and love parents enough to do
      what they ask them to do.
   c. Parents can say "no" and set limits on children's behavior
      when children are older if consequences will do the
      teaching.

3. Saying no and "making" kids take good care of their bodies
   may be self-defeating and lead to frustrations in parenting.
   Children tend to rebel in situations other than the three given
   above. Thus, the goal is to develop children who are self-aware
   and have self-control.

4. As children grow up to become husbands, wives, and parents
   they must have learned to take care of their own bodies, make
   wise choices, and accept the consequences of their actions.
   Those are the only things that work for successful adults; and
   it is best to start as early as possible, setting as many rules as
   necessary but as few as possible. Self-aware children who limit
   themselves appropriately are raised with the four basic Love
   and Logic Principles of building self-concept, sharing control,
   showing empathy before consequences, and sharing the think-

ing/problem solving. Start by being a Consultant Parent and giving choices as early in the child's life as possible.

5. Introducing creativity and fun also helps children accept limits. The attitude and perceptions of the parents rub off on their children. The examples in the chapter illustrate creative parents encouraging their children.

Chapter 4

No More "No!" Avoiding Power Struggles and Arguments

The thing I hate about an argument is
that it always interrupts a discussion.
—G. K. Chesterton (1874-1936)

Everyone knows that control battles and power struggles occur between children and their parents. However, your chronically ill child probably has many good reasons for engaging in more than the usual number of power struggles:

♥ Illness and chronic pain lead all of us to be more difficult to be around. People don't naturally become sweeter when they are hurting, worried, or scared.

♥ Chronically ill children forced into self-care

regimens, hospitalizations, and treatments show their need for control at times by becoming demanding.

♥ These children often can't participate in options available to other kids so, "It's just not fair!"

♥ When treatment regimens are absolutely necessary and medication routines are essential, it is understandable *parents become more demanding. Human nature says that when one demands, the other resists!*

So, given that power struggles are a fact of life and given that parents need to set firm limits even with sick kids, what can parents do to avoid big battles when limits are set? Love and Logic gives us several excellent tools to set firm limits in a loving way that minimizes and/or avoids power struggles. This chapter will cover these tools in detail and apply them to parenting kids with chronic illnesses and medical conditions. But before we start our discussion about power struggles, let's first clarify what power struggles aren't. Don't mistake a child's protest for back talk or defiance.

We all have the right to protest. In fact, the right to protest is protected in America and we need to protect it in our families too. Chat rooms are filled with parental concerns about a child's complaining attitude about doing medical treatments even as the child complies. It is almost as if some parents expect their child to be happy about taking the time out of his or her busy life to deal with medical issues. Children are as happy about doing medical treatments as their parents are about paying taxes and they often handle it the same way: with protest and compliance. The point is: Actions speak louder than words. When children mumble or complain about their treatments but go ahead and check their blood, take their shots, or hook up the breathing apparatus, they are often just asking for a bit of empathetic understanding. A wise parent responds with, "I know you don't like it honey. I understand that and I appreciate your doing it." Telling the child to quit complaining or commenting about their "poor attitude" is as effective as the government saying, "Pay your taxes happily." Sometimes when we hear parents complaining that their child complains, we can't help but wonder if the child is modeling what they see and the parent doesn't like looking in the mirror! This is not to imply that parents need to put up with chronic, loud, obnoxious complaining and whining. But occasional protest is to be expected.

So, what can parents do when their child crosses the line from protest with compliance to resisting a request with chronic arguing, whining, and complaining? Love and Logic teaches a very effective skill, the use of one-liners, for neutralizing arguments. This technique is taught early in Love and Logic classes because when parents start to change their parenting style, they can generally expect both arguments and resistance to the changes. The one-liner skill will help you implement those changes without raising your blood pressure, or your voice.

Master the One-Liner

The first step to neutralize arguing is: "Go brain dead." When parents realize they don't always need to directly address the child's complaints or arguments, it becomes easier not to think too much about what the child is saying. Why is this helpful? Because parents can easily get pulled into nonsensical dialogue by provocative, demanding, blaming, tattling, or run-of-the-mill obnoxious statements made by their children. Kids know exactly what buttons to push and they sure don't hesitate to push them! They especially seem to know that medical issues will push parental buttons faster than just about anything else. Usually the unhappy dialogue takes place when parents attempt to explain, cajole, defend, and clarify their own position. All such unwise responses invite a comeback from the child.

Some unhappy examples:

> *Child*: "If you loved me you wouldn't make me go to the hospital on field day."
> *Incorrect Response*: "I love you honey, but that's the only day the doctor could see you."

> *Child*: "I don't see why I have to take my treatment every day."
> *Incorrect Response*: "Ricky, we've discussed over and over how important your treatments are."

> *Child*: "Juliet keeps making fun of my headscarf."
> *Incorrect Response*: "Joyce, I'm tired of your tattling."

> *Child*: "You are always telling me what to do!"
> *Incorrect Response*: "Honey, that's because you need to do things other kids don't have to do. You just have to start understanding that."

The second step is: "Softly repeat a one-liner." The advantage of one-liners is that they accept the child's statement but leave no room for an argument or comeback. The disadvantage of one-liners is that they can be used in place of real dialogue. One-liners should not be used with a kid who wants a discussion. They should be used with a kid who is being obnoxious, demanding, or whiny, particularly if this behavior is repetitive. Let us see how the above responses could be handled with a one-liner that: (1) recognizes the child's feelings, (2) doesn't try to explain, and (3) leaves no room for an argument:

> *Child*: "If you loved me, you wouldn't make me go to the hospital on field day."
> *Correct Response*: "I'm sorry you feel that way."

Child: "I don't see why I have to take my treatment every day."
Correct Response: "It is hard to understand, isn't it?"

Child: "Juliet keeps making fun of my headscarf."
Correct Response: "That is a bummer."

Child: "You are always telling me what to do!"
Correct Response: "Seems that way, doesn't it?"

Some other commonly used one-liners are:
- ❤ "I know."
- ❤ "How sad."
- ❤ "Nice try."
- ❤ "I'll be glad to listen when your voice sounds calm like mine."
- ❤ "Probably so."
- ❤ "What did I say?"
- ❤ "What did the doctor say?"
- ❤ "I love you too much to argue."
- ❤ "(Kid says: "But why?") Response: "Why do you think?"

If the child continues to argue or whine, then softly repeat the same one-liner over and over. Most kids eventually get the message that arguing with you gets them nowhere! They shake their heads at this crazy parent and leave the room. If not, then the adult should calmly leave the room.

Remember that one-liners are to be used when kids question the obvious or are being obnoxious, negative, argumentative, demanding, whining, or complaining. Such statements would not be appropriate as responses to a sweet, respectful child or a loving spouse! There can be a dismissive edge to one-liners, so use them only in the right place at the right time. Let's see how this works:

Jacob

Jacob, an eight-year-old with CF, questioned the need for breathing treatments with the pulmonologist who patiently explained that breathing treatments on a daily basis would keep his lungs clean, just as brushing his teeth everyday keeps his teeth clean. "Do you want cavities in your teeth?" the doctor asked. "No," he replied. "Do you want cavities in your lungs?" "NO!" he replied. Mom thought the issue was handled very well. Jacob even took home an age-appropriate book about keeping his lungs healthy.

At home, Mom asked Jacob, "Would you like to do your breathing treatments before dinner or after dinner?" Jacob rolled his eyes and started arguing and whining: "But, Mom! Why do I have to do them?" "What did the doctor say?" "Well, I still don't wanna do them!" "I know, sweetheart, but what did the doctor say?" "This really stinks!" "I know, but what did the doctor say?" "Fine!!! I'll do 'em now just to get them over with." "Good idea! Would you like to play a computer game or checkers?"

Be aware of your body language, tone of voice, and facial expressions as you deliver your one-liner. This technique will only work when delivered calmly and without sarcasm or frustration. Practicing your one-liner in front of a mirror will help. Pick your favorites, practice them, perfect them, and stick with it!

Left unchecked, arguments and back talk can escalate into real power struggles. Wouldn't it be much easier to avoid them in the first place? Using choices, enforceable statements, and thinking words will help stop control battles before they even start. Let's learn about these important tools.

The Magic of Choices

Using *choices* is an excellent way to share control with our kids in ways that please both child and parent. It avoids power struggles and allows us to set limits. When we give lots of little choices as often as possible, we build up a "savings account" of shared control that can be withdrawn when it's really needed — like when the child has no real choice about certain medical procedures. When we give lots of choices in nonmedical areas of life, the resulting sense of shared control transfers over to the medical issues as well. Love and Logic's guidelines for sharing control through choices are as follows:

- ♥ Give choices *before* resistance, not after.
- ♥ For each choice give options that will be acceptable to you — and the fewer the better.
- ♥ If your child doesn't choose within ten seconds, you decide.
- ♥ Only give choices that are compatible with your value system.
- ♥ Never give a choice unless you are willing to allow the child to live with the consequences of his/her bad choice.

Love and Logic examples of choices for kids with medical issues:

- ♥ "Would you like your shot in your left or right arm?"
- ♥ "Are you going to do your nebulizer this morning or after school?"
- ♥ "Will you have your labs done by tomorrow or do you need an extra day to get them done?"
- ♥ "Are you having broccoli or carrots as your vegetable tonight?"
- ♥ "Are you going to re-wrap your bandages first or brush your teeth first?"
- ♥ "Will you be home at 10 p.m. or do you need an extra half hour with your friends?"
- ♥ "Are you guys going to stop bickering or would you rather pay me to listen to it?"

Here are some additional phrases for giving choices:
- ♥ "Would you rather ___ or ___?"
- ♥ "You can either ___ or ___."
- ♥ "Feel free to ___ or ___."
- ♥ "Are you going to ___ or ___?"
- ♥ "Will you be ___ or ___?"
- ♥ "Do you plan to ___ or ___?"

Choose Your Words Wisely with Thinking Words

Parents of kids with chronic medical conditions often have a hard time discerning between situations in which they do or do not have control. Parents may like to think they have control over medication compliance. When children don't comply, parents can feel out of control! The reality is, we only have control of one person — ourselves. We really can't "make" anybody do anything.

So how do parents set limits without bossing, nagging, lecturing, warning, punishing, etc? The key is to use *thinking words* instead of *fighting words*. Thinking words allow parents to set limits on children's behavior without telling them what they have to do. There is an implied choice for the child, which naturally minimizes power struggles.

Fighting words include:
- ♥ telling the child what to do
- ♥ telling the child what you will not allow
- ♥ telling the child what you won't do for them

Thinking words include:
- ♥ telling a child when he/she can do something
- ♥ telling the child the conditions under which the adult will do something
- ♥ describing the choices a child has
- ♥ telling the child what you will do for them

Fighting words: "Get those medical treatments done right now!"
Thinking words: "You are welcome to go outside when your treatments are done."

Fighting words: "You're not having second helpings of those fattening potatoes."
Thinking words: "Feel free to have as many helpings of carrots or beans as you want."

Fighting words: "I'm not driving you to the party because your blood sugar is too high."
Thinking words: "I'll drive you to the party as soon as your blood sugar levels are back down."

When dealing with chronically ill children who can understandably be resistant to the demands life has placed upon them, wise parents will emphasize to their child what they themselves are willing to do, and what they themselves believe, rather than what the child must do and what the child must believe. *Aggressive people tell others where to go, what to do, and how to think. Assertive people tell other people where they themselves stand, what they think, and what they are willing to do.* The first group almost always invites control battles, while the second group invites respect. When a mom tells her child the breathing treatment has to be finished before she leaves, it is unenforceable. She is telling her child what the child must do. However, if mom says, "I am leaving for the mall at six o'clock. If your treatment is completed, I'll be glad to bring you along and we can stop by the ice-cream parlor." That's enforceable! *Enforceable statements* are thinking words. They provide a powerful way for parents to take good care of themselves, set limits, and help kids learn to solve their own problems.

The use of enforceable statements encourages children to make wise choices. Instead of telling children what they have to do, we tell them what we are willing to do. The happiest people are those who take care of themselves. When they say what they are willing to do, they set a model for others. Using enforceable statements and taking an assertive posture is bound up in setting the right example. They all flow together. Common enforceable statements begin with:

- ♥ I'll be giving ...
- ♥ I'll be happy to...
- ♥ Feel free to ...
- ♥ I'll be glad to ...

Table 4.1 on the opposite page displays some ideas for the use of enforceable statements for medical issues.

Correct consequences are always enforceable; threats often are not. Understandably, parents feel that when they warn or threaten their kids they are taking good care of their child. Isn't it nicer (and easier) to just state a personal fact? Do any of these examples sound somewhat familiar?

- ♥ "If you don't pick up your dirty bandages, I'm just not going to help you with your dressing in the future!" (Notice this is said as the parent knows full well she will need to continue to help with the dressings in the future!)
- ♥ "If this bickering and fighting continues, I'm going to ask you guys to leave the living room."
- ♥ "If you keep bugging me for new crutches, you can bet I'm not going to buy them."
- ♥ "That's one, that's two, that's two and a half..."

There are four major problems with warnings and threats:

1. We often relent and teach our kids we don't mean what we say.
2. Threats back us into a corner because we have to carry them out or look like complete wimps if we don't.
3. When warnings are given, children generally know they can

Table 4.1 **Sample Enforceable Statements**

Ineffective Technique	Effective Technique
Get your inhaler and backpack ready.	I'm happy to go as soon as your inhaler and backpack are ready.
Stop banging your brother with your cast!	I only play chauffer to kids who don't bang others with their cast.
Quit being mean to your sister. I mean it!	My mouth doesn't respond when my ears hear snippy comments about your sister's condition.
I'm sick and tired of your complaining.	I drive when the company I'm driving with doesn't complain about their check-ups.
No TV until your treatments are done!	I am happy to turn on the TV when your treatments are done.
You need to take your insulin shot before you eat.	I'll serve dinner when you have finished your shot.
Make sure you bring your enzymes with you.	I am happy to take you places when I don't have to worry about your stomach cramps.
You can't go until you finish your IV meds.	You're welcome to leave as soon as your meds are done.
Watch that attitude with the doctor!	If all goes well with Dr. Anderson, I'll probably feel so relaxed I'll want to take us to a movie!

act up, act out, and act obnoxious, at least up to the point that the warning is given.

4. Warnings and threats may invite rebellion, particularly when parents word their threat or warning with, "Am I going to have to..." or "Are you going to make me..." Such statements simply recognize that the child has absolute control of the situation.

The truism "threats and warnings invite misbehavior" is clarified by the following: If we knew we would always get one warning each year for speeding before we received a ticket, wouldn't we drive like lightning until that warning was received? Most of us would obey the speed limit only after we received our warning for the year. When we became eligible for a "new warning," would we still be as careful to observe the speed limit? Probably not. It's human nature to "push it to the limit." Our kids do that, too.

Instead of using threats and warnings, parents can solve many problems and set limits by doing one of three things:

1. Remove the offending object:
   - "Paul, honey, I know you can't find your cane. I took it away because I was feeling hassled by your threats to hit Susan with it."

2. Remove the child:
   - "Jerry, I have decided not to take you with me this time because you caused such a problem when you were snapping your Ace bandage at your sister on the last trip."
   - "Guys, please go outside to resolve your argument. Thank you."

3. Remove the parent:
   - "I'm happy to make dinner when this mess is picked up. I'll be reading in my room until then."
   - "It's hard for me to stay in the room when you are having such a fit with the lab tech, so I'll just step outside until you are done with the blood draw."

If the "offending object" is a two-year-old having a tantrum on the floor, the parent can quietly leave the room.

Note that all of these ways of setting limits basically involve the parents taking good care of themselves.

In summary, great parents:
- ♥ Simply, quietly, and with respect take good care of themselves.
- ♥ Avoid threats and warnings.

♥ Take action when needed. They describe the limit once and follow through with actions instead of words.

Say It with Consequences

Love and Logic teaches that taking action is imposing a logical consequence. In Chapter 2 we learned the guidelines for natural and imposed logical consequences, which lead to "experiences" that are enforceable by parents. Natural consequences simply occur following a child's (mis)behavior, and allow parents to show empathy, to counsel, and to build an even stronger parent/child bond. Imposed consequences are generally accepted if they fit the "crime" and when parents lead with empathy. When dealing with medical compliance issues, imposed consequences may be more heavily relied upon when the natural consequences are too severe.

Logical consequences are a great way to avoid power struggles, especially appropriate natural consequences. One mom told the story of how her eight-year-old son loaded up his swim bag with 15 heavy dive torpedoes. She never said a word but then gave him lots of empathy as he carried the heavy bag by himself for two blocks to the pool. Now, he only carries two in his bag. She said, "If I would have told him to pack only two, I would have gotten a battle. I never said a word so we never got into a power struggle. I love it!"

In Love and Logic workshops, people often ask, "What is the difference between consequences and punishment?" Both consequences and punishment may involve parents taking exactly the same action; however, the parental attitude is very different and that makes all the difference in the world. The parental attitude in punishment is one of anger, frustration, severity, and sternness. The parental attitude in imposing consequences is one of empathy.

> *Punishment*: "Stop your whining and complaining about the doctor. That's it! No game tomorrow!"
> *Consequences*: "Gosh, Susie, this is really a bummer. I

won't be driving you to the game tonight because of the way you acted when I drove you to the doctor's office yesterday."

Punishment: "Paul, you make me so mad! Why can't you take your medicine without arguing? You're grounded!"
Consequences: "Oh, Paul, this is so sad. I am so worn out from arguing over your medicine I can't get off the couch to take you to Bill's big birthday bash."

Children who experience logical consequences are automatically forced into the problem-solving and decision-making process. They learn they are capable of making decisions. Children who experience logical consequences learn they are in charge of their own destiny. Good decisions leave us feeling good. Poor decisions leave us hurting.

Table 4.2 on the next page is taken from a *Love and Logic Workbook*. It shows the differences between logical consequences and punishment.

The Energy Drain Technique

One useful and versatile method of justifying the imposition of a logical and natural consequence is the delightful "energy drain" routine, first used by a foster parent in Dr. Cline's program. The annoying misbehavior of children makes life less pleasant for adults and disturbs the tranquility of the interpersonal environment or another person's psyche. In other words, misbehavior drains the energy of others!

We have emphasized the importance of being assertive and setting a model by taking good care of yourself. "Energy drain" is a powerful way of taking good care of ourselves by focusing most directly on our feelings and responses, rather than the child's misbehavior. One beautiful side-benefit to the energy drain routine is

Table 4.2 **Logical Consequences vs. Punishment**

Logical Consequences	Punishment
Offer an opportunity for the child to be involved in decision making.	The adult makes the decisions.
Allow a child to hurt from the inside out.	Child hurts from the outside in.
Child has no opportunity to displace his/her anger or hurt.	Adult provides the opportunity for the child to be angry and resentful, rather than working toward a solution.
Child has opportunity to develop a new plan of reacting or acting.	Child pays for his/her past deed.
Child does his/her own judging.	Adult is the judge.
Child sees the adult modeling problem-solving techniques.	Child feels the imposition of power (and learns to use power).
Adult voice is helpful and friendly.	Adult displays anger.
Child learns about the real world of consequences, cause/effect.	Child learns about the imposition of power.

that it avoids the nonproductive discussion that sometimes follows when a child says, "What did I do?" Again, when we talk about ourselves, it's unarguable. Let's look at an example:

Beth

On the verge of misbehavior all day, and now, in a misdirected attempt to gain attention, Beth loudly whines, "Ow, ow, ow," every time she unsuccessfully attempts to prick her finger with her glucose lancet. No kid ever had that much trouble with a finger prick.

"Beth, will you please go to the other room."

(Asking the obvious, and ready to argue about her behavior.) "Why, what did I do?"

"I'm not really sure, honey, but I notice I'm feeling an energy drain."

"But what did I do?!"

"Whatever it was, it has definitely drained my energy. And in fact, I feel my energy draining right now. I think it would work out better for you if you didn't drain any more of my energy. Just a thought."

"Oh, OK." (Beth stomps off to her room.)

When a parent's energy has been drained, there are innumerable ways kids can replace the energy. Energy replacement options include: mopping the kitchen floor, cleaning the garage, watching a younger sibling, preparing dinner, paying for a leisurely latte at Starbucks, etc. The ways to replace energy are only limited by a parent's imagination!

Although misbehavior drains energy, it is obviously more enjoyable when the child's great behavior puts energy back into the system. With good behavior, parents may feel so energized they decide to buy ice cream cones, pay for a movie, and stay up a little later reading extra bedtime stories. It is always to the kid's benefit to put energy into the system!

"Wow, you kids behaved so nicely today, I have lots of extra energy! Let's go see a movie tonight."

Problem Solve Together

Power struggles can be avoided by using the Mutual Problem Solving model which was thoroughly discussed in Chapter 2 as Love and Logic Principle 4: Share the Thinking and Problem Solving. Throughout this book we discuss how, when children have problems, it is very easy for the adults to give answers, become frustrated with noncompliance, and to get angry about their behavior, all of which invite power struggles. Mutual problem solving is simply a structured way of discussing choices and consequences with empathy and encouragement. Using the communication models for mutual problem solving can help prevent power struggles.

Encourage Responsibility

When children make wise decisions for themselves, take responsibility for their care, and are knowledgeable about their own health issues, control battles are much less likely to take place. Throughout this program we have emphasized the importance of:

- ♥ Helping children handle their own healthcare issues.
- ♥ Relating to children with compassion, love, hope, and concern, but not rescue.
- ♥ Responding with sadness for them rather than frustration and anger at them when they make poor health decisions.

The following remarkable account illustrates all the issues we have been discussing: choices, consequences with empathy, and encouragement. Sometimes the choices children are faced with aren't choices with a little "c" like carrots or broccoli, but choices with a big "C" as in life and death, like Laura.

Laura Scott Ferris is currently in her thirties. Even with a double lung transplant and diabetic retinopathy (which causes her blindness), she vibrates strength and resilience. Like Jack Kennedy, Christopher Reeve, Franklin Roosevelt, and so many others we could name, Laura is inspiring as she copes with chronic illness. Like the others, she would be remarkable, regardless of her health issues; and like the others, she is more than a survivor. She is a person who facilitates the success of others; she inspires hope in us all and is a flourishing woman who has lived a fulfilling and loving life.

Laura has authored a wonderful book called *For the Love of Life* and has given hope to audiences all around the United States. Success is always multidimensional and is often facilitated by loving people who form a trusted support group. It helps that Laura has a loving mother, husband, and close friends. But when we look at the successful lives of individuals who have coped successfully with chronic illness, one thing stands out. They are motivated, responsible people with a purpose!

Laura was not always motivated and responsible. There was a time, long ago, when Foster met Laura with her wonderful mother, MaryJane Eddy-Scott. At the time, Laura was a fairly resistant, non-compliant 11-year-old, who refused to take her medication. MaryJane brought her daughter to Foster's clinic because, after seeing a number of other therapists, Laura still refused to take her medication. Laura's pediatrician had warned her mother, "The next time we have to put Laura in a mist tent, we could lose her."

Foster recounts the therapy sessions with Laura:

Laura

Laura, with severe symptoms caused by cystic fibrosis, needed postural drainage every day. She was taking medication for her digestive system and lungs as well as medication to control the side-effects of the pulmonary medication. All in all, Laura was taking about 40 pills a day, and she decided she would quit. When I first saw Laura's mother, MaryJane, she was understandably weeping. I remember asking her, "Really, MaryJane, whose problem is this, ultimately?" She replied that she knew it was Laura's problem; however Laura was one of two beloved daughters, and her refusal to take medicine had caused understandable turmoil and frustration. I talked with MaryJane about laying all of the responsibility for taking care of herself on Laura's shoulders. I talked with her about giving Laura the decision to live or die. We discussed the fact that this could not be a "false choice" but had to be a real choice in order to give Laura the ultimate responsibility for her life. I explained that if this path was decided upon, I had some concern Laura might choose to die. And, this wonderful mother gave empathy and consequences a "blank check," for she replied, "Dr. Cline, Laura is going to die if things keep going the way they are. If you feel there is a chance of turning things around, even if she might die, let's take the risk."

MaryJane and I worked through ideas about how to "come through" with Laura. When Laura joined us, I asked her if she had seen other therapists before and she assured me she had. I asked her if she thought I had some things to say to her. She said she was sure I did. I responded that I had nothing to say to her, but her wise mother had been doing a good deal of thinking and she did have some things to say to her.

This wonderful mother laid it on the line:

"Laura, I want to apologize to you. In some ways I think I haven't been a very good mother because I have been messing around with whether or not you live or die. I have been thinking, and I realize that every 11-year-old has to decide for themselves if they are going to live or die. I want you to know I love you so much, if you do decide to die, I would put flowers on your grave every week."

Although this may sound harsh, what this mother was really saying is, "I can handle talking about very tough things. I can set the model of acceptance. By talking calmly about the choices, I am offering you full responsibility. By not becoming frustrated, upset, and angry, I can show you no longer control my emotions but you are in full control of yourself."

When MaryJane said this to her daughter, Laura's eyes became very big. In fact, they were like saucers. She could hardly believe her mother was talking like this.

Then it was my turn to talk with Laura. I simply told Laura she seemed like a very nice person, however, due to my hectic schedule, I would not have time to visit the cemetery very much. In fact, I would be lucky if I got out to the cemetery at all. However, barring a need to be at a workshop or something important, I would plan to attend her funeral. Ending with that, the mother and daughter left. The session with Laura probably took no more than 15 minutes.

Dr. Cline saw Laura and her mother the following week and at that time recorded the following conversation on a portable dictating machine:

Dr. Cline: OK, I'm here with Laura today. And we are going to have a "man-on-the-street" interview today and here in the studio with me is...

Laura: Laura....

Dr. Cline: Right and today we're going to talk about illness in children and medication and who should be responsible for the medication. Okay? I also have Laura's mother, MaryJane, with me. The first thing I wanted to ask you about, Laura, is the change in the way medicine has been handled in your home. Has there been a change?

Laura: Uh huh...

Dr. Cline: And do you want to tell our listening audience how change has come about and who is responsible for your medication right now?

Laura: I am responsible for my medication right now.

> *Dr. Cline*: Was that more your mother's idea or was that more your idea?
>
> *Laura*: It was my mom's idea because she got tired of reminding me to take my medication all the time.
>
> *Dr. Cline*: Well, do you like the new method better or do you like the old method better?
>
> *Laura*: I like the new method better.
>
> *Dr. Cline*: Why is that?
>
> *Laura*: 'Cause now I get to decide for myself whether or not I'd rather live or I'd rather die.
>
> *Dr. Cline*: And do you have it figured out you'd rather live than die?
>
> *Laura*: (with pride) Yes.

Isn't that something! Here is a little girl, on death's doorstep because she refused to take her medication, and a week later she is proudly taking responsibility for herself and making a conscious decision to live.

This example raises a very difficult problem. How much responsibility is "too much?" In the above case, Laura could just have easily chosen to die. It wasn't too difficult to give Laura the choice of life or death in this case, because she was already making the choice for death by her refusal to care for herself. Laura's mother had been accustomed to making Laura's choices for her for many years and it had just not worked out.

What a difficult issue! In general, we give children choices for two reasons:

1. We can give them a choice as a manipulation, and when they make the wrong choice, refuse to honor it. That method may work a few times as long as the child makes the choice we wish. But it's not long before they catch on that the whole choice routine is basically a lie, the parent/child bond is negatively impacted, and the situation worsens.

2. Or, we can give children a choice because that is the way the

real world operates; because most people, given freedom, make good choices most of the time; because we believe in our child's ability to cope if they make the wrong choice; and because if they make the wrong choice their life and limb are not usually in danger.

Let's be honest: *No parent can give children choices if the parent is unwilling to allow the child the consequences of the poor choices.* And when a wrong choice endangers life or limb, as it did in Laura's situation, then most parents, understandably, are unable to truly allow their children the freedom of choice. The choice itself then becomes another power struggle and grounds for manipulation leading to a vicious cycle that, in the case of children with serious medical issues, could have life-and-death ramifications.

Even with non-life-and-limb choices, some parents are unable to let go of their illusion of control and allow their child to have free will. "Rescuers" or "Helicopter Parents" have a hard time giving their children choices. It goes against their nature because they need to be needed rather than taking the healthy stance of wanting to be wanted. Rescuers like to have people dependent upon them because being needed can provide them with a sense of purpose and meaning. However, they are crippling the very people they are rescuing and when things don't work out as planned they often become guilt-provoking martyrs with their too-familiar mantra being: "Don't I do everything for you? Why do you treat me this way?"

Figure 4.1 on the opposite page compares the difference between giving a child true freedom of choice versus giving a choice as a manipulation.

Figure 4.1 **Power Struggle Paradigm**

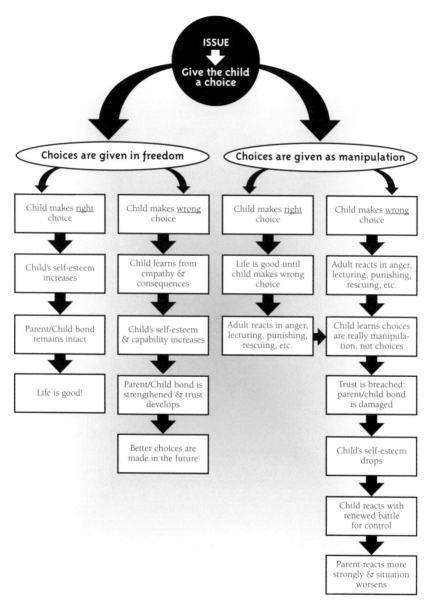

Jose learns to make wise choices:

Jose

Jose, a 13-year-old boy with epilepsy, takes medication three times a day to control his seizures. His mom, Gloria, had been making sure he took his meds on schedule since he was diagnosed as a young child. She came to us frustrated at Jose's lack of responsibility in remembering to take his meds. After determining that missing a dose did not have life-threatening implications, we advised her to let Jose know she would be turning over full responsibility to him to manage the afternoon dose of his meds, and that she knew he could handle it just fine. When Jose had a mild seizure at school because he forgot to take his medication and was embarrassed by the attention (the paramedics were called by the concerned school administrator), his mother responded with empathy and consequences.

Jose had rightly expected particular toys for Christmas. His mom helped him figure out which ones he could do without to help pay the paramedic bill. It turned out to be an excellent learning experience! Jose turned to his mother for ideas on how "he could better remember to take his meds." They had fun brainstorming good ideas and silly ideas alike (pasting a sticky note on his forehead was one discarded option), and their bond was strengthened. His mom said in a note, "Jose may not yet be absolutely perfect about taking his meds right on the dot, but he sure takes it seriously now and I don't think he has skipped a dose since then. The best part of it is he comes to me now for brainstorming sessions about other issues he has at school and with friends. I think this experience has made us better friends."

Julia fails to learn to make wise choices:

Julia

Julia, 16, has a severe case of irritable bowel syndrome (IBS). If she doesn't watch her diet, stress level, and general health carefully, she could be bedridden for days with a very painful "episode." Her parents, who had already missed a great deal of work caring for her when she was sick, were frustrated with her apparent lack of concern about her diet. She would respond for a while, as long as Mom or Dad prepared her meals or nagged her; but then life would get busy and she would slip into a "fast-food lifestyle" and end up in agony at home for a few days, disrupting the whole family, including her siblings. Mom and Dad attended a Love and Logic conference and loved the concepts of choices, responsibility, etc. They decided to "go for the gold" and lay Julia's health issues squarely on her shoulders. They let Julia know "the new plan" and gave her the freedom and resources to manage her own diet at lunchtime.

For a while Julia did okay and things went along just fine. Her parents thought, "Wow! This choice thing really works!" and everyone was happy with the new arrangement — that is, until Julia got stressed out with finals and careless with her lunch plans. She became very sick and missed several days of school, including some finals, which added to her stress. Mom had to miss several days of work caring for her and they were right back to their old pattern. Mom feared for her job and was very angry. She yelled at Julia, grounded her for two weeks, and was not very pleasant to be around during those sick days. Dad gave Julia a "real good talking to" and Julia's siblings were upset about missing some important activities. One night, the whole family erupted in an uproar of anger and frustration directed at Julia and her careless attitude. Once again, the whole family circled around her, gave her lots of negative attention, and took care of her while she was sick. There were no logical consequences for Julia, only predictable punishment.

When Julia recovered, she found her lunchbox sitting on the counter waiting for her each morning. Life was back to normal. Her parents had decided that "choices just don't work for us" and felt very frustrated and hopeless. At the same time, they continued to rescue Julia and control her diet. Julia felt pretty hopeless herself, calling herself an irresponsible loser and wondering if she would ever be able to take care of herself.

So, what went wrong?

1. Julia's parents reacted to Julia's mistake with anger, frustration, and rescue.
2. The whole family punished her with their anger, and she was grounded rather than being allowed to suffer the logical consequences of her bad choices.
3. Julia's parents disrupted their lives to rescue Julie and reacted to her mistake based on the same old scripts.
4. Her parents gave up on her and took back the small amount of control they had given her.

What could have made this experience an effective learning opportunity for Julia?

1. When Julia became sick, her parents could have reacted with genuine sorrow and empathy for her suffering rather than anger and frustration.
2. Julia's parents should have made a plan to successfully handle a potential, and likely, poor choice by Julia. She is old enough to stay home alone with some creativity around getting her needs met for care, such as having a neighbor check in on her to make sure she has food and drink readily available or hiring someone to spend part of the day with her at Julia's expense.
3. Julia herself could come up with the solution to her problem once the parents laid it back on her shoulders by saying, "Sweetheart, we can't miss work anymore, so you'll need to figure out how you can get your needs met while we are at work. We are happy to brainstorm ideas with you if you'd like. Let us know your plan by the end of today or we'll take care of it ourselves." Of course, the parents would be prepared to do so by hiring someone at Julia's expense.
4. The siblings need not have missed their activities. Once again, Julia could have paid for a taxi service to a game, etc.
5. All of these options could have been delivered to Julia in a calm, caring manner.

In summary, we need to make something very clear here. Are we saying every child is able to handle *all* of the responsibility for his or her severe illness? Of course not. However, we *are* saying many children can be much more responsible than their parents realize! And the more responsible the children are in coping and handling their medication and illness, the more responsible they are likely to be as human beings in general. It works the other way as well; when children are responsible in general, then they are more responsible in handling their medication and illness.

Chapter 4 Key Concepts

1. There are many reasons kids with chronic illnesses engage in power struggles with the significant adults in their lives.
   - Those who are ill or experience chronic pain can be more difficult to be around.
   - The lack of control caused by illness causes kids to show their need for control at times by being demanding themselves.
   - The children can't enjoy a lot of the freedoms and options available to other kids, so "It's just not fair!"
   - Parents often become more demanding when treatment regimens are absolutely necessary. Human nature says that when one demands, the other resists!

2. Effective tools help avoid these ultimately unconquerable battles for control and help parents set limits that avoid power struggles. One-liners neutralize arguing because they accept the child's nonsensical and frustrating dialogue but leave no room for an argument or comeback. One-liners should never be used in place of meaningful discussion but are used to gently "shut down" a negative, argumentative, demanding child.

3. Giving a child lots of small choices when things are going well builds up a savings account of control that can be withdrawn when really needed.

4. Thinking Words and Enforceable Statements allow parents to set limits on their children's behavior, without telling them what they must do. There is an implied choice for the child, which naturally minimizes power struggles.

5. Natural and imposed logical consequences lead to experiences that are enforceable. Threats often are not. Natural conse-

quences simply occur following a child's (mis)behavior. Hopefully, an ill child's poor decisions have natural consequences, for then parents cannot be blamed or resented. Natural consequences allow parents to show empathy, to counsel, and to build an even stronger parent/child bond. Imposed consequences are generally accepted if they "fit the crime" and when parents lead with empathy. When dealing with medical compliance issues, imposed consequences may be more heavily relied upon because the natural consequences are often too severe to allow to occur.

6. A common way to impose consequences that make sense is to use the "my energy is being drained" technique. Giving frequent warnings is never as effective as simply allowing or imposing the consequence directly and quietly, but with empathy.

7. Mutual problem solving is a structured way of discussing choices and consequences with empathy and encouragement.

8. When children make wise decisions for themselves, take responsibility for their care, and are knowledgeable about their own health issues, control battles are much less likely to take place.

Chapter 5

From the Inside Out: How Children Really Learn

Leadership is based on inspiration,
not domination; on cooperation, not intimidation.
—William Arthur Wood

All we have said so far about parenting, good management, good government, and wise counseling are simply subsets, explorations, expansions, and explanations of the five great Es of Love and Logic: Example, Experience, Empathy, Expectation, and Encouragement. Why is all of leadership and life wrapped up in these five?

- ♥ They cannot be forced.
- ♥ They can only be offered from the outside.
- ♥ They are the major aspects of all interpersonal exchanges.

Our children learn by the example we set, the experiences we allow, the empathy we demonstrate, and the expectations we show.

Set the Example

An unknown author once said, "People are changed, not by coercion or intimidation, but by example." This can be translated into: "Wise parents model the behavior they want from their children." Dads who sink toilet paper ships in the toilet, and moms who have fun fixing dinner, enjoy drawing architectural plans, mowing, and sewing all set an example for their kids. In front of the kids, everyone has fun doing his or her job. When an ill child is present, parents are afforded even more opportunities for setting an example.

♥ Jimmy had to have one arm amputated after a severe streptococcal infection. His dad, Henry, often has fun doing things one-handed in front of his son. "I'll race you doing that as a monopod (one-armed)! If you can do it so well one-handed, so can I! But maybe I will never be able to do it quite as well as you do it!"

♥ Cindy takes her daughter Robin with her when she goes for her own blood tests.

♥ Dennis has no medical problem, but he pricks his finger and uses the glucose meter in front of his diabetic son, saying, "I love medical technology. I always wonder how sweet my own blood is. It's interesting to find out! It really helps me keep track of how my body is working. Of course, John, I don't get to keep track of my blood as much as you get to keep track of yours. I guess my blood chemistry just isn't as important as yours right now. But it will be when I get older!"

Allow New Experiences

We need to allow our special children the latitude to make their own decisions whenever possible. Good judgment, self-awareness, self-confidence, and self-reliance grow when children make their own decisions and are allowed to experience the results. Despite the challenges, life still has to be led. Just as wives and husbands may attempt to control a spouse's health decisions, it is understandable parents may believe only they can truly separate their child's "probably shouldn'ts" from the "must nots." With some illnesses, this is a gray area that changes from day to day. The fact is, parents can't live in their children's bodies. Kids often have a better sense of their own capabilities.

♥ Jane notes, "It's one thing for a mother to allow her child to learn by letting her go without a coat. It is an entirely different matter to allow the child not to take her pancreatic enzymes and risk the pain that results. But sometimes that is what it takes. However, I would rather Jenni learn through a medication that prevents stomach cramps than through the medication that keeps her breathing. I believe every mistake can be a learning experience, and that's the thought that has kept me going some days."

♥ Katelin's mother reminisces, "She wanted to play in that state meet so badly but her asthma had been bothering her. I knew the dust on the field could make it harder for her but, you know, she was a bright little 12-year-old. She knew the risks. Some mothers always think they know more about their kid's body than their kid does. But not me; I trust her judgment. She played that game and scored two goals. She had some increased wheezing, but through it all she assured me it was worth it."

♥ A mother tells how her son, despite severe lung damage from CF, jumped motorcycles, competed in stunt-riding, and even rode when he needed an oxygen tank strapped to the bike. The day before her son was hospitalized for the last time, he rode his beloved bike. The mother is so glad she was not over-protective and that she encouraged him to do what he could, while he could. She finds comfort in the fact that her son loved and enjoyed life until the very end.

Demonstrate Empathy

What happens when parents react to their child's mistakes with empathy and understanding, rather than anger and frustration? The child feels encouraged, supported, and learns from mistakes. But there is more! Empathy provides love and respect, even as it locks in the learning experience. As we've discussed previously, empathy is a cornerstone of Love and Logic. Empathy is the "love" in Love and Logic. Rather than reacting to our child's mistakes with anger and frustration, parents are taught to react with empathy before delivering the consequences. Elisabeth Kübler-Ross (1926-2004) was one of the twentieth century's great psychiatrists. She aptly pointed out: "We need to teach the next generation of children from day one that they are responsible for their lives. Mankind's greatest gift, also its greatest curse, is that we have free choice. We can make our choices built from love or from fear." Responding with empathy, rather than anger and frustration, helps children make good choices based on love instead of fear.

When children deal with extensive medical issues, they are bound to have times when they are simply mad, sad, or scared. Empathy, rather than sympathy, is generally the appropriate response, and, of course, apathy is never the correct response. Parents show empathy by focusing on a child's feelings. The only way people know we understand how they feel is to reciprocate the feeling they are expressing. Therefore, it is more effective to say, "I bet it makes you angry to have to go to the hospital to get shots when the other kids are out playing," than to say, "I understand how you feel about taking your shots." It is even more effective when we paraphrase their statement and use a synonym for the feeling word. For instance:

Child's Statement: "I hate having my braces tightened."
Correct Response: "I bet you get really upset when it feels like your whole jaw is being squeezed."

Child's Statement: "John always gets whatever he wants."
Correct Response: "You feel pretty left out when he gets all those toys just because he was in the hospital for three days."

Generally, this method is more effective than sympathy. Sympathy says, "I feel sad, too, when you feel sad." Empathy says, "I feel sad *for you* when you feel so upset." Sympathy allows the other person's feelings to rub off on us; we can become overinvolved with another person's pain. Empathy is the thoughtful understanding of another's feelings. In the case of controlling or blaming children, sympathy can be manipulated to control others. Empathy can't be manipulated, so if your ill child is psychologically healthy, it is safe to be sympathetic, but if your ill child plays victim or tends to manipulate, empathy works best. Empathy can also be applied when events take an unfortunate, unexpected turn, as a mother demonstrates here:

Jeff

Jeff was set on participating with the scouts. They were going rock climbing and I was very concerned. With his condition (hemophilia) I felt it was simply too dangerous. However, he was very persuasive about the safety of the situation. The scoutmaster and Jeff's friends all knew of his condition and wanted him to participate. In fact, they all emphasized how careful they would be. Life has to be lived, so I decided to let him go. Even in those early days, I had to sign massive liability releases. Nowadays, the Scouts might not even risk climbing with a child with hemophilia. Of course, he fell, and his knee joint was soon the size of a softball. The scoutmaster and everybody else were scared stiff. So was Jeff. The hardest thing for me was to keep my mouth shut. I wanted to say, "I told you so." I felt awful, but I decided to focus on his feelings with the empathy you talked about. When I met him there in the ER, I simply held him and told him how sorry I was that his climb had been ruined. Before I could even think of saying he had made a poor choice, Jeff looked at me and said, "You know, Mom, I think other sports are more my style. Just don't force me into rock climbing anymore, promise?" We both laughed and I knew he would never go rock climbing again. He never did.

The mother's response with hugs and humor is packed with loving empathy rather than sympathy. Here are some more examples of sympathetic vs. empathetic responses:

Sympathy: "Oh, Jennifer, I feel so bad about your tummy hurting. You didn't take your enzymes at lunch. Let's go lay down on the couch."
Empathy: "What a bummer. I'd also be frustrated if my tummy hurt so much I couldn't practice."

Sympathy: "I feel so upset when Mrs. Franklin expects your homework to be done while you are in the hospital."
Empathy: "I can appreciate how angry you feel about Mrs. Franklin's expectations."

Sympathy: "I feel so sorry you can't play in the state meet."

Empathy: "Honey, I bet you feel awful about being unable to play."

It's possible for sympathy to border on rescue, which is another danger of overusing sympathy with children. Too much sympathy can provoke a parent to move quickly from sympathy to nagging/lecturing to rescue. Empathy is more likely to help the parent to lovingly keep the problem on the child's shoulders.

Since empathy is a thoughtful understanding of another's feelings, it is helpful to "put ourselves in his or her shoes." Sometimes other adults or older kids can help us see life from our child's perspective. With understanding comes compassion.

And perhaps one of the best things about using empathy with our children is that they learn to be empathetic toward others and themselves.

Show Your Expectations

Wise parents "vibrate out" high but reasonable expectations. The smiles, hope, and love that accompany the expectation will lead most children to try harder whenever they fall short. High expectations given with demands (rather than smiles, hope, and love) result in feelings of inadequacy in a child when he or she does not meet these expectations. And then, of course, the parent-child bond is injured.

Troy

After Troy first had his arm amputated, before we could get the prosthesis, he insisted on going back to school right away. I think he was shocked at how mean some of the kids could be. Nobody wanted him on their team. One kid called him "armclops" (a word play on cyclops). He was always a strong kid but some of those remarks brought him to tears. I was so mad I wanted to go and wring those kids' necks. I wanted to talk to the principal and teachers about helping the other kids become more understanding. I wanted to do something, anything, to make the situation better but I remembered the Love and Logic class.

I remembered our facilitator saying, "Every time we rescue our kids from a situation they could have handled, we weaken them." So, I empathized with him, and discussed ways he might handle it and model coping for other kids who will face problems in the future. We even practiced a few sentences. We decided if someone somewhere had to have an arm amputated, the world was luckier it was him, because he was one of the kids who could handle it. Wow, what a difference it made to his demeanor. When one of the kids made fun of him, he laughed and said he was going to "armclop" him. He even told one kid he could understand why the other kid didn't want him on the team. Then he told me he kidded the boy by saying, "It could be upsetting if I played better with one arm than you do with two. But, I said it to him nicely, kind of like kidding him, Mom, and it worked!"

The interface between protection and high expectations changes as illness and coping abilities fluctuate. Parents should always give their children the "can do" message, as Rebecca Hill shows so eloquently in her writing, *The Need to Fly*:

I am watching my son play in the yard. Our playground is pretty safe with wood chips and padding. My son wears a helmet but I still feel my heart speed up as he climbs the seven-foot tower to get to the slide. "Sage, careful!" I call, in spite of myself. I sit back down next to John, my co-worker and friend. "I just can't do another hospital trip," I sigh.

"Did I ever tell you," he says, "that I used to play with this kid who had hemophilia?"

"Really," I say.

"Yeah, he was really sick. I mean he was in a wheelchair."

"When was this, like the sixties?"

"Yeah, late sixties. I guess the treatments weren't that great back then."

"No," I said. "They weren't."

"Well, anyway, this kid, he was in wheelchair, and he used to just sit on the playground during recess, and just watch everybody else play."

"That's sad."

"Yeah. Eventually, though, we became friends."

"Really?"

"Yeah, and I used to push him in the wheelchair. We'd go really fast, and he'd yell, 'Faster, faster!' And I would go faster; we'd build up so much speed as we crossed the yard."

John was quiet for a moment, smiling at the memory.

He turned back to me. "One day, though, we hit a rock."

"Oh geez," I gasped. "Did he get hurt?"

"Well, he went totally airborne. He was banged up a little, but he was okay. All the teachers came running and they really freaked. He kept saying, 'I'm okay, I'm okay.'"

I sat back and watched my son hanging off the monkey bars.

John continued, "It's like it was worth it to him,

you know? Just that moment of freedom, of going fast. It was worth the risk of getting hurt."

I am taken with the image: a little boy willing to risk pain and medical procedures for just a moment of freedom, and his friend who understands his need to fly.

"Mama!" Sage calls, from the top of the slide. I wave and smile. And I silently resolve to never, ever forget his need to fly.

—© 2006 Rebecca Hill. All Rights Reserved

Offer Encouragement

Of course, parents want to control their children's healthcare issues. When children are in their baby, toddler, and early childhood years, this is obviously appropriate and necessary. However, as the child grows older and parents continue to control the child's healthcare issues and hit resistance (which is absolutely normal), frustration creeps in as parents start to realize they *can't* control their child's responses to their illness but somehow still think they *should*! So, how can parents stop this pattern of power struggles, frustration, and feelings of inadequacy? By turning over the responsibility for healthcare to the child in small, steady increments, starting in the early elementary years. This is where the Love and Logic tools are so helpful. Simple things, like a parent saying, "I bet you are proud of yourself," rather than saying, "I'm proud of you," are easy to learn and are especially helpful when working with chronically ill kids. When parents see the right words modeled, they can quickly learn to use them with their child naturally. These are words that put the problem on the child when he or she is resistant and words that give the child the "glory" when they make good decisions:

- ♥ "I bet you would be unhappy if you have a hard time breathing this afternoon..."
- ♥ "You must be pretty upset with yourself when there's that much wheezing..."

♥ "You must be proud of yourself right now. Gosh, I bet you could blow up a hot-air balloon the way you've taken such good care of your lungs."

Most people intuitively know that one of the key elements in the development of a high self-image is a feeling of accomplishment in a job well done. Therefore, adults naturally concentrate on a child's job and want the child to feel good about it, especially when a child is already struggling with self-image issues because of a disability or illness. The easiest and perhaps most common adult response is to praise children in the belief or hope that they will accept the adult's praise and feel better about themselves or the job. This is understandable because praise works well with very young children and has some positives:

♥ Praising another person makes *us* feel good!
♥ Praising a child is helpful if:
  • The child accepts we have the ability to judge his or her responses.
  • The child *wants* us to feel good.
  • The child is in a receptive frame of mind or mood.

However, praise is a double-edged sword; the very things that make it work cause it to be ineffective with many children.

Seth

At the hospital for a two-week CF "tune-up," Seth is annoyed about having to be there in the first place and is half-heartedly attempting to entertain himself with artwork. The nurse walks up and says, "What a beautiful painting!" Seth replies, "I don't think so!" "Why not?" "The nose is too big." (Now, the judgment of the evaluator is being questioned so the argument begins.) Nurse: "I'm not so sure that's true." Seth: "Well, it is..."

"I don't think so!" "Is too!" "Is not." And so the nurse leaves the room frustrated with her unsuccessful attempt to connect with Seth and Seth is even more irritated about being "stuck" at the hospital.

Praise is built on three assumptions:
1. That the evaluator and those evaluated have a good relationship or at least have mutual respect.
2. That the person being evaluated is in a receptive frame of mind or mood to be evaluated.
3. That the evaluator is in a position to judge the "goodness" of the person or result.

When any of these assumptions is not true, praise falls flat. When children have a poor self-image, praise almost always causes the child to act out. That is, the praising comment does not fit with the child's self-image. The child then acts worse to instruct the adult about the "real situation." And so it is, the doctor says, "This morning was Seth's best morning yet at the hospital, but this afternoon was the worst he's ever had!" If a child is generally very negative but actually did a good job on a blood draw, the encouraging evaluator might say, "Gee, if I handled my blood draw like that, I'd probably feel better about myself than you often seem to... but everyone is different."

Even when a child does a bad job, some adults will make the assumption that praise is called for. I, Foster, remember going once to the park and a father was watching his son fly a model airplane. The plane would crash with great frequency after increasingly short flights. And after each flight the father would exclaim with false joy, "What a great flight." I know the kid had to feel as I did, that:
1. The dad was blind.
2. The dad was lying.
3. The dad really didn't know what a good flight was.
4. The dad assumed the kid was blind.

5. The dad assumed the kid didn't know what a great flight was.

So it is that false praise almost always leads to disrespect.

So what to do? How does one encourage children without praise? Love and Logic teaches that praise and encouragement are very different. Wise parents encourage a high self-image with questions rather than statements. This has the advantage of massively reducing the adult's need for the expression of both joy and disappointment. Therefore, resistant children are unable to control the adult's emotion. The adult emotion shown is *curiosity*, which is satisfied whether the child is doing great or blowing it. In either event the adult can respond, "Gee, that's interesting." Adults can always show pleasure that their curiosity is fulfilled.

> "Um, that's pretty interesting. So, is it your thought
> you'll live a long time?"

The beauty is that this response works, whether children are taking good or poor care of themselves.

Encouragement has several advantages:

- ♥ It makes no assumptions about the relationship. It can be bad, neutral, or good.
- ♥ It does assume that children can judge their own behavior or output and make decisions on how to modify things in the future if necessary.
- ♥ Encouragement always accepts the evaluation of the child — even if the self-evaluation is too harsh.
- ♥ Encouragement accepts (and may explore) the child's responses at face value.

Seth

The situation previously described concerning Seth's artwork is different when encouragement is used. The nurse exclaims with a happy and encouraging voice:

"Wow, what do you think of your picture?" Seth replies, "I don't like it." "Why is that?" "The nose is too big." "Really! How'd that happen?" "I have trouble with noses." "So how will all this turn out?" "Great, 'cause I'm practicing 'em and I'm getting better."

Love and Logic teaches that curiosity and interest almost always trump worry and concern, just as ideas and thoughts trump advice, suggestions, and pleading. Questions give resistant children less adult emotion to manipulate and show curiosity and interest. For example, asking a difficult child, "How do you always manage to remember to take your medicine?" is generally more effective than, "Good job on remembering your medicine."

Table 5.1, on the opposite page, shows the differences between using curiosity and interest, aka encouragement, with children rather than praise.

An effective way to commend your child for an accomplishment is to use descriptive praise as taught by Charles F. Boyd.[5] Descriptive praise focuses on who your children are, and not necessarily on what they do. We describe a child's behavior, personality traits, and character, rather than just his or her accomplishments. For example, instead of saying, "Good job doing your breathing treatments today," we would use the following approach:

- ♥ *Describe what you see.* "Charlie, I notice you are very diligent about doing your breathing treatments on time every day."
- ♥ *Describe how you feel.* "It's such a pleasure not to have to worry about your breathing treatments because I know you have it handled!"
- ♥ *Give a short description of the positive strength.* "That's what I call being responsible and dependable."

As a modified form of praise, this approach does assume a good, respectful relationship with the child and a receptive frame of

Table 5.1 **Praise vs. Encouragement**

Issue	Praise	Encouragement
Location	Good feelings from the outside	Builds good feelings from the inside
Technique	Statements	Questions
Assumes	Child and adult have good relationship Child is in a receptive frame of mind or mood to be evaluated	No assumptions about relationship No assumptions about receptivity or mood
Content	Judgmental	Nonjudgmental
Results when child has a good self-image and likes the adult	Feels good about job and adult	Feels more competent in making decisions Feels good about self
Results when child's self-image is poor or when child is depressed	Discounts by: "He's just trying to make me feel better..." "He doesn't really know me..." (acts out negative behavior to prove how bad he really is)	Feelings toward adult unchanged May be better able to self-evaluate In no case does behavior worsen if asked nonjudgmental questions
Examples	What a great job! You did so well! I'm so proud of you!	How do you think you did? Why is that? How did you figure that out? How do you think you will handle it next time?

mind, but it is helpful at times to give children useful information about their performance, accomplishments, and, most importantly, who they are.

With plenty of encouragement and the judicious use of descriptive praise, you'll find your children glowing from the inside out, rather than needing approval from the outside to feel good about themselves.

Is Criticism Ever Constructive?

This section wouldn't be complete without addressing the opposite of encouragement, which is criticism. Understandably, most parents dealing with the rigors of important medical procedures fall, to some degree, into the criticism trap. With the stakes so high, it is obvious that many medical procedures must be done right. Failure to do so can have life and death consequences. The problem is, criticism damages a child's self-image; it's a "spirit killer." Well-intentioned parents can kill the spirit of the one they love the most, their own child, with constant criticism. Another potential danger is that constant criticism, which borders on nagging, may cause the child to tune-out or rebel. The spoken words, "You'd better watch your blood sugar more carefully" can be said in a loving, demanding, or judgmental way. When our children are not taking good care of their health needs, it's understandable that elements of all three may be present when parents express their concern in such sentences. So, how do parents make sure the child "does it right" when dealing with critical medical procedures without coming across as critical?

An antidote to criticism is asking questions (as we just examined during the discussion of praise vs. encouragement). Couple your question, which shows curiosity and interest, with wording that implies a meaningful possible negative consequence for the child's poor decision. This is usually quite effective. Some of these examples that follow may appear harsh, but really they are simply honest. They are asked not in a "witness stand" manner but with genuine interest. This leads the children to consider the outcome carefully, knowing they have full responsibility for their situation.

♥ "I'm wondering if, while you are young, it really doesn't seem that important to worry about blindness or loss of a foot, which could be years down the road."

♥ "Are you feeling that perhaps the hassle of possible blindness just isn't worth the time it takes to measure your glucose three times a day?"

♥ "Is there anything I can do that might help you stave off the possible sad physical disabilities that we've talked about? If you become blind, I'd feel more comfortable if I knew I did everything you think might be helpful to help you remember the important stuff."

It is effective to ask questions expressing curiosity and interest coupled with possible outcomes because such a combination strongly implies not only concern, but the belief that the child can make good decisions and is aware of the possible results of poor care. Expressing curiosity and interest doesn't scream the overinvolvement that angry criticism can often convey. It's nearly impossible to rebel against honest curiosity and interest delivered lovingly.

Chapter 5 Key Concepts

1. Our children learn by the example we set, the experiences we allow, the empathy we demonstrate, and the expectations that we show.

2. Example, Experience, Empathy, Expectations, and Encouragement must form the foundation of all good leadership and management, be it parenting, teaching, or governing. Although they must be developed, they cannot be forced from the outside.

3. Children learn by the *Example* parents set, as they model the behavior they want from their children.

4. Children learn by the *Experiences* parents encourage and allow. Responsible children, though ill, may understand their bodies, their limitations, and their abilities more than parents may give them credit for. They should be given as much latitude as possible to make their own decisions. From this, good judgment, self-awareness, self-confidence, and self-reliance grow.

5. When parents show *Empathy*, rather then anger and frustration, following their children's mistakes, the children feel encouraged and supported and learn from their errors. Empathy provides love and respect, even as it locks in the learning experience. There are important differences between sympathy and empathy.

6. Children with chronic illness must receive high but reasonable *Expectations* given with smiles, hope, and love, rather than authoritarian demands. Children meet expectations, but demands often result in self-destructive, noncompliant decisions.

7. It is necessary for parents of infants and toddlers to control their children's healthcare issues. However, frustration creeps in as children grow older and parents start to realize they can't control their children's responses to their illnesses but somehow still think they should! Parents can stop this pattern of power struggles, frustration, and feelings of inadequacy by turning over the responsibility for healthcare to the child in small, steady increments, starting in the early elementary years. Correct wording puts the problem on the resistant child, while providing the child a sense of accomplishment for making healthy decisions.

8. The power of *Encouragement* is great. Simply saying, "I bet you are proud of how you remember your medicine" is more effec-

tive than saying, "I'm proud of the way you take your medicine." Effective communication is easily learned and especially effective for kids with special healthcare needs.

9. Praise and encouragement are very different. The better the parent/child relationship, the better praise works, but praise can be used to manipulate both sender and receiver. Encouragement through questions puts the healthcare issues and results directly on the child. Questions promote a high self-image and allow the adult to express joy and disappointment while encouraging the child to think. Love and Logic teaches that *curiosity and interest about self-care issues almost always trump worry and concern*, just as ideas and thoughts trump advice, suggestions, and pleading. Questions give resistant children less adult emotion to manipulate but do show curiosity and interest.

10. Descriptive phrases help children focus on and evaluate their accomplishments, treatment decisions, and results, rather than provide the child with outside judgments. Resistant children can easily negate nondescriptive praise for a number of reasons. "I notice that..." is a good way to begin a descriptive phrase.

11. The criticism trap can often be avoided by expressing parental concerns as carefully worded questions. These should be asked with curiosity and interest coupled with the potential negative outcomes for noncompliance with medical procedures.

Chapter 6

Now What?
Tips for Parenting from Infancy to Adulthood

A child only educated at school
is an uneducated child.
—George Santayana (1863-1952)

The First Years

Illness, the treatment of illness, and or/physical trauma in the first years of life can profoundly affect the afflicted child's unfolding personality, possibly playing a role in lifetime character and personality traits. Intuitively, we might wonder, "How can such things affect my child when she can't even remember them?"

This is how.

The development of the human personality occurs in stages. Each stage is built upon the foundation of the earlier one. When infantile development and health is atypical, so is brain growth and development. An infant's world becomes painfully unpredictable when he or she suffers from chronic pain, experiences numerous separations from mother, or lives in a world where unfolding, unpredictable responses and pain are possible or probable. This child has an entirely different experience than one whose infancy and experiences as a toddler are usual, predictable, and not painful. Just as living in full sunlight without protection would affect the normal development of the skin (the body's largest organ), so an environment of pain, separation, and loss burns and affects the brain.

In the first year an infant's brain goes from a relatively smooth mass with little gray matter to an amazingly complex masterpiece of tissue with a gray, convoluted surface beneath which are literally trillions of new neurons reaching out to others. If we could take a time-lapse photograph of the surface of an infant's brain, we would see waves and ripples of development across the surface that would rival the beauty we see in the time-lapse photograph of a rose opening.

Views provided by the wonders of electron microscopes clearly show the axons of developing neurons reaching out to those of others in a choreographed symphony of connections. The melody of external experience impacts and changes the chemistry and connections that go on far beneath the surface of the brain.

Why do external circumstances play such a pivotal role? It is because all higher-order thinking is routed through midbrain switching centers that are intimately connected with emotions. So adults who have had a bad experience may say something along the lines of, "I just don't want to think about that!" when asked to think about the tough time. However, the adult's decision not to think about the situation is volitional. It's not that the adult really can't think straight about the issue; the adult just prefers not to. However, research by the early investigator John Bowlby and many others since has shown beyond a shadow of a doubt that trauma and loss in early life experiences can affect the ability of the developing brain to think clearly. It's not that the child makes a decision not to think. It's as if the child, like an adult with a temporary depression, really can't think. When the developing midbrain switching center is flooded with negative experiences during development, then higher-order thinking may be affected. This includes cause-and-effect thinking, the development of impulse control and trust, and the ability to focus without fragmentation. These specific issues impact the level of ease or difficulty in living with, and controlling, the child. After all, a parent's control of her child depends on the child's ability to love, trust, respond, and think.

While the brain's hardware is developing its neural connections to handle emotion and thinking, the early software programming is concerned with forming trusting and loving relationships. In fact, a most amazing cycle takes place dozens of times in the first week, rolling around every time a baby is fed, and locks in Basic Trust and the foundation beliefs. This can be clarified by imagining the baby being able to tell us, "Hey, this is a great time of life because my brain is learning that:"

- ♥ "I can be taken care of."
- ♥ "Other people can do great things for me."
- ♥ "Life is often better when I cry, and mom arrives and responds."
- ♥ "When I'm really unhappy or hurting, she comes along and makes it all better."
- ♥ "I'm figuring out that when she's around, even if it takes a while for the bottle to get warm, the situation will improve. And my neurons are learning:
  - • To love and trust others.
  - • To handle some frustration.
  - • To wait.
  - • To anticipate what is coming.

> • To lay the foundation for my awesome, and essential, cause-and-effect thinking."

The cycle that locks in all this early foundational learning is illustrated in Figure 6.1 on the opposite page.

Notice that the infant's unhappiness and hopelessness (the components of rage) are relieved when the mom gives four essential gifts that for the rest of life will be associated with love: eye contact, touch, food, and smiles. In fact, the memories of a mother's early presence and her provision of love and food have led healthy people to use names for their loved ones that are related to pleasant-tasting carbohydrates or other foods. Typical examples are: Honey, sugar, sweetie, apple of my eye, jellybean, pumpkin — and heaven knows what other nutritional delights! And when we meet new people, we invariably use a pleasant meal in a cozy venue as the facilitator for a good interpersonal connection: "Hey, let's go out for dinner," or "I'll meet you for a drink," or "We are having a backyard barbecue. Want to come?"

Food, love, trust, and appreciation of others are learned in infancy and run like an invisible thread tying together adult relationships. Thus, when chronic illness, pain, deprivation, or parent/infant separation takes place, these foundational responses, which involve clear thinking, love, and basic trust, are impacted. And these affect how easily the child responds to love and authority.

This is not to say infants who have experienced chronic illness, hospitalizations, pain, separations, and deprivations must turn out to be more difficult than the average child. Genetics, parenting, length of the problem, and subsequent life events all play important roles, making each child's individual response unique. However, children whose early years have been disrupted or painful are at risk of experiencing interpersonal difficulties or disrupted thought patterns not experienced by children with more normal infancies.

These "at risk factors" can easily be visualized and understood

Figure 6.1 **Oral Cycle of Bonding**

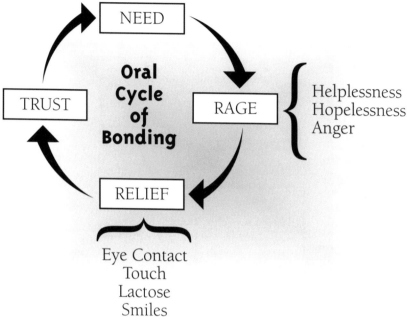

when we see what takes place when the normal cycle, shown in figure 6.1, is disrupted between the Rage and the Relief responses. This is demonstrated in figure 6.2 on the following page.

In times past, difficult adults were said to have a "colicky personality." This term may have been an unconscious recognition that the seeds of an individual's problems, which surfaced as an adult, were sown in infancy because, after all, infants have colic, not adults.

It is not uncommon for the parents of children who earlier in infancy suffered from infantile pain and hospitalizations to say something like, "This child is a real pistol. And things that worked on my other children don't seem to work on Jimmy!" Sometimes these children are diagnosed with mild, moderate, or severe Attachment Disorder.

Figure 6.2 **Disruptions in the Bonding Cycle**

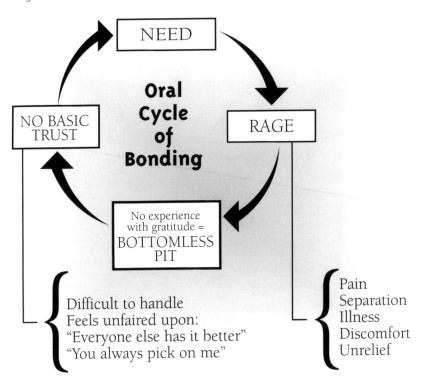

When a child's infantile disruptions occur in the life of the couple's second or third child, at least the parents have had a history of normal responses to their parenting. When the problem child is the first child, it's understandable that mothers or fathers could wonder, "What am I doing wrong?"

Common reactions to first- and second-year of life hardships are:

- ♥ The child is unusually demanding.
- ♥ The child appears entitled (slow to show meaningful thanks and appreciation).
- ♥ The child easily feels as if he or she has been treated unfairly and complains, "That's unfair," or "You always pick on me."

♥ The child may have food problems (hoarding or gorging food).

♥ The child does not act like his mom is his "sweetie."

♥ Temper tantrums, impulsive behavior, and control problems are present.

Remember, these problems are not present in all children who have had difficult early years. And even if these problems are present, there are good reasons for hope and responses that help!

One mother's story is typical:

Jackson

When Jackson was an infant, he cried much of the time. The doctors didn't know why. Finally, when there was blood in his stool, they diagnosed a lactose allergy. I was nursing and took all milk products out of my diet. The problem went away but he had about six months of severe abdominal pain.

During Jackson's second year of life, he threw severe temper tantrums and at times I felt as if I was at the end of my rope. But now, at the age of 7, he is a great kid, and I know he will have great relationships in life. Still, however, when he is under the weather or outright sick, I recognize indications of his old, "life's-not-fair" attitude. There were a number of factors that saved the situation.

I learned from Dr. Cline that Jackson's behavior was not my fault. I really wasn't doing anything wrong. That discovery was a profound help.

Furthermore, Love and Logic attitudes and tools brought a screeching halt to vicious cycles that could have been set in motion.

When Jackson had temper tantrums, I didn't take them personally. I didn't get mad or feel guilty but just lovingly understood. I gently rocked and held him if it helped but lovingly deposited him in his room if he didn't settle down with holding.

When Jackson became demanding, I ran through all the good Love and Logic response tools. Sometimes I told him, "I love you too much to argue." Sometimes I simply said, "I'm sad that you're having such a hard time. I'm sure your bedroom would appreciate your attitude more than I do right now. I'll see you when you can be sweet." At other times I would help him recognize he had been draining my energy and we would have fun together doing the jobs that put energy back into my system.

My mantra during the times I held him and the times he was recovering in his room after a fit was: "Poor little kid, he's had a tough early life. I hope he gets over it." All I am responsible for is providing him with the environment where he can learn best to cope. It is hard to express how liberating it was to feel blameless in the face of his turmoil.

In summary, when separations and pain take place in a child's infancy and during the second year of life, typical and sometimes lasting responses are predictable. These responses are often a combination of personality (software) responses and problems in causal thinking and impulse control (hardware issues). The suggestions given in this book and other Love and Logic materials will ensure that dysfunctional and destructive cycles between parent and child do not occur.

With corrective parental attitudes and tools, the problem often improves with age. If this is not the case and the child continues to stress the parents' ability to respond correctly and to cope with behavioral problems, there are a number of resources that are available on the Web. Therapists trained in these specific issues and support groups may be located when searching for resources that deal with attachment problems.

Preschool Children

Invariably, parents are devastated when they learn that their infant or toddler has been diagnosed with a chronic illness. The ensuing emotional turmoil can be characterized by soul-searching, wakeful nights, and weeping, and it is understandably difficult at times to implement the tools and techniques we recommend in this book. But if such parents persevere, they will find life much easier as the child develops. Parents can provide very young children with information in a hopeful, encouraging, age-appropriate manner that will promote good decision making. The very best time to become a Consultant Parent and allow your child to face the consequences of his/her own decisions is when the child is young. You will be setting a foundation for your children's lives that may end up saving them. Love and Logic's tools and techniques must be modified for toddlers and preschoolers, and this chapter will address these modifications with respect to handling medical issues. General parenting issues are expertly addressed in Love and Logic's early childhood books and audio and video resources. The modifications we discuss in this chapter are based on the following facts:

- ♥ Parents form the young child's whole world.
- ♥ Children unconditionally accept parental attitudes and belief systems.
- ♥ Toddlers generally mirror parental emotions exactly.
- ♥ Toddlers have neither the experience nor the neural development to question adult decisions or statements.
- ♥ Toddlers understand the world though pictures and gain mastery through manipulation and play.

A thoughtful eight-year-old may be able to say to a friend, "Yeah, my mom gets too mad." Or, a third-grade girl might confide to a friend, "This is the kind of thing my mom freaks out about." You won't hear any toddler talking like that! When a mother shows anger towards a two-, three- or four-year-old child, the child doesn't think, "There she goes again!" He or she will simply feel bad or scared, cry, and run to their room.

Now all of this is good news and bad news. It means toddlers can be easily led down a healthy garden path, be reassured, and persuaded to buy into the belief they are "big boys and girls, and can handle it." At the same time they understandably need even more hugs and encouragement than children of other ages. Often they need extended periods of rocking-and-holding time.

When an infant or toddler is crying out in pain, every parent in the world would like to take that pain away. But with many chronic illnesses, that's simply impossible. So, fighting back their own frustration and tears, wise mothers and fathers simply rock and sing to their unhappy children. Showing anger and impatience, driven by the frustration of not being able to take the pain away, simply makes the situation worse. And while holding and rocking a child may not alleviate the pain, it nevertheless is necessary and beneficial to a relationship that is already stressed by the illness.

During the early months of life, a child cannot be overcomforted or held too much. However, "normal" children can become spoiled and demanding by their first birthday, when parents attempt to meet every whim and demand issued during the last four months of the first year. By their first birthday, some children have learned to be real terrors of the high chair, as mothers become retrievers fetching thrown bottles. However, when an ill child is hurting and in pain, the holding and comforting needs to be extended, even though an increased willfulness may result. Low-grade, "spoiled-child" behavior is easily corrected later with good parenting skills but bonding issues are not. It is always better to err on the side of love and nurture.

After a child's first birthday, the sense of determination, optimism, resolve, and hope the parents show is downright contagious. A hopeful parent generally raises a courageous child. A pleased parent raises a child with a high self-image, and an encouraging parent raises a child who copes. Parents who model coping and determination in the face of difficult diagnoses raise a far different child than those who exude worry and sorrow.

Optimistic and positive parents, at the very least, are comforted in knowing that when worry, sorrow, and fear do show themselves in their children's eyes, those feelings originate from within the children themselves and are not simply a reflection of emotions the parents can't keep to themselves.

In the second year of life most parents help their children learn by doing what comes naturally; that is, showing their children books with pictures, matching pictures to words, and helping their children build both vocabulary and concepts. These pictures are important. Toddlers are visual and kinesthetic learners. They make sense of their world by seeing and doing. It is important for parents to also realize that not only are pictures necessary in their children's learning about dinosaurs and dump trucks, they are needed to talk to their kids about illness and self-care issues as well. The DVD version of this program demonstrates how to interact with little children around pictures that they (or their parents) draw to illustrate their illness and treatment.

Following are a few possible scenarios of parents and children interacting as they use crayons and paint:

- ♥ Father and daughter interact around a picture that shows insulin molecules (blue dots) making the brain spark and making sugar molecules (yellow dots) disappear.
- ♥ A mother and son laugh together over a poster picture of lungs, where the boy draws bugs (red dots) down in the bottom of the lung. Those bugs experience a sudden and agoniz-

ing death when medication (blue crayon puffs) snuffs them out after flowing down the trachea and bronchioles.
♥ A four-year-old girl laughs in glee, bending over her mom's drawing in which mad, ugly-looking, fat molecules are torn to pieces by digestive enzymes.

The conversations that can take place around such drawings not only clarify the issues but also give children a feeling of mastery over the illness. For instance:

> "And then, Troy, what happens when the medicine hits the bugs?"
> "They scream. They die."
> "Well, what helps the medicine get down there to knock them off?"
> "Keeping all the tubes in my lungs clear..."
> "And what are they called?"
> "Bronchioles."
> "Right! And what keeps them clear the best?"
> "My thumper machine that pounds 'em open..."
> "Good thinking! So I guess using that every day is really important, right?"

Little children generally don't come to understand their illness when parents use only words to teach them. They certainly don't gain understanding when using the metaphors and analogies that are so helpful with preteen and older children. Small children live in the world that Piaget called "concrete operations." Perhaps the most concrete help of all are pictures of the illness that the children themselves have drawn. Parents can interact around these pictures to help them understand their illness and make good self-care decisions, even at a very young age.

In summary, parental emotions are completely contagious. Small children can easily be led down the path of fright, fear, or fight, or the path of understanding, acceptance, and hope. It all depends on the parents' attitude. Let's read how one wonderful mother, April Lloyd, uses these concepts to achieve "happy compliance" as she works with her two young children with CF:

Max and Madeline

When my newborn son and my two-year-old daughter were both diagnosed with cystic fibrosis, it was an overwhelming time. One thing I knew from the very beginning was that if I had to wrestle my kids to complete CPT or nebs or force my kids to take their medicine at every meal or snack, I would be a very tired mom with very unhappy kids. We have tried many creative ways to encourage happy compliance with these treatments.

My son Max was diagnosed when he was born and has had the benefit of treatment from birth. This is nice because he has never known any different way of doing things. He is two years old now and has a wonderfully sweet and resilient personality, with a touch of stubbornness thrown in. He loves to run away during CPT, sometimes turns his head away from inhaled medications, and has been known occasionally to spit out his enzymes. But with constant praise for his positive actions and a lot of crazy songs and stories we invent for his amusement, he now enjoys his treatment times and takes his medicine willingly.

My daughter Madeline was diagnosed and started treatments at around two years old. She could talk and understand more things than our new baby could. She has always had an exceptionally obedient nature and thrives on praise for her good behavior. We praise her bravery during clinic visits and tell her what a champ she is whenever she completes a treatment. She is four years old now and needs explanations of what will happen at the doctors and why she needs certain medicines. We use books and pictures to explain what is going on. Cartoon-like drawings of how medicine is taken into the body and used have been a helpful tool. Her favorite is a teddy bear showing her how to use her Albuterol inhaler and spacer. In the picture she can see the medicine drops going into the spacer and then into teddy's lungs. Our most helpful tool has been finding real-life pictures or videos of other kids doing the same treatments she does. Seeing other kids going through similar things helps her feel comfortable and relieves the fear of new treatments or tests during visits to the doctor. These tools give her the determination to comply. We mix them with a lot of silliness to help the time go by.

Both of my children respond to rhythm, music, and poetry really well. When we do CPT, I make up silly stories or adapt humorous folk tales that are told in rhythm to the tapping on their bodies. At other times, we listen to a CD or watch a DVD of a favorite children's singer and tap to the beat as they sing along, laughing at the wobbly voices they have from the tapping and shaking. They dance and move within the limits of their therapy of course. Poetry is my favorite tool because classic poems like Wynken, Blynken, and Nod transport us to a different place, and the repetition and rhyme envelop us for a little while. We do not force compliance. We teach happy compliance.

These tools have helped turn our treatments into a

happy time of day. They have turned cystic fibrosis into an outpouring of love, learning, silliness, and strength. At times I still get sad or tired. But when I hear my daughter happily reciting Wynken, Blynken, and Nod to herself as she drifts off to sleep, or my son humming snippets of Beethoven as he scoots his trains around the floor, I know these treatments are not only keeping them healthy, but this special time also keeps them happy. What more could we ask for as parents?

Elementary School Years

Parenting may seem deceptively simple during the elementary school years. Children who have successfully navigated their way through the early childhood developmental stages should be reasonably ready to enjoy several years of relative peace and emotional and behavioral stability. This is not to say there aren't challenges but, compared to the toddler and teenage years, these years are generally trouble-free. In fact, these "latency" years can be so deceptive that parents can be lulled into a false sense of security with the often mistaken belief that no matter what parenting style they use, it is universally effective and will "work" even into adulthood.

During the elementary school years, the child's brain is still operating in concrete operations mode, which means the world is fairly black and white in the child's eyes. Children understand they are supposed to obey parents and they usually do. For the most part, elementary school-age children adore their parents and want to please them. Parents can "muscle" their elementary age kids into undergoing almost any medical treatment with loving, power-parenting, but if this continues unchanged as the child matures, power-parenting can come back to haunt parents when the child approaches the teen years.

As children transition from preschool to elementary ages, parents are also transitioning from the necessity of providing for every need to encouraging more independence. However, parents are often both competent and accustomed to handling everything, particularly a child's medical needs, and it is very hard to know what to let go of and when to give responsibility to the child. It is easy for a parent during these ages to continue using this pattern of telling the child what to do, and when and how to do it. This may happen with respect to homework and peer issues, but especially medical issues. Most parents, naturally, continue to handle most of the details of their child's medical care. The more serious the care needed, the harder the parent holds onto control over it. Slipping into Helicopter and/or Drill Sergeant parenting styles is so easy to do, but it can have a deadly result when the child with significant medical issues becomes a noncompliant or rebellious teenager. The elementary-age years are the best years for the Consultant Parenting approach to be fine-tuned, as families prepare for possibly turbulent teen years.

Let's take a close look at the important differences between the styles of Helicopter, Drill Sergeant, and Consultant Parents as they apply to kids with chronic illnesses.[6]

Helicopter parents hover, search, and protect. The messages they send say:

- ♥ You are fragile. You can't make it in life without me.
- ♥ You need me to run interference.
- ♥ You need me to protect you.
- ♥ *You can't make it in life without me!*

An example of a Helicopter in action:

> *Mom*: "It's time to get started on your IV antibiotics."
>
> *Eva*: "No! I don't want to do it now."
>
> *Mom*: "You know we need to start them now. You won't get better if you don't keep the schedule the doctor prescribed."
>
> *Eva*: "I'm not gonna do it right now. I don't want to!"

> *Mom*: "Well... okay. You can wait for a little while this time, but next time you'd better do it on time. And, I mean it!"

Drill Sergeant parents say: Do it! Do it now, or else! The messages they send say:

- ♥ You can't think.
- ♥ I have to do your thinking for you, boss you around, tell you what to do.
- ♥ *You aren't capable of making it in life.*

An example of a Drill Sergeant in action:

> *Dad*: "For crying out loud, how many times do I have to say it? Sit down and let's get that inhaler started. NOW!!"
>
> *Chuck*: "I don't want to start it now."
>
> *Dad*: "We are going start it right now even if I have to sit here on top of you to make you do it. Plus, I'll take your TV away for a whole week."
>
> *Chuck*: (Tries to leave the room)
>
> *Dad*: "You get over here right now, young man! You should appreciate having great meds. Other people aren't that lucky, you know..."

Consultant Parents are always there to give advice and let the child make the decision, with the idea they will let the child make as many mistakes as possible when the price tag is affordable and when the consequences, medical or otherwise, are not life-and-death issues. The message Consultant Parents send says: You'd best do your own thinking because the quality of your life has a lot to do with your own decisions. Consultant Parents take very good care of themselves in front of their kids because:

- ❤ They prefer to give options, rather than tell their children what to do.
- ❤ They get better results by saying what they're going to do.
- ❤ When confronted with a problem, Consultant Parents use meaningful actions and few words. They wrap consequences in a loving blanket of empathy.
- ❤ The message they send says: *You are capable and can handle whatever challenges come your way in life!*

An example of a Consultant Parent:

Mom: "Would you like to start your treatment now or in 10 minutes?"

Tara: "Neither! I don't want to do it. I'm sick of this."

Mom: "Yeah, it is tough, isn't it? I wish you didn't have to do it but the doctors said you need to kill those nasty little bugs in your lungs. What do you think might happen if you don't do it on time?"

Tara: "I don't know."

Mom: "Would you like to hear what has happened with some other kids who didn't listen to the doctor?"

Tara: "I guess."

Mom: "Well, some kids with CF who don't stick to their treatment schedule get very, very sick. Other kids have to go to the hospital for two weeks to take their antibiotics because the docs can't trust them to do it at home. I sure hope these things don't happen to you because I love you so much and I hate to see you suffer. Give it some thought, and I'll be back. (Gives a little kiss and walks out of the room)."

Mom returns in ten minutes:

Mom: "Tara, are you ready to start your treatment now?"

Tara: "Fine, I guess. What a hassle! I hate doing it."

Please note here that although Tara has a poor attitude toward her treatment, she is complying, and she decided to do so on her own. Mom didn't muscle her into compliance, nor did she simply let Tara off the hook. With a really resistant child, there are other techniques that can be used to create some logical consequences for Tara's lack of compliance. For instance: Mom could have an energy drain, which results in no "chauffeuring services" for the weekend.

Table 6.1 on the following page, shows Love and Logic's Three Types of Parents.

Becoming a Consultant Parent will increase the odds that your chronically ill child will live as long as medically possible. Your parenting style may not only determine the quality of life but the quantity of days. Luckily, Drill Sergeants can learn to enjoy parade-ground rest, and Helicopters can learn to fly a more effective course. Becoming a Consultant Parent simply takes desire, practice, and patience, and it's never too late to start. Even adult children benefit from the consultant parenting approach. Let's now look at an example of how parents used the Consultant Parent approach to work with their resistant six-year-old.

Tommy was six years old when amblyopia was diagnosed. This is a condition that can cause loss of vision when the eyes do not focus together. Treatment requires patching of the good eye and strengthening the "wandering eye." The doctor informed Tommy's parents that keeping the required patch over his eyes might be a long, and perhaps difficult, process. At first, Tommy kept his patching glasses on for short periods; however, it wasn't long before his parents found that most of the time, when they turned their backs, Tommy ripped off his patching glasses. Both parents were frustrated. Tommy's vision was slipping from 20/30 to 20/80.

Pauline, his mother, wrote an e-mail to Dr. Cline noting, "We have tried several things to get him to keep his glasses on, without any success at all. I am sure we show some of our frustration as his vision is dropping from 20/30 to 20/80 but, as you know, it will not

Table 6.1 Types of Parents

	Consultant	Helicopter	Drill Sergeant
	This Love and Logic parent provides facts concerning healthcare and gives guidance and consultation.	*This parent hovers over children and rescues them from, or ensures no negative consequences for, any healthcare decision.*	*This parent commands and directs all aspects of the child's care.*
1.	The Love and Logic Parent provides messages of personal worth and competency.	Provides messages of worry about ability and doubt about the child's healthcare decisions.	Provides demanding messages that may easily lead to low personal worth and resistance.
2.	The Love and Logic parent very seldom lectures or talks about responsibilities.	Makes excuses for the child, but complains about mishandled responsibilities.	Makes lots of demands and shows anger about possible lack of responsibility.
3.	The Love and Logic parent focuses on his or her own health needs, often in front of the child, setting an example of good healthcare.	Emphasizes and worries about the child's responsibility in healthcare.	Tells the child (perhaps with threats or anger) how he/she should handle responsible healthcare.
4.	The Love and Logic parent shares personal feelings, joys, and sense of accomplishment about self-care issues.	Protects the child from any possible negative feelings.	Tells the child how he/she should feel.
5.	The Love and Logic parent provides "time frames" in which the child may complete self-care responses, chores, and treatments.	Provides no structure, but complains, "After all I've done for you..."	Demands treatments and/or responsibilities be done *now*.
6.	The Love and Logic parent models a sense of accomplishment and joy at achieving healthcare success.	Whines and uses guilt: "Why can't you do this yourself?"	Issues orders and threats: "You take your medicine right now! Or else..."
7.	The Love and Logic parent uses lots of actions but very few words.	Uses lots of words and actions that rescue or indicate the child is not capable or responsible.	Uses lots of harsh words; very few actions.
8.	The Love and Logic parent allows the child to experience negative healthcare consequences that will *probably not* affect long-term functioning or life.	Protects child from healthcare consequences, whether or not there are probable, or even possible, poor lifetime consequences.	Uses punishment or humiliation as a primary teaching tool.

get better without patching. We have also tried the drops but this did not work for his situation. We would appreciate your suggestions."

In an e-mail response, giving precise instructions, Foster emphasized the following:

- ♥ Showing frustration always makes things worse.
- ♥ Children need to be given choices.
- ♥ Parents need to show encouragement around whatever choice a child may make.

Paradoxically, this works better, as we are about to see, if the child's first choice is really a poor one. Usually, when children make a poor choice, they expect a lecture, admonishment, frustration, new suggestions, and possibly even new orders. All kids can rebel against these but they can never rebel against encouragement. And, if the choice is a poor one, whether or not there's encouragement, most children (in fact almost everyone) rethink the choice. Why? Because most people want to avoid the pain and suffering that often accompanies bad choices.

When parents can "have fun" with a poor choice situation, *without making fun of the child*, it plops the whole problem onto the child's shoulders.

Tommy

Following Dr. Cline's instructions, the parents had this conversation with Tommy:

"Tommy, we apologize for hassling you about your glasses. Lots of people grow up with poor vision, and they do fine. In fact, lots of people are blind and that does not slow them down a bit. Perhaps you could be one of those great people who overcome such challenges."

"However, Tommy, because you are not wearing your glasses, you are going to grow up without seeing very well and we realize we are not preparing you for adulthood. It would be good to get used to having really poor eyesight now so, as you grow older, you will be accustomed to it and do great as a nearly blind person. So we have a wonderful idea we hope you will find very helpful. At dinner tonight Dad and I are going to give you some little glasses we brought at the drugstore, and we're going to smear a bit of Vaseline over the lenses. That ought to blur things up quite a bit. It will be perfect for you because that's the kind of really poor vision you're going to have. Lucky for you, this will be a big help 'cause you'll get used to seeing poorly now, and it won't be a big deal as your eyes deteriorate."

At dinnertime, the parents globbed Vaseline onto the lenses. Restraining their giggles, they enjoyed doing a great job of encouraging Tommy:

"Oops, you missed your plate. Don't worry. Feel the edge of it there. Good job! You got all the beans on the plate except one. Don't worry about it. I'll pick that one up... Oops, you got the salt shaker instead of the pepper. Don't worry about it, kiddo. I'm going to put a little sticker on the side of the salt. There, see how different it feels? Now you can feel the difference. No problem!"

Toward the end of dinner, Dad said with real enthusiasm, "Tommy, you're going to do great as a partially blind person! I think you're going to be a real inspiration to others!"

In addition to allowing Tommy to make his own choices, his parents added a little incentive should Tommy decide to make a different choice. They had a discussion in their bedroom they knew Tommy would overhear from his bedroom:

"You know, dear, I was thinking of buying Tom a new bicycle, but now that he is choosing to go through life partially blind, I guess buying the bike would be kinda foolish. But you know, dear, if Tom did decide to wear his patch and decided not to go blind, I'd like to paste up a star for every day he wears his patched glasses. When he collects enough stars, he'll have a whole bike. I think it would only take a dozen stars or so to earn the handlebars. That's not much. That's less than a couple of weeks of wearing his patched glasses."

After wearing his Vaseline glasses at the dinner table for the second time, Tommy decided that, all things considered, although he would make a perfectly good blind person, and even though he might be an inspiration to others, he'd rather not be partially blind. Tommy realized this decision might be slightly rough on his parents, as they had been looking forward to the encouragement he could be to other blind folks, but they swallowed their disappointment and acceded to his new choice.

The ophthalmologist was impressed by the turnaround in what had appeared to be a fairly rebellious little boy. He asked the mom to write out the program, so he could give it to other parents, and she agreed to our sharing it with you.

Using appropriate humor, without making fun of the child, can be a most effective strategy with strong-willed children and ensures that the process is fun for the parents.

School Daze: Handling Medical Issues at School

Starting school will bring on many new experiences and challenges for children and parents. Internet message boards and chat rooms are filled with the laments of those who struggle with formidable problems at school because of medical issues.[7] Complaints include inflexibility with bathroom privileges, problems with medication distribution, bullying, and people who are seemingly insensitive to the special needs of these children. Individualized education plans (IEPs) and 504 plans abound.[8]

Public schools teach children by grouping them together into classes. By definition, a "class" is defined as a biological group with similarities. Living organisms are organized as phylum and class. But really, many kids don't fit the "class" definition. In fact many Special Ed classrooms might better be defined as a bio-diverse "glen" of children rather than a "class" of children. Schools and teachers understandably have problems responding to unique situations in a class of thirty children. From first-hand experience, we know that in spite of its best efforts, the public system has trouble accommodating special needs and unique situations, whether the children are experiencing a death in the family, the special requirements of chronic illness, or even the scheduling needs of Olympic training.

There can be many physical and emotional challenges which arise when school-aged children have special healthcare needs. Down the road, children with chronic illnesses may be small for their age and physical development may also lag. Girls with respiratory and other illnesses might curve out a year or so behind their peers. Boys, too, may be slower to bulk out and experience secondary sex changes. When social development lags, it might be a blessing that the children experience the temptations of drugs and driving a year later than their peers but plenty of other parenting challenges make up for it!

As silly as it seems now, parents who were given an enrollment choice years ago tended to push their kids ahead a year and enroll them as early as possible, somehow believing this would give them a year's jump on life. Today, parents of even "normal" children are savvier about the advantages of waiting a year before enrolling their children in kindergarten, believing that the extra year's maturity will give their kids a real advantage in the competitive academic world. They may be right, but this has resulted in classrooms that more commonly have children with as much as a twelve-month age difference! This puts the children at the younger end of the spectrum at a clear disadvantage and puts the younger children with health issues at the greatest disadvantage of all.

Taking all this into consideration, we believe children with chronic medical issues may be much better served by waiting an extra year before being enrolled in school. When school must be missed to accommodate medical treatment or emergencies, children with an extra year behind them may have greater maturity and be able to handle the backlog of homework or missed lessons more easily.

Here are some general guidelines for handling medical issues at school:

♥ *It is generally helpful to be frank about the child's illness*: Secrecy almost always encourages the few children who learn about a problem to tease mercilessly. A matter-of-fact openness about why there is a prosthetic leg or why peanuts can be dangerous allows for the caring and understanding majority to give their support. In Spokane, WA, a ten-year-old girl told an entire school assembly how she had been born without a fibula, and openly displayed her prosthetic leg, which was decorated with pictures of kittens. Playing show-and-tell with the insulin pump or inhaler for asthma can be most informative. Take an extra moment and let other children explore it and see how it works. Just as guilt encourages blame, embarrassment about an issue encourages complementary shunning and judgmental responses.

♥ *Help your child learn to give facts in an age-appropriate manner*:
The situation is facilitated when you encourage your child to
talk easily about his or her medical condition in an age-appropriate way. "Well, I'm pretty much like all of you on the inside,
but I'm certainly different on the outside!" It should be
explained that the condition is not contagious. If certain precautions have to be taken for a fragile immune system, or if
there are special dietary requirements, be open about the reasons for those special precautions. Nature abhors a vacuum
and it is quickly filled with speculation, innuendo, and gossip
when a condition is not fully explained. If your child could
have a seizure, it would be good to explain this in a matter-of-
fact manner to the class before it occurs. For example: "Most of
the time, my brain works just like yours. But sometimes it gets
a little too active, so I take medication to pull in the reins. And
sometimes my brain ignores the reins, blacks me out, and
takes my body for a real ride. Then I shake all over. If this happens, just get a grown-up and don't get all shook up your-
selves. I'll probably do enough shaking for both of us!"

♥ *Medical requirements often necessitate increased appropriate
parental involvement*: Parents must train their child and school
personnel to recognize and properly handle a potential medical emergency concerning the child's special issues. Frequent
practice sessions at home and playing "What if?" will ensure
your child knows how to handle his or her health issues properly. The child's age and ability are, as always, critically important in determining how a problem will be handled. As
necessary, parents can ensure the school has a supply of blood-
and urine-testing supplies, an emergency supply of juice, or a
kit to handle an anaphylactic reaction to food. Federal laws
and some state laws protect diabetic children at school by
requiring schools to accommodate their special needs through
the Individuals with Disabilities Education Act.

Appropriate parental involvement with the school also means avoiding overinvolvement that takes too much responsibility off the child and may alienate school professionals. Such overinvolvement may lessen the odds of ensuring that your child receives the necessary individualized responses (sort of like the story of "The Boy Who Cried Wolf"). If a young child has Type 1 diabetes, fluctuations in blood sugar can cause vision problems, drowsiness, mood changes, concentration problems, and trips to the bathroom that lead to missed class time. Parents can educate teachers about these reactions so they will recognize them when they occur. Before approaching the school it is best to be prepared: know your rights, and be sure to cultivate a nondemanding but assertive relationship that embraces consultation and mutual respect:

> "Robert has some severe dietary allergies, and I'm wondering how we can best work together to ensure that if he has a severe reaction you are prepared. Robert knows very well how to avoid most foods that contain peanuts, but sometimes they slip unexpectedly into some products. How would you like to handle that with the dietary staff? Can I help with that? I have some information that other schools have found helpful..."

Many parents encourage academic individualization by choosing private or home-schooling options. Both options are universally present, and home schooling has flourished with the availability of support groups on the Internet and hundreds of sites packed with lesson plans and tutorials which simplify home schooling and make it a very viable option.

Sandy

Sandy was twelve when she started having real problems at school. The sixth grade curriculum, homework, and special projects were hard to keep up when she had to spend at least two hours a day attending to medical treatments to manage the effects of CF on her lungs. She started missing more school that year, too, with several hospitalizations and sick days at home. CF was clearly progressing in her body. She tried her best to keep up with the work and the school was very supportive, but she knew she was always behind and it started to affect her self-esteem. It didn't help that she was very small for her age, despite the night feedings with her G-tube. The other kids treated her okay but she still felt like she didn't belong. She wasn't able to participate in sports much, and when she was well they still didn't pick her to be on the teams. Sandy and her parents felt as if they were always playing catch up but were never quite getting caught up!

After much investigation and discussion, they decided to try home schooling for one year. The administrators at the public school supported the decision and assured the family they would "always be there." Sandy and her mom found much support, training, and friendship in the local home school community. Sandy discovered she was able to complete a week's worth of work in half the time (she was a really bright kid after all!) and began to feel better about herself. With the reduced stress and more time to take care of her body properly, her health improved too. The whole family was less frustrated and more relaxed and soon realized how much of their lives had revolved around Sandy's challenges at school. Sandy was home schooled through the rest of her school years and even began college classes in her junior year. She had become a much happier,

healthier young lady with a bright future in bio-
physics.

Wise parents consider the many educational options now available.
Decisions such as Sandy's should be made by the parents *and the
child* in order to empower him or her to "buy into" the process.
Although tempting at times, home schooling based largely on
parental fear and overprotection is generally unwise. Wise parents
encourage their children to live as normal a life as possible.

Problems at school concerning a child's medical issues will arise.
It is only a matter of time until a child gets a teacher who is hassled
by unrestricted restroom breaks or one who will require a child to
go to the principal's office for pancreatic enzymes at snack-time.
When such challenges arise, parents must model the coping skills
they wish their child to show. Set the model of effective problem-
solving skills, which include cooperation, patience, creativity, and
negotiation — even when it may be tempting to respond with frustration and demands. Always encourage your child to take the lead
in effectively solving his or her school issues.

Preteens and Teenagers

Kathleen, who is wise beyond her 15 years, stated it so well when
she said, "I am not a disease!" Regardless of your teen's medical
issues, he or she is first of all a teen. That alone has far-reaching
implications for healthcare. Although books emphasize the "turmoil of the teen years" the fact is that while most teens live a busy,
somewhat fragmented life laced with new experiences, times of self-
doubt, and risk-taking behavior, good research shows the average
teen is not as unhealthy, impulsive, difficult, and rebellious as many
believe.

Before examining chronic illness during preteen and teen
years, it is good to look briefly at an overview of pre-teen and teen
development.

Generally, the pre-teen years are characterized by physical and mental change. "Little William" becomes big, hairy "Killer Bill," pride of the junior varsity team. Sweet little Kathryn becomes "Kat" whose daily outfits show plenty of skin between her shirt and the jeans that hug her body tightly. At this age, kids search for their identity in a sea of change. Girls mature first. Seventh grade girls generally think abstractly, worry endlessly about their appearance, spend hours IMing each other with text messages, and live in a world quite different from the active playful world of seventh grade boys. But change is in the air for both sexes as they search for some kind of shoal in a sea of change. Their primary concern is, "How do I fit in?" One mom gives an example: "I was taking Jenny to school the first day, and after we stopped the car, she sat in silence and looked at all the kids going into junior high. After about 30 seconds she asked, 'Where is the secret store where all these kids buy their clothes? And, how come I don't know about it?'" Each child consciously or unconsciously starts to realize he or she is no longer just Mr. and Mrs. Smith's kid, but a unique individual, who will have to make his or her own place in the world. In the late elementary school and preteen years, supervising adults preach conformity and compliance, so there is a general feeling among most kids most of the time that "being different is bad." It is no wonder peer acceptance becomes essential. Even as the child transitions from the preteen into the teen years there can be subtle changes:

- ❤ In the preteen years, before school, it's not cool for your mother to kiss you goodbye. At high school graduation, appreciating the love and energy of parents is accepted and cool.
- ❤ In the preteen years, fitting in is essential for many kids. In high school, being unique is generally accepted.
- ❤ In the preteen years, it's important to "merge with the herd." In the high school years, kids often strive to stand out in the group.

That said, what makes adolescence a difficult time for some parents and children? The main stumbling block is the fact that teens can actually think like adults. That is, for the first time in their lives, they can understand analogy and metaphor and thoughtfully weigh situational ethics. This "higher-order" thinking also lays the foundation for children to question adult value systems that were previously unquestioned when loving authority figures presented them.

In the pre-teen and teen years of developmental turmoil, chronic illness may add another important ingredient to the stew of life. *When a child is ill, the illness itself modifies and impacts all of life, including the "usual" teen issues.* Therefore, a pre-teen may be embarrassed about the appearance of his insulin pump; another may be resentful about his friend's lack of understanding concerning dietary restrictions; another may be resentful about the limitations imposed by asthma, and another copes with a friend's responses to her skin problems. Some chronically ill children face the challenge of rejection by a peer group during their teen years because of a genetically inherited condition that may affect their looks or ability to function on the same social or sporting level as their peers. Because peer acceptance is vital at school, some teens battle with these issues; others often handle them with more acceptance. Kathleen Burke is a great example. She is a remarkable teenager with CF who wrote, directed, and produced a play with her friends called *One Step Closer*, which is included on the DVD version of this program. She successfully copes with difficult issues by reaching out to her community and communicating how teenagers with CF handle their emotional storms.

Although it would take a whole book to reasonably clarify parent/teen issues and the problems/issues related to integration and adaptation of kids during their teen years, we can give you a few ideas that will be helpful when dealing with your chronically ill preteen or teenager. The tools and techniques needed to reach teens effectively through consultant parenting are the same, whether a child is dealing with decisions around thoughtfully using insulin or the car; whether the child is considering college choices or making health decisions. Before we look at these tools and techniques, let's first understand the role chronic illness plays during these years.

During the preteen years, chronic illness sometimes affects and slows the development of children who may be both small for their age and less physically developed. Children who feel scrawny, less mature, and are a lot shorter than the other kids simply can't "herd-merge." This can affect both self-image and general feelings of security. Some girls may have delayed breast development and be slow to start menstruating. Others, such as girls with Turner's Syndrome, may have serious growth and developmental problems because of a genetic predisposition towards small stature. For some girls who are emotionally dependent on peer approval and always in the front-line of peer pressure and conformity, this can be devastating. They feel different and alone. Other children can be cruel. Kids who don't fit in can become the object of bullying and ridicule (especially if they don't belong to one of the "in" groups).[9] These issues can be aggravated in a chronically ill child whose academic life or ability to engage in school activities is impaired by the constraints of his or her illness — such as regular visits to the hospital, surgical procedures, or the side-effects of life-altering daily medication.

Children may have bone, pulmonary, or GI involvement that limits their sports, extracurricular activities, and the amount of peer time available. Taking time out for treatments and medication leads kids to feel "different" during the time that they yearn to be like others.

During their teen years children start thinking about the future. The mating dance haltingly starts to take place, and these young emerging adults start asking themselves, "What am I going to be when I grow up?" For the first time, the long-term reality of a possibly life-shortening chronic illness starts to really sink in: "Maybe I won't have time to have kids... Maybe no one will want to marry me... Maybe I ought to have as much fun with sex while I can."

The children's realization of a possible or probable shortened life impacts the lives of their parents. During these years parents, realizing they can no longer "manhandle" children into compliance, now start urging them to think about what is best for their lives: "You need to start thinking about what (...a felony, poor grades, using drugs, noncompliance, getting pregnant... etc.) could mean for your future."

And even when the parental relationship is good, it is understandable when the ill child's angst-producing retort is: "It doesn't matter anyway!!!" And one mom said, "And then I don't know what to say."

Whether it is because of attempts to fit in, a response to feelings of hopelessness about an uncertain future, or outright rebellion, pre-teens and teens may make self-destructive choices. Some react by not taking their medicines and hiding this fact from parents who only later find out that their children with CF have been feeding enzymes to the garbage can. Young girls with CF, aged 10 or 11 and already thin, may become more severely underweight, "But, mom, everybody else is eating carrots and celery for lunch, why do I have to eat lasagna?" No amount of parental haggling or reasoning will change the preteen need to conform to his or her peer group.

So how can parents best help their preteens and teenagers navigate the challenges of these stages of life?

First, nothing can take the place of a good foundation of general knowledge about parenting preteens and teens. The recently updated *Parenting Teens with Love and Logic*, by Foster Cline, M.D., and Jim Fay, will give you a good start. When parenting pre-teens and teenagers who have chronic medical issues, parents must keep the following points in mind:

- ♥ Parents must increasingly rely heavily on giving facts and options about disease and healthcare, rather than giving demands and orders. Wise parents encourage their children to become educated about their illnesses and to become thoughtful consumers by accessing informative Internet sites packed with information. Curiosity and interest always trump worry and concern, especially with this age group.

♥ Chat rooms, summer camps, mentoring programs, and websites encourage communication between children who have the same illness. These provide an invaluable resource for those who face the same choices and care issues and help fill the identity and belonging gap.

♥ Parents find that encouraging their children to be "upfront" and educate classmates about their illness is often helpful, and most children are responsive and supportive with increased understanding: "Once the kids knew that just one little peanut could send me to the hospital, they didn't think I was so weird for reading the labels on all the food in the cafeteria. I thought they would think I was weird if I told them, but they thought I was weird because I hadn't told them."

♥ Teens may retort verbally or show by their attitude that, "It doesn't matter anyway" when contemplating their future. The more the parents show upset, angst, and pain, the more it validates the child's attitude. And in the case of parent/child conflict, it gives the controlling child more power over the parent's psychic life and emotional well-being. Thus, it is best to indicate a caring, loving, nonangry, and nonfrustrated response, such as, "I'm so sorry you feel that way." Nothing can take the place of simply caring and listening. A child (or any person) is generally helped by relating to someone who listens and understands without being bent out of shape. It's up to the parents to ensure the child's negative feelings are not contagious or magnified back onto the child. Often a small dose of encouragement may help: "I always knew you were the sort of kid who would set an example for how tough issues could be handled."

💜 It does not work to respond to the teens' feeling of hopelessness or anger by indicating:
   • "You disappoint me."
   • "You don't really mean it."
   • "Well, get over it."
   • "You'll feel better tomorrow."

💜 Help your child fit in where possible and appropriate. For example: If your daughter's peers are wearing make-up, don't ensure your child feels even more isolated by insisting it's too early. When dealing with teens, pick your battles wisely.

💜 Expectations are important. If you expect your child to be a problematic teen, he/she will be. If you expect these years to be fun, enlightening, and joyful, the odds are they will be.

💜 Encourage your child's strengths and normal activities. Generally, it is better to follow your child's lead on activities when he or she feels able to participate in them, even if you have your doubts about their effect on health.

In addition, wise parents accept the following truths about teenagers with medical issues:

💜 Teens will be secretive and hide some poor healthcare decisions from parents.

💜 Teens will resent their parents' overinvolvement in healthcare decisions. Most teens are generally open to the observations and thoughts of parents and others if they are not given as absolute directives or demands. Thus, they appreciate parental ideas but not advice or suggestions about how to handle issues concerning their medical condition.[10]

💜 There will be days the teen will wonder if the effort of taking care of his or her illness is really worth it, just as many adults wonder this, too.

- ♥ Teens always make mistakes.
- ♥ Teens may respond to "facts" but become either rebellious, sneaky, or both when threatened (i.e., when told, "Do this or else.").
- ♥ Teens often respond much better to information presented by a peer or a trusted, respected adult like a coach or doctor than by parents, particularly if the parent/child relationship is fraught with conflict or has reached a "stalemate."

In essence, to reach most teens *parents have to consider the responses that would be most effective with most adults!* This is often difficult for both parents and for the teen because both parties have been interacting in a parent/child relationship for years. Looking at their teen, most parents see in the back of their minds the little girl who always needed guidance, or the little boy who responded to firm control. And the teen may see the parents as people who have *always* tried to call the shots and make him or her shape up. Sometimes, then, it is important to sit down and overtly and realistically discuss the new relationship:

Trevor

Marge and Tom's only son, Trevor, was diagnosed with juvenile diabetes when he was 13 years old. On top of that he was subsequently diagnosed as having gluten intolerance and celiac disease. Trevor took these diagnoses poorly, saying he might as well die. He threatened suicide when responding to Marge, who had always tried to make every problem along life's path better for Trevor. She noted, "This is the first time Trevor has had problems I can't fix, or at least attempt to fix." Marge felt guilty about her previous overprotectiveness, which had resulted in a child who couldn't cope when faced by real problems. Her husband, Tom, was always a loving, somewhat demanding dad who demanded that Trevor "shape up" and showed understandable anger, mixed with his own sorrow about Trevor's medical issues.

During a consultation Foster emphasized that Marge and Tom should treat Trevor's medical problem in a matter-of-fact manner and that the more they offered consolation and overreassurance, the more Trevor would feel free to push in the other direction with angst and hopelessness. Although their overreassurance, demands, overconcern, and anger were understandable, they gave Trevor the message that the problem was theirs, not his. The parents took notes during the consultation, reviewed them over a dinner together, and then set up an appointment with Trevor. During this meeting they succinctly hammered home the following points, without embellishment or overconcern:

- "Trevor, when you were a child, we treated you as a child, giving guidance, helping you make decisions, and sometimes telling you what to do and how to handle things. Parents do that for little kids."
- "Now you are a teen and you think like a teen. God has provided you with some things that can either crack you or build your character; that can either lead to an increased awareness of life and its beauty or to unhappy decisions that will lead to death. We are both interested and curious about which path you will take." Now note here, dear reader, that these are parents who had previously emphasized love, angst, concern, suggestions, and admonitions. If the parent's love and support were in question, then this

"matter-of-fact" and "we-are-curious-and-interested" approach would need to be softened.

- "Perhaps luckily for you, Trevor, you have illnesses that only require self-control and awareness on your part. You don't have cancer, a wasting neurological disease where you will end up paralyzed and unable to breathe, or a brain hemorrhage. Your illnesses are perfectly designed for building character, should you choose to go that route. Sometimes when the going gets rough, some people keep hiking and become stronger. Some quit. It's your decision."
- "It's been great talking to you Trevor. Thanks for listening. We sure are looking forward to future great vacations and fun times with you should you decide to take a life-fulfilling route."

The parents wrote Foster that after their talk, Trevor made a complete turnaround.

In summary, if you are having trouble relating to your adolescent, there are many great resources available. But one and all generally emphasize the fact that teens reach a point where they ignore directions or rebel when given demands. At this juncture, thoughtful discussions outlining possible consequences become very effective.

Do all you can to encourage your special pre-teen and teen to pass through these years with a sense of purpose, connection, acceptance, and belonging both to family and friends. Mentoring, summer camps, and support groups can provide this critical peer-to-peer support. Ana Stenzel, an adult with cystic fibrosis, shares a pivotal life experience as she struggled to come to terms with her disease:

Ana

Until the age of 11, I grew up thinking that my twin sister and the three other children I knew at the hospital were the only ones in the world with CF. It was an isolating and difficult experience. Then, at the age of 11, I started going to a Cystic Fibrosis summer camp in Southern California and met dozens of other CF kids of all racial and socio-economic backgrounds coping with CF in different ways. I saw a disease that spared some but wreaked havoc on others. I saw teenagers and adults with CF who had jobs, went to college, and were even married. I saw adults with talents and goals, who could find joy, purpose, and camaraderie in a supportive community while facing a life-threatening and high-maintenance disease like cystic fibrosis. This gave me an invaluable hope that some day I too could live to adulthood. It was at camp that I felt normal and I "woke up" to learn what it meant to have CF.

I saw what happened to some of the teenagers who didn't take care of themselves — they suffered immensely and ultimately died. It was a harsh reality of what lay ahead and how much of surviving this disease was in my control. I recognized the impact that my choices, both good and bad, would make on my health and my life. After seeing the sicker kids, I rarely missed a treatment. I saw what medications the other children took and what kind of treatments they did, which was very different from the treatment I was receiving. After camp, I went back to my doctor and begged him to give me the better medicines that the other kids were taking. In essence, it was a life-changing and highly educational coming-of-age experience to be around other children and adults with CF for one week every summer.

Children with severe health problems need the support of peers. We can become each other's saving graces, especially as the disease progresses. One gains a sense of normalcy when interacting with those who live in the common culture of a particular disease. We all speak the same language, have the same lifestyle, and take similar medications; we also have similar hopes, fears, and dreams. I hope that all children with chronic illnesses find the same camaraderie that has fueled my will to live since the age of 11.

Finally, it may be reassuring to realize that whether teens are healthy or ill, there are no guarantees when parenting them. Wise parents who provide children with the general tools and techniques we have emphasized throughout this work have the best chances of raising functional and responsible citizens who make prudent, thoughtful life decisions, including those concerning self-care issues.

Into Young Adulthood and Beyond

So, your teenager has graduated from high school and is ready, with great anticipation, to go out into the big world. You've been preparing him or her all along for this transition. After all, isn't that a parent's ultimate role? Like the mother bird who cares for and nurtures her young until they are old enough to fly and then gently nudges them from the nest after removing a twig at a time, your job is to remove, where possible, the twigs of dependence so your child can fly in life and make the life-saving decisions required of an adult with a chronic medical condition.

Parents of healthy children are often proud but worried when their kids leave home. The parents of chronically ill children are often doubly proud *and* doubly worried. These times are filled with parental doubt. "Will my child take good care of herself? What will happen if she gets sick at a college across the country? Who will make sure she is following her treatments or taking her medications? What if she gets too busy at college and forgets to take good care of herself? The doctors won't give me any information now that she's eighteen! How can I find out if she is doing okay?" These are all very real, valid concerns, taken right out of the mouths of parents who are going through this as we write.

Life is filled with transitions. This may just be one of the toughest, but there are good resources for parents and children traveling this path.[11]

It is difficult to give precise information on handling this phase of life because each young adult's transition after leaving home is unique; and when medical conditions are thrown into the mix, the situation is often very complex. Naturally, how the young adult handles this transition to adulthood depends not only on the type and severity of the illness but upon prior self-care, attitudes, abilities, and expectation levels. For some children, their illnesses are so severe that a transition out of the home is impractical; other children in relatively good health may decide to stay home for financial reasons.

Regardless of the situation, there are predictable problems for family members when children transition from the home.

One predictable outcome is that family dynamics change. Although an illness may have been a difficult issue for all to cope with, it nevertheless may have been a defining factor for family roles and patterns of interaction within the family. If Mom has been a primary caretaker, her whole job description is thrown into chaos when the child leaves. If a father is present, he may suddenly have different and more personal expectations of his wife. Other children in the family, who may have been no problem previously, now start having difficulties. It is as if they are saying, "Hey, now you have to focus on me!"

Paul and Henry

Paul is the younger 11-year-old brother of Henry, a teen with hemophilia who graduated from high school and went to college. Suddenly Paul found himself under the unwelcome scrutiny of his mother. After a soccer game, in a therapy session with nearly tearful intensity, he pleaded, "You've got to get my mom off my back, Dr. Cline. She watches me like a hawk. If I fall or if I trip, it's like it could be the end of the world. I tell her, 'Whoa, Mamma Mia, *I'm* not the one with hemophilia. Whoa. Back off.' But it is like she's *there*. After the soccer game, I had this little scratch and about four drops of blood. Four drops! The way she was screaming around, you would have thought I needed clotting factor!" While Paul complained bitterly about the increased attention, one could not help but wonder if he protested too much and whether, underneath it all, he enjoyed being the focus of maternal concern for the first time in his life.

Paul's mother, Angie, was thoughtful and introspective but still had a hard time controlling her behavior. "I've had to be hyper-vigilant for 18 years. What am I supposed to do; just turn it off? Just, click and it's off? No. I know I have to turn it off, but it's hard. You would think, after Henry left, I would feel, 'Now there's freedom!' But it's like I've never been so depressed in my life. And then I get depressed about that! I still worry about Henry and how he's doing at school and it's all I can do to keep from phoning him about his knees!" She laughs knowingly. "But I can turn that off if I spend a little more time worrying about the shortage of clotting factor and how he can get it up there (in college). I just have to be more choosy about my worry quotient."

(Sigh) "So, I suppose I do express my concern to Paul more than before." (Laughing) "Foster, so just tell me to stop, okay?"

Obviously, there will be identity issues whenever a child leaves home, and this is especially true for families living with ill children, who have been primary actors in the family's play of life. All those left behind as children leave home simply must find new activities, interests, and interaction patterns that healthily fill the void.

Another predictable outcome when children leave home is that they must carry the primary responsibility for their own healthcare issues. Hopefully this responsible adult behavior has already been cultivated throughout the teen years.

Henry

Henry says, "So you are writing a book about kids leaving home? Honestly, I have friends who are shocked when they step right into the new college world simply because they have to do their own laundry. I'm not kidding. Mom isn't doing their laundry, and they can't figure out how long to leave the clothes in a dryer. Well, hello!!! I wish I had that kind of problem. Mom always used to worry about the shortage of clotting factors for *us*, or she'd worry about new medications *we* might try. She always referred to my illness in the plural. Like, 'How are *we* going to handle that problem?' Now, I *still* think, 'What are *we* going to do?' But there is no '*we*!!!' There is only '*me*!' That is my wake-up call. *So I would say the most important thing is to make sure kids take care of themselves completely and do a good job of it before they leave home."*

Whether the young adult stays at home or leaves, wise parents must have a conversation to clarify expectations around relevant illness issues. Of course, such a conversation should take place about nonmedical responsibilities too.

- ♥ The young adult has the responsibility of ensuring that ICE (In Case of Emergency) has been keyed in on the phone (a space in front of ICE ensures it will be FIRST on the contact list); that insurance information is readily available; that emergency telephone numbers are available; and that all relevant issues pertaining to the particular health issue have been covered with backups, if necessary. Important information about the child's illness should be carried on a card in his or her wallet or purse.

- ♥ Parents need to clarify, "If you have a shortage of money or have problems getting drugs, do you plan to tough it out or call us?"

- ♥ "If you had seizures, diabetic comas, severe bleeds, or severe breathing problems, would you tell us about it, or feel like you didn't want to worry us and just let it pass?"

- ♥ "How would you handle your problems and symptoms at school or in a distant city?"

- ♥ "If you got into a financial jam and couldn't pay for care, would you feel okay about calling us to talk about it?"

- ♥ "If you make a mistake in handling your medications, breathing treatments, or blood sugar levels and decided to contact us about it, do you think we would be disappointed, angry, helpful, or what?"

Let's face it. All wise parents understand that some children just aren't going to be able to do an adequate job of taking care of themselves and that they can't be truly self-sustaining. This realization is hard to face but it's not really the main parenting point. The main point is, *Do we as parents wish with all our hearts to raise our children to be responsible and self-sufficient, and do we do all we can to encourage them*, or are we bound up in the trap of needing to be needed?

Particularly at this age, sharing the control, providing empathy before allowing the consequences to occur, sharing the thinking and problem-solving, and being a Consultant Parent will all contribute to the child's chances of being independently successful.

If children have been thinking for themselves all along and taking responsibility for their own healthcare, then they should be able to spread their wings and take flight after leaving the nest.

Illness in Adult Children

Throughout this book, we have emphasized the tools, techniques, and loving responses that will be most effective in raising children who cope with the tough issues brought about by chronic illness. When the subject of ill children crops up, we naturally think of youths — of little kids and the guidance, love, and encouragement they need. However, the grim master of chronic illness respects no age. The results of effective parenting don't really shine until children are adolescents and young adults. Generally, the glow of great parenting shows in grandchildren who reflect the "respectful, responsible, and a joy-to-be-around" attitude that was expected in their own parents' childhood. However, effective parenting is most apparent in the character of adult children as they face the possibility of a terminal illness or a threat to a spouse's life.

Wayne (43) and Betsy (40) are the loving parents of two beautiful children in the fourth and sixth grades. Wayne loves the outdoors, and on an August hike he noticed his right leg seemed weak. He had also been plagued by some night twitching and stiffness in both legs. Expecting a minor problem that could easily be sorted out, he was shocked when nerve conduction and other tests revealed he was one of 30,000 other Americans who have Lou Gehrig's disease, a fatal condition also known as ALS (Amyotrophic Lateral Sclerosis). The first people Wayne and Betsy turned to for support were Wayne's parents.

Moms and dads never quit being mom and dad, no matter how old their children are. But when an adult child has problems, how sweet it is to know that our adult child:

- ♥ Can cope with his illness but would *be appreciative* and able to use parental love and support.
- ♥ Will make thoughtful and wise decisions that will truly reflect what is in his or her family's best interests.
- ♥ Will be able to weep with his parents, while remaining thoughtful and realistic.
- ♥ Will be able to plan for the future with his folks' input.

Wayne's mother epitomizes parental love flowing out, irrespective of the child's age.

Wayne's Mom

It's heart-wrenching when something like this drops out of the blue. But it is, perhaps, God's blessing that as a family we have time to prepare. A car accident doesn't afford that opportunity. We have sold our home and helped Wayne and Betsy find a one-story home near the one we have bought. There will be a time, soon it seems, when stairs won't be helpful. In the next two years that are statistically left, we are going to enjoy every moment with the kids and grand-kids. We take the kids once a week for Wayne and Betsy's night out together. We all intend to pack a life-time of love and time together into the next 700 days, or whatever we are blessed with.

In this mom's response, the empathy, the ability to cope, the sense of loss, and her continuing support for an ill child are evident. What a gift of courage, comfort, and hope she has given to her child and to his family.

Chapter 6 Key Concepts
Chronic Illness in the First Years

1. Illness, treatment, and trauma can have a lasting affect on the developing brain and personality of the child. During the first year of life, a sense of basic trust normally develops as infantile needs are met. Causal thinking develops when the world is predictable. Thus, when chronic pain is present and the world is unpredictable, both basic trust and causal thinking may be negatively impacted, leading to behavioral problems in an ill child. The trust cycle and bonding problems are diagrammed and explored. The symptoms of attachment disorder and possible parental responses are examined.

2. During the second year of the child's life, parents are encouraged to use stories, drawings, and other examples to help the child visualize his/her illness and its treatment. The techniques advocated in this book should begin when the child is a toddler.

Chronic Illness in Preschool Years

♥ Generally, the younger the child, the less lasting and less painful the consequences of poor decisions will be. Starting with young children, parents can give information in a hopeful, encouraging, age-appropriate manner that will promote good decision making based on factual information. This chapter addresses these modifications with respect to handling medical issues.

Chronic Illness in the Elementary School Years

1. The elementary school years can be deceptively smooth, and parents can be lulled into a false sense of security when they use parenting styles that will not be effective in the teen years and during young adulthood. Therefore, Consultant Parenting, which is optional during the elementary years, should be practiced and perfected. It is the only style that works well during and after the teen years. Explanations and examples of Consultant Parenting are given in this chapter.

2. The start of school can present the potential for a multitude of parenting challenges. There are many options to consider as children and parents navigate these challenges together.

Chronic Illness in the Preteen and Teen Years

1. During the preteen years, a desire to fit in with a peer group becomes a primary concern. Medical problems can lead to a child feeling different, isolated, and the target of negative and painful remarks. Children with compromised functioning and/or a shortened lifespan may realize their differences. Physical changes in brain function cause children to transition from the concrete thinking of childhood to the adult ability to conceptualize. Children who were once unquestioningly obedient start questioning adult authority and disagree with dearly held parental values and ideas. They may no longer accept parental responses at face value. Therefore, providing children with good information about their condition, treatment, and possible long-term outcomes is essential. Information and peer-support groups can be helpful. A primary job for parents is to help their children maintain high self-esteem, while accepting their differences and giving them tools to effectively respond to, and educate, peers.

2. During the teen years, parents should choose their battles wisely, only "fighting" those issues they know they can conquer — and often these battles do not involve their children's healthcare issues. Wise parents learn to respond to their adolescents as they would to any other adult. Rebellious teens may try to manipulate and control home environments with self-destructive behavior. At such times, wise parents let their children know that, beyond a shadow of a doubt, they must care more about their health than the parents do. Parents must continue with loving, nonangry, nonfrustrated, and caring responses that don't exude worry or concern. Teens often respond well to information presented by other teens with whom they can identify because of their common ages or similar illnesses. Information from adults who have coped well or poorly and learned important lessons during their own adolescent years is helpful. This chapter covers responses that are not effective and provides an example of a corrective conversation with a rebellious teen.

Into Young Adulthood and Beyond

1. When children transition from the home, family dynamics and the higher expectations for responsible adult behavior can cause turmoil. Ways to address these transition issues are discussed.

2. When children leave home, parents may be faced with a "hole" in the need for habituated responses. "Nature abhors a vacuum," and this hole can be filled with either healthy or unhealthy patterns. Thus, it is not uncommon for parents who had a need to provide their children with a great deal of guidance and support to feel depressed, rather than liberated, when their children leave home. Well siblings may assume the role of being a "sick" child, with the onset of behavioral or other

problems. Parents face the choice of either developing healthy new interests, patterns, and plans for the future within the couple's relationship and with the remaining children, or continue being overconcerned and overinvolved. This may result in adult children who continue living a dependent, enabled, dysfunctional, and lonely lifestyle.

Illness in Adult Children

♥ When adult children are diagnosed with a terminal illness, effective parenting becomes most apparent in their character as they cope with tough situations and handle them in a healthy manner with their own spouse and children. An example of coping and acceptance is given.

Let's Wrap Up Basic Training

Congratulations! You've made it through Love and Logic Basic Training. This section presented Love and Logic's curriculum as it addresses challenges common to all parents but with a medical focus. We hope you have found these techniques to be effective, enjoyable to learn, and easy to implement. The next section will delve more deeply into specific difficulties that arise when parenting children with health issues. The major points in this section are emphasized in this personal and encouraging note written by a very special mother, Jeannine Bailey:

Jeannine

When we were parenting our two children in the 1970s and '80s, we had very little access to formal parenting support. Matt and Greg were born with cystic fibrosis, and parenting was a special challenge. I received one handout from the local children's hospital, which recommended that we give our children as much control over their lives as we could since they had so little control over their illness. Simple and great advice! Other advice from their pediatrician was to avoid refereeing at all costs; that they needed to work out their own conflicts with each other. Another piece of great advice. I heard somewhere the idea of natural consequences and loved that idea. I had support from friends who also were facing the challenges of parenting, although none of them had children with special healthcare needs. It seemed that we were all facing the same dilemmas; mine were simply more intense than most. One of these friends lent me a book that was helping her through the crisis of her husband's mental illness. That book taught me how to focus on "what is" and not to dwell on the "what ifs" of cystic fibrosis. I also was drawn into the care ministry of our church, and there I received a lot of training in listening and compassionate care. The emphasis was to be simply a loving presence. My own experiences as a child with good parents helped immensely. My dad was long on logic. As I have become acquainted with Love and Logic, I am impressed that the curriculum brings together the bits and pieces of my parenting philosophy, which worked so well with dear Matt and Greg.[12]

These various resources gave me a foundation for parenting, but I also needed energy. Matt was diagnosed at 14 months while I was pregnant with Greg, and when Greg was a year old his diagnosis was confirmed. I had a baby and a toddler and was learning about therapy, mist tents, and enzymes. My sorrow was deep, and the future looked bleak. My first strategy was to pretend while the boys were awake that life was great and to do my grieving while they slept. And one day, while weeping into the lunch dishwater, I heard very clearly in my mind the message that all I had to do was love them. Their care was overwhelming, and sometimes I wasn't able to do everything expected of me by their pediatrician. Loving them became my focus — loving them constantly and deeply and caring for them the best that I could. I had the energy to love them, and life became more manageable. Eventually, even doing two therapies twice daily became routine. And quieting my worries by focusing on the current moment helped. Most days, the "what is" was that the boys were well, and we were having a lot of "normal" in our lives. Other days, I needed to call the doctor; and then some weeks, we needed to hunker in and endure a hospitalization, or at-home antibiotic therapy.

We have great memories of our time with Matt and Greg. Greg, our youngest, lived to be 17, and Matt lived to be almost 24. I have many stories about these two. We did love them deeply and constantly. Refusing to get involved in their conflicts with each other enhanced their relationship; they were the best of friends. And we did give them as much control of their lives as we could. Messy rooms were ignored, what they wore was their own choice, their participation in extracurricular activities up to them, etc. They made good choices, and parenting was pretty easy. Their medical care was more challenging. Being that compassionate presence when they were grieving was a rare gift, although witnessing their grief as they adjusted to the progression of their disease was heartbreaking.

As I reflect on the years of parenting Matt and Greg, one of my favorite stories about parenting involved Greg and friends in junior high, when experimentation often begins. One weekend morning, Matt and Greg were quietly talking in our living room. That in itself was unusual. I heard Matt say to Greg, "You need to ask Mom." Greg gave him a hiss that meant shut up. Matt, louder yet, repeated his comment. Greg hissed again, and again Matt, louder and louder, told him he needed to ask me...something. So I sweetly called into them, "Ask me what?" They came into the kitchen, Greg grumping at Matt, but then telling me that at the sleepover with his buddies that evening, they were planning to sneak out and he wasn't sure about it. He had been asking his older brother for advice. Matt was relieved to pass the responsibility for guidance on to me. I asked Greg what he thought his friends had in mind. He wasn't sure. I asked if he thought they might be thinking of toilet papering a friend's house or going skate boarding in the moonlight. He didn't know. I told him it might be fun, but that it could also lead to trouble. Egging a car or a house would be vandalism, and if they were trespassing they might get shot at. I told him he needed an escape plan if things got a little wild. He thought that was a good idea. Matt thought I was violating my job description as mother and couldn't believe I was giving Greg permission to be out in the night. I suggested to Greg that he needed a buddy who would have his same comfort zone, and that they could put together a plan to return to the sleepover or to call me. He decided that his friend Chad would be a good buddy. He had a plan. And it turned out that they didn't sneak out. I had counted on the mom hosting the party to be on top of the details, and evidently she was.

At all the future sleepovers or parties, Greg knew he could call me. I would often get a call about 10 p.m. and it would be Greg. He would simply say a very quiet hi, and I knew he was sneaking a call home on the house phone. I'd ask what was up, and get a quiet grunt. Then I'd ask, "Staying?" "Nope." "Ten minutes?" "Nope." "Twenty?" "Yup." "I'll be there." His friends would be very surprised when I would arrive, and wonder why he couldn't stay. I'd tell them he was "busted," their term for grounded. They would look at him with a mixture of respect and amazement for getting into trouble, and Greg would give me a look of gratitude that would make my day.

When Matt was in junior high, I had forbidden him to attend a ninth grade sneak his crowd was planning; they were going to skip school and go swimming at a friend's house, with no adults present. I had told him no. He had pleaded, and I had stuck with my no. He went anyway, and I still have my regrets about how I handled that. Another of my parenting guidelines was to never put my kids in a position where lying to me was tempting. I put Matt into that position. How I wish I had walked through the whole issue as I did when Greg presented a similar challenge.

My hope for all of you with special children is that you will use your energy to love them with a passion, and that you will care for them the best that you can given all of your circumstances. And that you will have hope for tomorrow and for their life in eternity, where all of our children will realize their full potential and we will get to enjoy them forever. Have faith.... A community of people filled with a commission to love is a great place of shelter for you and your children.

Part 2

Advanced Love and Logic Applications

Chapter 7

It's Not Birds and Bees: Talking with Kids about Life and Death

Hope is the thing with feathers,
that perches in the soul.
And sings the tune without the words,
and never stops at all.
—Emily Dickinson (1830-1886)

Although the issues around chronic illnesses and medical challenges are special, we still use Love and Logic communication tools to handle these special problems. Ordinary parents with their "run-of-the-mill" kids can be taken aback by questions that, on the spur of the moment, are difficult to answer. Such questions might be, "How often do you and dad have sex?" Or "Did you do drugs when you were a kid?" Those with chronically ill children have even more difficult questions. Our kids might ask, "When am I going to die?" Or, "Am I really going to go to Heaven?" Or, "Will my disease kill me?" These questions require really thoughtful responses. Let's examine how Love and Logic says we can handle children's questions about very difficult issues:

1. Before we give answers, let's ask ourselves, "Whose needs am I addressing — mine or my child's?"
2. Consider whether we are giving more information than the child wants or needs to hear.
3. Be open to our children talking with us about anything and everything.
4. When we are not sure how to give the answer, ask more questions.
5. Recognize that sometimes our children try to "protect" us.
6. Show acceptance even when we can't show approval.
7. Every answer dealing with life-and-death issues should leave room for hope.

Let's look at each of these considerations more fully in the context of dealing with chronic illness:

1. **In giving answers, we must ask ourselves: "Whose needs am I addressing — mine or my child's?"** It's often difficult to separate our needs from the child's needs. Sometimes in divorce situations, parents, unconsciously meeting their own needs, destroy their children. Yet they honestly believe they are only doing what is best for the child. Another example: many parents pop a pacifier in a toddler's mouth, not because the toddler needs it or even requests it. It simply makes the mom feel more "motherly."

   When our children ask about death and dying, we need to ask ourselves if our answer is an attempt to reassure ourselves as well as reassure the child. Is the answer honest? Does it leave room for hope? Is the answer something that will decrease or increase our child's character development or ability to cope? When a parent reacts with terror or fright about a particular subject, the child will feel the same fright and terror, too. This immediately inhibits discussion, which means there will be less chance of the child coping successfully. Children model their own coping skills on those of their parents. Parents who cope well are more likely to have children who cope well.

2. **Are we giving more information than the child wants or needs to hear?** Parents wonder when to give their children information about difficult subjects. Unless the children are protecting the parents, there is an easy answer: When children are ready for the answer, they will ask the question. However, parents often need to simplify their answers. Once there was a child who asked her mother, "Where do little birds come from?" Mom gave encyclopedic information about the sex act and how it was different in mammals and birds. Really, the answer the little child was searching for was much shorter: "Eggs, dear." When a child is small and asks, "What is wrong with my lungs?" A sufficient answer is, "There is icky stuff down there that needs to be cleaned out." Later on, a child may ask why they have icky stuff there in the first place. Then genetic predispositions can be discussed. And even later the child may benefit from knowing about recessive illness when he or she asks, "Why don't you and dad have CF too?

3. **Do we encourage our children to talk to us about anything and everything?** Are we able to set the model by radiating an attitude that implies, *"Nothing is too scary for me to talk about. I'm able to talk about anything with you."* Great parents project this kind of acceptance laced with strength, and it's a quality that varies from parent to parent. Projecting acceptance is more than simply saying, "Honey you can talk to me about anything." It is putting that statement into action by not over-reacting; asking thoughtful questions about the child's percep-

tion; giving acceptance but not necessarily approval; and providing eye contact and a body posture that says, one way or another, "That's an interesting subject. First give me your thoughts and I'll give you mine."

4. **When we are not sure how to give the answer, ask more questions**. When we are at a loss for words and really don't quite know what to say, it's best to ask another question. Often, when we explore an issue further, we find that what the child really needs to know and gain insight into is precisely what and how much she or he can cope with. Truly, most counselors seldom need to know exactly what to say when first confronted with a tough issue. They simply need to know what questions to ask, allowing the client to find his or her own answers. Invariably, almost automatically, folks then thank the therapist for helping them come up with answers they discovered themselves!

While showing genuine curiosity and interest, here are some common questions a parent might ask children about their illness:
- "How much do you know about your illness?"
- "How worried are you?"
- "How are you handling it?"
- "What can I do to make things easier?"
- "Is there anything more you need to know?"
- "How important is living longer to you because you take good care of yourself?"
- "Is your illness increasing your awareness of each day's opportunities?"
- "What special things can you offer others that healthier (or most) kids can't?"

5. **Recognize that sometimes our children try to "protect" us.** Sometimes children don't ask certain questions because they want to protect their parents or they respond in a manner they

feel will shield their parents from facing difficult situations. We really do need to understand that children sometimes will not bring up difficult subjects out of concern for the parents. Children want to make adults happy most of the time. Let's look at an example.

Eleven-year-old Gracie accidentally overheard two nurses in the hallway of Children's Medical Center talking about how the medications were no longer effectively fighting her cancer and how short her life might be. Nevertheless, Gracie's parents told her that the new medication seemed to be melting her tumor. She smiled sweetly at her mom and said simply, "That's good news, Mom." Only upon reading Gracie's journal after her death did her parents realize the extent and accuracy of her knowledge about her illness. Later her mom commented, "I can hardly believe how she fooled us and how out of touch with her reality we must have seemed. Now I wish we had made fewer statements, given less reassurance, and asked a lot more questions!"

6. **Show acceptance even when we can't show approval**. Even if we don't approve of our child's beliefs, responses, or concerns, are we able to show acceptance? Wise leaders and parents know this very important difference between approval and acceptance. Human hearts yearn for acceptance, but not necessarily approval. Great therapists can radiate acceptance without approval, as does a Catholic Priest when he listens in the confessional. When acceptance is shown, communication always continues. Judgmental responses and lack of acceptance always stop communication. Often, after a workshop, people ask Foster questions about how to handle a particular problem they are experiencing with a child. Many times he says, "Go home and ask your child that same question — the question you are asking me — being careful to ask it with the same tone of curiosity and interest."

When an accepting person shows love to an individual who knows the other does not approve of the behavior, it brings the two closer together. It is a bonding experience. This is the power of Grace!

7. **Every answer dealing with death, disease, and illness should leave room for hope**. During times of trial and tribulation, at one time or another, adults and children alike wonder if life is worth living. For people of all ages, illness is one of the major reasons for suicide. Once a little girl named Laura decided she was simply done with taking 40 pills a day, and though there may have been an element of rebellion in her decision, there was no doubt there were also elements of hopelessness and helplessness. It is these two elements, hopelessness and helplessness, that cause many parents to attempt to sidestep communication when living with children with special medical needs.

Hopelessness is best avoided when parents model a hopeful attitude. Hope is God's great balm for tough times. The life-changing benefit of faith is the hope with which it fills people's hearts. Providing hope does not mean blithely reassuring children everything will be okay. It is certainly not saying, "Don't worry about that" when children talk about their fears of illness, death, and dying. Many times, ill children find it easier to talk about their own death than their parents do. Understandably, it is incredibly difficult for parents to hold the hand of a child they love and talk about death and dying. However, when *anyone* is at death's door, this is a subject that often fills the mind. How sweet it is when a loved one is strong enough to discuss death and intimately share in the lonely and, sometimes, scary thoughts that occupy the minds of the parents and child before one passes through the portal.

Bobby

Beth began working in a pediatric surgical ward after graduating from nursing school. Bobby, a beautiful seven-year-old boy, was scheduled for a second open-heart surgery. Beth knew it would be a very challenging operation, especially because scarring from the first operation made the second much more risky. Nevertheless, when Bobby frequently asked, "Am I going to die?" Beth always answered, "Of course not!" However, Bobby never made it off the operating table. His little heart finally gave out just as the surgeon was closing his chest up after a long and difficult operation. Beth reflects on this difficult experience:

"As I look back on it, I realize I could have been so much more help to Bobby. However, at the time, my own son, Jess, was seven, and also a brunette, brown-eyed boy. I think that may have played a role in my denial. Bobby's death devastated me but I learned from it. Now, when a child asks if they are going to die, instead of saying, 'Of course not' and closing down the conversation, I give hope but I explore their fears. Because of what Bobby taught me, I have had so many heart-to-heart conversations with sick and dying children over my career. I wish with all my heart every parent could have that type of conversation with their child but I realize sometimes it is just too hard for them."

Helplessness is avoided by focusing on providing children with choices and control. When children feel emboldened to participate in decisions around healthcare and have the responsibility of carrying out those decisions, helplessness is banished. Even when a child is extremely disabled, helplessness is avoided when that child is allowed to make decisions about when treatment is given and how it is provided. Far too often a child's wishes and thoughts are steamrollered by parental and hospital schedules. Here is a good example:

Ginny

Eleven-year-old Ginny suffered severe burns. Changing her dressing was a painful experience. She often asked her nurse, Janet, to change her dressing half an hour later than was scheduled. Janet's response was, "No, this has to be done on schedule." The fact was, it didn't have to be changed exactly on schedule. Janet later admitted, "I feel so bad when I look back on it. Finally, one day, in exasperation, I asked Ginny why it was so important to wait half an hour. She said, '*Seventh Heaven*, my favorite TV show, starts half an hour after my dressing is changed. If you could wait until then so I could watch it while you are changing my dressing, I think it would take my mind off being hurt so much.' Of course I changed her dressing half an hour later. Sometimes I think we get so wrapped up in getting the job done, we just don't listen to these kids in the hospital."

All good relationships depend on good communication. However, as we have noted, good communication may be difficult when illness, death, and dying are part of the picture. Some parents are able to do it naturally more easily than others but anyone can improve their communication skills using the inspiration, examples, and practices we advocate.

Before looking at an example of communicating about difficult issues with an older child, let's first review the foundational concepts for communication presented here:

♥ We listen to our child with acceptance, but not necessarily approval.

♥ We ask further questions to probe what our child needs or wants to know.

♥ We let our child know we can talk about anything.

♥ We do our very best to separate our child's needs from our own and meet his or her needs, not ours.

♥ We always leave room for hope.

With these concepts in mind, let's eavesdrop:

> "How did school go today, John?"
>
> "Not so well, I guess."
>
> "Want to talk about it?"
>
> "Well, today I had one of my really bad coughing spells. One of the kids asked, 'What's wrong with you?' Then, a kid named Robert said, 'My mom says he has a real bad lung disease and he's going to die early.'"
>
> "And, you feel pretty upset. What upsets you the most? What the other kids say or the kid himself?"
>
> "What he said."
>
> "What are you thinking?"
>
> "I'm thinking about when I'm going to die."
>
> "Would you like some information?"
>
> "Yeah."
>
> "No one knows when they are going to die. Lots of people look forward to a long and happy life and suddenly die in a car accident. Every day, people are dying in thousands of car accidents and many more die of one thing or another. But the truth is, you could die before a lot of your classmates."
>
> "Like when?"
>
> "Well, right now, many people die when they are in

their mid 30s, but people with cystic fibrosis are living longer and longer. What do you think the doctors are doing right now, even as we speak?!"

"Working on cures."

"Good thinking! Yes they are. Do you have any idea of how much progress they've made?"

"Not really."

"What's your guess?"

"A lot?"

"You said it, kid! People are living longer all the time. Just a few years ago, kids with cystic fibrosis didn't live 'till their 30s. So, what are your thoughts now?"

"Well, I hope they work on it really hard. Because I'd like to live a long time."

(Smiling) "Well, I'd like that too. May I share some of my thoughts on this?"

"Sure, Dad."

"Often when people suspect they might die early, each day and each week becomes particularly precious. Such people live life to the fullest. They make every minute and every day count. I think you might be a person like that. See, in doing this, these special people set a wonderful example for all the other ordinary people who may waste time in their lives. I guess, John, for me it's not a matter of the size of the cup, but the value of the drink. It's not a matter of how long we live but how well we live the life we have. In fact, Mom and I always thought of you as being more like lightning than moonlight. Now don't get me wrong. Moonlight is great. But it's pretty ordinary; everyone expects it, and there's not a lot of marvel in it, if you know what I mean. But the crack of lightning! Wow! It may not last as long as a moonlit evening, but everyone pays attention to it, that's for sure. And they tell others about it, and forget even mentioning the moon- light. I wonder if you see yourself more as focusing on how long the life you live will be or focusing on how tightly you pack the values you put in it?"

"Maybe more on how tight I pack it."

"That's what I always figured too. Thanks for talking with me about this, John. If you have more questions, what do you think I would really appreciate?" (Notice that the dad accepts the "maybe" in a positive light and doesn't ruin the moment by saying, "Only maybe?" or pressing for a more positive statement.)

"Talking to you?"

"You better believe it!"

"Thanks Dad."

The Trouble with Statistics

As we've just seen, answering a child's questions about the course of his or her illness can be difficult. And how can parents answer their child's questions with hope if they have not come to a good place themselves? The child will almost always take the parent's cues. Let's take a close look at the inherent difficulties when relying on statistics for medical predictions.

When a child is first diagnosed with a medical condition, espe- cially a life-threatening one, the first question many parents under- standably ask is, "How long does my child have to live?" Medical professionals respond by quoting the statistics. Statistical predic- tions are ubiquitous and necessary. They help with individual and corporate planning. They form the foundation for an insurance company's viability and thereby ensure the availability of insurance programs for everybody. Statistically, all illnesses have a somewhat predictable course. Statistically, life-shortening illnesses have an "average life expectancy." But statistics based on the group norms may be very misleading and even disabling when applied to individual children. A statistical "average" simply means that sixty percent, more or less, fall within a standard deviation of the norm. A third fall outside that deviation and it's very hard to predict who will be among the many who "beat the odds." At a recent Cystic Fibrosis Research Inc. (CFRI) meeting in California, many attendees with CF were well over 40 years of age, despite the current median life expectancy of about 36.

Historically, medical professionals have been known to advise parents of children with cystic fibrosis not to worry about saving for their children's college education. And parents have been known to lower their expectations concerning their children's performance in school, sports, or other important matters relating to the future and living a "normal" life. This lowering of expectations, with its suggestion of a "What's the use?" attitude does a great disservice to children. It encourages them to become both entitled[13] and to feel hopeless within themselves. Achievement and self-image both suffer. The average life expectancy for many diseases is increasing at a fairly rapid rate due to medical advances. What might be an accurate statistic today probably won't be tomorrow. While it is important to understand the statistics, it is not helpful to be governed by them. The Nash family knew this to be true:

Liz

When Liz was diagnosed with cystic fibrosis in 1973, her parents were told not to expect her to graduate from high school. She did much more than that. Liz earned a PhD in molecular genetics and went on to become a research scientist in CF. She did an internship at Johns Hopkins University and post-doctoral work at the University of California, San Francisco. She volunteered as a mentor to teens with CF, who struggled with thoughts about their future and medical compliance. When she could no longer work full time as a bench scientist, Liz continued her fight as chair of the Research Advisory Committee of Cystic Fibrosis Research, Inc. (CFRI). When Liz died at nearly 33, CFRI honored her by renaming their post-doctoral research funding as the Elizabeth Nash Memorial Fellowship Program.

Liz was optimistic, enthusiastic, and passionate about her life's work and interests. She shunned the limitations imposed by CF. As captain of her college ski team she refused to give up the sport when oxygen became necessary. She simply skied with a backpack filled with portable oxygen tanks. As an inspiring individual, Liz was selected to carry the 2002 Olympic Torch through Union Square in San Francisco. Liz's family established a foundation to honor her spirit and continue her lifelong fight against cystic fibrosis.[14]

With many medical conditions, there is a strong correlation between good self-care and longevity. Parents can use statistics to inspire hope and spark an "I can beat this" attitude. Parents who give off positive, "we can beat this" vibes generally raise kids with the same determined spirit. We have met many CF parents and patients who demonstrate this indomitable attitude. Boomer Esiason (of NFL fame) and Jerry Cahill are great examples of positive, motivating individuals who inspire and, in fact, challenge, those living with CF to "beat the odds."[15] Boomer vowed to eliminate the threat of cystic fibrosis after his young son, Gunnar, was diagnosed with the disease in 1993. The Boomer Esiason Foundation raises millions of dollars every year to fund CF research and promote awareness and education about CF. Jerry Cahill, who has CF, recently celebrated his 50th birthday and hosts award-winning podcasts, which help many families, patients, and professionals learn about CF issues. He notes:

"Compliance, nutrition, exercise, and determination are the keys to having a great quality of life with CF."

Wise parents handle statistics and medical predictions by:

- ♥ Emphasizing that significant medical progress is being made in almost all areas, and that health and longevity are increasing for almost all illnesses.

- ♥ Realizing that for *all* individuals, the future is unknown. Many lives are shortened by unexpected illness and traumatic events.

- ♥ Encouraging their children to believe that they have every chance of being one of those children "who fall on the high side of the bell curve because you take such good care of yourself."

- ♥ Understanding that the quality of a life is measured not by its *length*, but by the amount of love, accomplishment, and giving that fills it.

- ♥ Understanding that worrying about the future and chewing on the mistakes of yesterday rob both today and tomorrow. The resulting hopelessness, negativity, and worry can shorten lives and certainly diminish the quality of life.

- ♥ Believing that those who bravely face life's obstacles build a character that not only leads them to be more capable people and leaders, but sets an example that enhances the lives of all with whom they come in contact.

Lisa Greene shares her experience of "becoming a statistic" when she was struggling to accept her newborn son's diagnosis with CF:[16]

Lisa

I began to see another world that exists alongside the one in which I had lived up until now. This "other world" is the one lived in duality by those who have children or loved ones with severe, chronic, or terminal illnesses, and/or special needs. This world encompasses Down syndrome, autism, AIDS, cerebral palsy, cancer, diabetes, leukemia, muscular dystrophy, birth defects and the list goes on and on. The number of people who live in this duality of existence must really be staggering, yet we rarely see them when we are out and about living our lives each day. It is only when we are *ready* to see them that they appear. Now, I see them everywhere: the kid in the wheelchair; the little one with a bald head and big eyes; the autistic child's unresponsive stare; the Down syndrome kid so happy to be alive; the little boy with a prosthetic sticking out of his blue-jeans. It touches me each time I see them because I know the struggle each family endures to overcome the realities they face.

I used to cry each time I went to the Children's Hospital because of the suffering I saw there. Now I try to smile as they pass by because there really is hope for all of us, once we can see past the pain. Sometimes it's the kindness of a stranger that gives one the strength to make it through the day. And now it's not just *"they and them"* but *"me and us."* We, too, are one of the statistics. We, too, are now a part of this "other world." But we're going to be just fine. We will make our home here, appreciate the blessings we find, and get to know our new neighbors. Together we'll beat this thing. We may be one of the statistics but we don't have to become just another statistic.

When We Don't "Beat the Odds"

As this is a program dealing with chronically ill children, unfortunately an early death will be an outcome for some. Guiding our child through the process of dying is probably the hardest thing a parent will ever have to do, yet it can also be the most profound experience for the parent, child, and others whose lives are touched. How a parent handles a child's impending death can impact the parent's psychological state for years later, perhaps permanently. Feelings of guilt, characterized by such questions as, "Was I there for him in the end?" are very common. For this reason we will frankly discuss the communication options concerning a child's impending death, which are:

1. The child is open to communicating about death, but the parent is not.
2. The child is not open to communicating about death, but the parent is.
3. The parent and child are both open to communicating about death.
4. Neither the parent nor the child are open to communicating about death.

Obviously, the least "troublesome" scenario is when both parent and child agree on how to communicate about death (options 3 and 4) but it is not always easy to discern where a person stands. It may take some time to figure it out. Later in this section, we'll give some helpful "probing questions," which will help you determine the level of communication your child is open to. There is no easy answer to the question of whether it is better to be openly communicative about a child's pending death or to soften the fact with denial. We can't answer that for you, but we can help you explore the options.

In her observations of children with leukemia aged three to nine, Myra Bluebond-Langner shows "how the children came to know they were dying, how and why they attempt to conceal this knowledge from their parents and medical staff and how these adults in turn tried to conceal their awareness of the child's impending death." The causes and consequences of this "mutual pretense" is the subject of her book. She concludes with the statement that the question may not be, "Should I tell the child he is dying?" so much as, "Should I *acknowledge* the prognosis with the child?" since all of these children already knew they were dying, even without direct communication of the fact. Myra says (of hospitals), "The answer lies in devising a policy that allows the children to maintain open awareness with those who can handle it and at the same time to maintain mutual pretense with those who want to practice it. The children know both what their parents know and what they want to hear. They are more concerned with having parents around than with telling them the prognosis."[17]

In essence, there is no one, right, fit-all answer because every family member is different. What is right for one person could be damaging for another. What is perfectly clear is that *it is always best to allow the child to "direct the show" when the child is in the process of dying.*

Parents must take their cues from the child and support the child in the way he/she wants to be supported. The parents' job is to overlook their own "stuff" and ideas about "the best way" and be there for the child in the manner the child needs during this time. This is obviously not easy. Parents are going through their own emotional hell during their child's dying process. It is usually helpful, if not essential, for the parent to get support and comfort from *outside* the "child's circle of circumference" so when they are with the child, they can truly be there for him/her.

Here are some guidelines to help you navigate difficult communication decisions:

1. Let the child take the lead in setting his or her "desired level of denial" by asking questions:
   - "What are your thoughts about your health situation right now?"
   - "What are you thinking about what the doctor has said?"
   - "Do you have any questions about what is happening with your body?"

     If the child is not willing to discuss these issues, drop it. He or she may not be ready to deal with them head on or may never be ready. It is not absolutely necessary for a person to know their death is imminent. For some people, never knowing may be the most peaceful and compassionate way of passing on and may be the best gift to give your beloved child.

Because of the complexities involved in the parent/child relationship, it may be the child is comfortable talking frankly about his or her death with someone other than the parent. Medical personnel can help a parent pick up on these cues. Parents need not "take it personally" if the child wants to talk about these issues with others. Sometimes the child's own pain and the parents' pain are just too heavy for the child to handle. A child needs the space and opportunity to open up with whomever he/she feels comfortable and safe.

Myra Bluebond-Langner says this: "Children will do whatever is necessary to keep their parents near, but they would often like to share their knowledge with someone else as well. That person should listen to what the children are saying, taking cues from them, answering only what they ask and on their terms."

In the course of a child's chronic illness, many children will develop a certain affinity and trust in a particular healthcare worker (doctor, pediatrician, nurse, specialist), and this trust can be a bridge that will enable the child to share his or her heartfelt concerns about his/her condition and longevity. Conversely, there are healthcare professionals in whom a child will simply not confide on any level, and a parent's awareness in this regard is paramount.

2. If the child wants to deal with death directly then answer the questions in an age-appropriate manner while providing hope. Here is one way of offering the hope of life after death to a child by using a concrete visual example (if it fits with the par-

ent's belief system). Such analogies help younger children understand difficult concepts:

The parent lights a candle and shows it to the child, saying, "Meagan, this candle is like your body and is made of carbon atoms, but instead of flesh and blood, the candle's carbon atoms are wax. And, like your own physical body, the candle itself is not all that important, but the flame is. Holding that flame is what the candle is all about. For you, the flame is like the spark in your eyes, the sparkle in your smile, your thoughts, and your personality. (Believing parents may explain that the flame is the soul.) That candle's flame is like the real you. The flame is not the body at all but your body holds your sparkle (soul) just like the candle holds the flame. If you lost both legs and arms, that sparkle would be just as bright inside you. No matter how the body might be injured or the candle carved on, the flame still burns. If I cut off the bottom of the candle, it doesn't affect how brightly the flame burns. However, all candles burn down. All bodies wear out. When that happens to a candle, keeping the flame going is very important, so that the flame is transferred someplace else, like to a new candle, or to a lamp."

At that point, the parent lights a candle and transfers the flame to another candle, then blows out the first. Then the parent places the second burning candle out of sight, behind a chair in the room. If it suits the parent's belief system, she or he might say, "I believe that when people die, the real them, the sparkle in their smile, the flash in their eyes and personalities still exist. Those are simply out of sight, and people who are alive can't see them any more because these personalities are in a different place. But look, Meagan. We can still see the glow of that candle even when it is out of sight. That glow is the joy, memories, and love you have given us all. As you burn brightly in another place, we will continue to feel and love you."

Other ways of offering hope may be to suggest the prospect of the relief of pain and suffering and being in Heaven together one day (again, depending upon parental beliefs). Stories of other people who have experienced similar trials can also be encouraging to adults and children alike.

3. If the child has expressed curiosity and is open to discussing death and what happens afterwards to the body, with sensitivity express curiosity and interest about what the child's wishes might be for his or her funeral service, effects, etc. After asking the child's permission to discuss these issues, encourage her or him to participate. If it fits your belief system, let him or her know that you know he will be watching from a better place and that "we want to make sure you have it just the way you like it." A discussion like this, hard as it is, can help ease children into peacefully letting go when it's time, knowing that the important things in their lives have been taken care of. Children, like adults, appreciate deciding who will get their favorite belongings. This also gives the child an element of control over their own passing.

Now, we'll move onto another subject that is difficult to discuss with children: suicide. Sometimes parents are reluctant to talk about suicide with their children because they "don't want to put ideas into their head." However, the fact is, if parents wonder about a child thinking such thoughts, it is almost certain the child has. It seldom makes things worse to open such discussions by asking:

- ♥ "Do you sometimes feel like life isn't worth living?"
- ♥ "I'm wondering if you sometimes think this hassle just isn't worth it?"

If the discussion about the child's potential suicide appears relevant as the child becomes more open, other things to ask might be:

- ♥ "Who would find you if you died?"

- ♥ "Who would take care of your pets?"
- ♥ 'Who would you want me to call and tell about your death?"
- ♥ "Have you attempted suicide before?"

Sometimes parents are unaware of previously unsuccessful attempts at suicide so, if at all possible, find out if a child has tried to commit suicide before. If a child is contemplating suicide after a previous sincere attempt, this is an indication of serious intent and "success" is a likely result at the next attempt. *If a child has previously attempted suicide or appears to be seriously contemplating it, find professional help immediately.* There are also suicide hotlines available in many cities.

At times we have found it productive to discuss with teenagers the fact that they can always commit suicide as a very last resort. This is an option that is always open for everyone. Even when a person loses both legs and an arm, he can easily commit suicide if he so chooses. Furthermore, suicide is the *one* decision people can make and never have the ability for a change of heart or mind. We can change our minds about almost every other decision in life, so we encourage children to always focus on other options first! Surprisingly, this "You can always do it, let's look together at other options, first," routine has helped many children delay a suicide decision to the point they no longer consider it a viable option.

On other occasions it may be relevant to let a teen know that depression is like a tunnel. Though it might not seem possible in the midst of the darkness of the moment, everyone gets over depression sometime. There is always light at the end of the tunnel. However, suicide turns that tunnel into a cave.

If your child starts writing goodbye letters, gives away his or her personal possessions to other children, hints about, or overtly expresses thoughts of suicide, it's time to explore the difficult issues and help your special child make wise decisions. It is also time to seek professional help.

In summary, wise parents:
- ♥ Avoid feelings of helplessness by giving children as much control as possible.
- ♥ Give their children hope by modeling a hopeful attitude.
- ♥ Are open to communicating about difficult subjects.
- ♥ Meet their children's needs for communication, not their own.

Chapter 7 Key Concepts

1. A communication model is provided for discussing difficult issues with children. These issues may involve medical conditions, death, depression, and suicide. Seven guidelines are explored:
   - In giving answers, we ask ourselves: "Whose needs am I addressing — mine or my child's?"
   - Are we giving more information than the child wants or needs to hear?
   - Can our child talk with us about anything and everything?
   - When we are not sure how to give the answer, ask more questions.
   - Recognize that sometimes our child may try to "protect" us.
   - Show acceptance even when we can't show approval.
   - Every answer dealing with life-and-death issues should leave room for hope.

2. With many medical conditions, there is a strong correlation between good self-care and longevity. Parents can use statistics to inspire hope and spark an "I can beat this" attitude. Parents who give off positive, "we can beat this" vibes generally raise kids with the same determined spirit.

3. Guiding our child through the process of recurrent illness and

death is incredibly difficult. How a parent handles a child's impending death can impact the dying child's experience as well as the parent's psychological state for years. Although there are no easy answers, options and examples are provided in this chapter. It is best to allow the child to "direct the show" when the child is in the process of dying.

4. For some families, not telling the child at all about their impending death is appropriate. For others, it is best to give the child honest, open facts and emotional support. Here are some guidelines to help you navigate these difficult decisions:
   - Let the child lead us in setting their "desired level of denial" by asking questions.
   - If the child wants to deal with death directly, then answer their questions in an age-appropriate manner, while providing hope.

5. Suicide is another difficult issue in which the same rules of communication must apply. If a child has previously attempted suicide or appears to be seriously contemplating it, find professional help immediately.

6. Wise parents:
   - Avoid feelings of helplessness by giving children as much control as possible.
   - Give their children hope by modeling a hopeful attitude.
   - Are open to communicating about difficult subjects.
   - Meet their children's needs for communication, not their own.

Chapter 8

You're Not Alone: Psychological Issues Presented by Medical Challenges

Human beings, by changing the inner
attitudes of their minds, can change
the outer aspects of their lives.
— William James (1842-1910)

This chapter will address complex psychological issues, such as grief, guilt, and denial, and we hope to pare them down to size for you. There are volumes of books written by specialists on these subjects. However, recognizing the ruts in the road will help parents avoid them, or at the very least, navigate them better. Here we simply provide brief glimpses into these issues as they apply to parenting kids with special healthcare needs. If these issues are deeply affecting your parental responses, relationships, and healthy functioning, counseling would be advisable.

Dealing with the Stages of Grief

Taking her for granted, we run through Life expecting her blessings. And then, suddenly, we find her standing hand-in-hand with the Grim Reaper. Through the haze of initial shock, we hear him sometimes whispering, sometimes shouting, "You are about to experience a devastating loss." Then we embark on a haunting journey, during which our feelings and attitude pass through what Elisabeth Kübler-Ross described in her 1969 book, *On Death and Dying*,[18] as five "stages." There should be a better word than "stages," because this implies something almost linear (a succession of emotions following one after the other). However, as this great physician noted, grieving folks shuffle through one stage to another and then return back for a look-see to places previously reconnoitered. During this unpredictable journey, they subject themselves to an almost involuntary self-examination: "What's wrong with me? I've already been here; I didn't like it in the first place; and I like it no better this time around!" The Five Stages of Grief (now called the Kubler-Ross Model) by which people deal with tragedy and loss are:

1. Denial and isolation: "This can't be happening to me (or my child)."
2. Anger: "You can't do this! How dare you!" (Referring to God, the cause of the medical condition, accident, etc).
3. Bargaining: "Just let my son live one more year."
4. Depression: "I just can't handle this anymore. It's not worth it."
5. Acceptance: "Okay, I'm ready (to accept God's will, to die, to forgive, let go, etc). I don't want to struggle any more."

Kubler-Ross taught that these stages do not necessarily come in order, nor are all stages experienced by all people; but the point is that people experience a normal process of grieving before reaching acceptance, and it is an individual, often lonely, journey.

Living with chronic illness is like swimming against a current all the time — a current that most folks never experience when they float down the river of life. No matter how strong one becomes fighting that current, each new loss stirs up the old feelings. The losses may include loss of good health, loss of dreams, loss of finances, for some the loss of a child, and always the loss of control. There are constantly new challenges to deal with in the cycles of progressive chronic diseases. A positive bacteria culture, again! The blood sugar out of control, again! Insurance hassles, again! These recurrent issues make arriving and staying at the stage of acceptance very hard indeed, for the train of feelings always returns and beckons us to hop in and chug off to a place previously visited.

When parents experience the turmoil of anger, depression, denial, and isolation it is very difficult to be calm, ever empathetic, and ever available as loving parents know they should be. It is particularly depressing to not be able to get through the depression! "I'm not handling this well. Why can't I get over this?!" Snapping at the children, being out of sorts, and even blaming them for things out of their control are unhappy but normal responses. Lisa Greene notes:

Lisa

I know of a man whose two children were diagnosed with CF several years ago, and he is still very angry. I *so* understand his anger, having been there myself when our own babies were diagnosed. Anger is a normal response, but we have to pull ourselves out of it somehow or our children will either be angry. too, or blame themselves. This poor dad's response to CF is polluting the flavor of life for three people, not just for two kids, who could really be living a happy, even if shortened, life. It's so sad.

It's been liberating for me to learn that not feeling normal at times is normal. Knowing about the way stations of grief and that they are simply points of interest in my life's journey and that they are not a permanent residence helps me cope. When I go back to a dark spot for a visit, I know I'll be off again soon to someplace brighter. It is probably one of the major things that gets me through.

Understanding these stages also helps me give other family members more grace as we struggle through challenges together. Sometimes our kids experience those same "points of interest" and are scared, out of sorts, and angry. Simply responding with, "Honey, feel free to stay with us as long as you can be sweet" seems a little too simplistic and rejecting at those moments. There is certainly the right time for all the great tools Love and Logic teaches, but there are also those times when I need to just fold my child into me and say, "You know what, sweetheart? I feel exactly the same way sometimes. Come here my mad little friend and let's hug each other a while."

Childhood Illness and Parental Guilt

Rational Guilt can be a necessary but unwelcome blessing that helps us to change our ways. It is a wake-up call from our conscience, ideally suggesting a possible apology or offering a door to a learning experience. It provides the opportunity for different behavior in the future. Then there is a real bugaboo, *Irrational Guilt*. It does no good at all. It hangs around and makes us feel badly about ourselves when we either don't deserve it or there is nothing we can do to make amends or change the situation.

Colleen

When attorney and single-mom Colleen was working 70 hours a week she didn't have enough time to give the required attention to eight-year-old Susie's complex nutritional needs. When Susie continued to lose weight and needed a feeding tube to get back on track, Colleen felt guilty because she knew if she had been home more she could have taken better care of her daughter. Colleen had a serious talk with her boss, and they worked out a 50-hour working week arrangement so she could care for Susie appropriately.

Colleen's healthy, rational guilt, well-founded in reality, caused her to make much needed changes in her lifestyle and priorities. Once she had made these changes, she let go of her guilt, knew she was doing the best she could at the time, and moved on. Colleen handled her guilt in a healthy way — she solved the problem and let go of the guilt.

Irrational guilt is often not based on reality or it is magnified disproportionately. When people deal with such heavy issues as chronic illness, guilt may play a significant role. Whenever something goes wrong, our rational side starts shadow boxing with the irrational. We say:

- ♥ "What have I done to deserve this?"
- ♥ "Is God testing me?"

It's paradoxical that our rational side can come up with guilt-producing irrational responses in its search for reasons. If bad occurences have reasons, then life becomes more predictable and controllable, so we tend to look for reasons like something we could have done differently. It might be a little crazy, but "finding" reasons gives us a feeling of power and control. This is the point where guilt comes crawling around the corner of our feelings because somehow we then feel responsible for the bad situation. For example:

Liz

Liz blamed her son's congenital heart defect on her bad decision to ignore the need for pre-natal care. Although the two issues were completely unrelated, it provided her with a "reason" for his, and her, suffering. And it caused her much guilt.

Guilt causes problems in parental responses:
- ♥ Guilt often causes the adult to give the child a tacit "okay" for misbehavior: "They're acting this way because of a choice *I* made in the first place."
- ♥ Parental guilt leads to parental inaction. "How can I expect more of my child? I'm responsible for his acting like this! It wouldn't be fair for me to require different behavior." *When parents feel guilt, the children often respond by blaming the parent.* They go together like bread and butter.

So, that's a quick snapshot of "guilt." Now, for the important part — how to deal with it:

1. Recognize whether the guilt you are feeling is rational or irrational.
   - Is this situation something you clearly have direct control over?
   - What can you do to correct it? Even baby steps and a game plan can help ease the feeling of "guilt running rampant."
   - Counseling may be needed to help with the inability to discern the difference or if you are having a problem taking the necessary corrective action.
2. When the guilt is justifiable and "not correctable" by action, it's

helpful to understand that, given our genetics and backgrounds, most people do the best they can, moment by moment. Retrospectively judging ourselves and others is generally a destructive waste of time and energy. Every parent does some things wrong. However, few set out thinking, "Today, I'm going to do things to upset my life and the life of my child." It is a very rare parent who sets out to do things wrong intentionally. Character and growth occur when people look at their mistakes and learn from them, rather than wasting psychic energy wringing their hands about things that can't be changed.

3. Much guilt is irrational. Simply recognizing that fact can help put it into perspective.

   • Facts provide a reality check. If a person feels guilty about "giving" their child a genetic illness (surprisingly, some do), then perhaps some basic, scientific information about the way genes work may help ease the sense of false responsibility and guilt for "causing" an illness.

   • Forgiveness and acceptance are the antithesis of blame and guilt. Daily ten-minute meditations thanking God for the moments of acceptance that we do have helps those moments grow exponentially.

   • Sometimes, irrational guilt may be driven by fear. Journaling can help ease our fears; so can confiding in a trusted loved one. Counseling may be needed to help work through guilt and fear that is having a negative impact on our ability to function and relate to others in healthy ways.

When parents feel guilty, children almost always respond with blame. When children blame parents, it is best for parents to sincerely respond by saying, "I'm sorry you feel that way and I hope you get over it." Of course, this needs to be said gently and lovingly but any other response simply validates the child's blame.

No matter the source of our guilt, finding and having faith may be comforting. God forgives when we have difficulty doing so.

Illness and Denial

Denial is a very tricky thorn that snuggles unseen and unfelt into our minds. It ensures that reality is distorted. Generally when we ignore a feeling or issue, we can at least 'fess up to it: "I don't like looking at that!" However, denial causes us to say, "I am *too* looking at that," when in fact we're not! *An individual might be chock full of denial, yet it can only be seen by an outsider — another person.* And when the other person brings it to our attention, we are almost certain to reply, almost always with a bit of anger, "Well, that's just not true!!"

Denial often tries to sneak in whenever there is a chronic problem that requires time and energy or is very difficult to control. It "protects" from feelings a person might have great difficulty in controlling, even if recognized. Denial is often present in families and individuals who struggle with medical challenges. As noted, we might not recognize denial in ourselves but recognize it in others. Thus, overweight parents often worry about what their children eat. A diabetic parent may be more concerned about his child's blood glucose than his own. A parent in the midst of an affair may be overconcerned about the sexual activity of a chaste, dating daughter.

A person who sees folks living right on top of the San Andreas fault line might say, "How can they be so unaware? Why would anyone live there?" Perhaps this person passing judgment is 25 pounds overweight and is thus more likely to die an early and unnecessary death than the person perched happily on the fault line. While busy focusing on the fault line, this person is in denial about his own health issues.

Parents can become frustrated by the denial that it is normally present in children. There will be times when children deny the importance of treatment; ignore the importance of diet; doubt the truth of medical findings.

Confronting denial is difficult. There is absolutely no doubt that hitting denial head on with a, "You are wrong about this" approach builds the wall of denial even higher. The approach that has a much better chance of tearing down the wall is a simple statement that begins along the lines, "I guess I see things differently..."

Denial can be healthy when a person can do nothing to prevent or change a catastrophic happening over which he or she has no control. At the time of this writing, there is a good chance that a global plague as destructive as that of 1918 may be just ahead. But for the average person who is not involved in developing vaccines and first responses, a refusal to dwell upon what could be inevitable may be an understandable and protective response.

Denial may be a healthy way of dealing with a potential outcome of some chronic illnesses. For instance, it does no good to "stew" in the fact that some children with CF will die by their thirties; with new medical treatments, early death is not inevitable. However, it is important to recognize the *potential* of early death so that care is taken to comply with health and medical requirements. It is critical to stay well grounded in reality and remain balanced. *Denial becomes a problem and must be addressed when the child (or an adult for that matter) refuses to face the seriousness of a situation and take the necessary actions to correct it.*

Judy

Judy is a teenager with CF. Like most other teen girls she is concerned about her weight, so she diets, partly to be like her friends. Judy is already at the low end of the growth curve but instead of being concerned, she is glad CF causes her to be much thinner than her peers. Now she appears somewhat anorexic. There is a direct correlation between lung health and healthy weight levels. Judy is in denial about her need for healthy weight gain. Her mother realizes the danger: if

Judy gets a lung infection, she could lose weight very rapidly, which could (at her already low body weight) plunge her into a potentially life-threatening situation.

Judy's mother nags her, threatens her, and begs her to eat well and stop dieting. When Judy's mom discussed the issue with a doctor, he told her to give Judy a choice: give up dieting and get her weight up to an acceptable level, or get a feeding tube. Judy's mom responded with, "Oh, a teenage girl would never accept a feeding tube. I just can't do that," and was unwilling to approach Judy in this way. The doctor said later, "Judy can either face reality now, on her own terms, or she will face reality later when she is very sick in the hospital and a feeding tube will be put in then." The doctor wonders, "How can I make the parent understand this? She just won't face reality. How can Judy face reality when her mother won't?"

Despite the doctor's well-meaning concern, Judy's mom is correct and not in denial. She recognized the danger Judy was putting herself into and also realized that forcing a basically healthy child to be tube-fed could lead to even more rebellion. She thought about the issue long and hard. Judy's mom realized that teens sometimes listen to other teens so she asked the doctor to see if one of his teen CF patients would talk with Judy. A mother of another patient was willing to help out.

A conference call was set up (to avoid cross-infection issues) and all four participated. Judy listened wide-eyed to the other teen's "near-death" story, and how she had experienced hospitalization and been tube-fed because of her weight loss. Judy's mom noted with surprise and satisfaction that her daughter had a chocolate sundae for dessert that evening. Judy's mom realized an important fact: peer counseling is often effective with teens.

Unfortunately, teens and adults often learn best by the college of hard knocks. When rehabilitation and treatment are forced by loving others the recidivism rate is high, and although there may be short-term gain, there is often long-term pain.

In summary, a child's refusal to accept the importance of medication should be addressed by a discussion focusing on facts. "The way I see it is...." The help of others whom the child may look up to can be enlisted. But a child's denial about approaching death should probably be honored if he/she is taking appropriate care of him/herself:

Henry

Eleven-year-old Henry is a seemingly cheerful boy with CF. He tells his friends he has asthma. He obviously likes to tell himself he has asthma, too. When Joyce and Annette, two student nurses, see him in the hospital, his fingers show clubbing, an indication of compromised oxygenation and lung capacity. When asked if he researches information about CF on the Internet, he says, "No, I really don't care about that." Does he know the average life expectancy? "No." Does he care? "No." Due to his compromised pulmonary functioning, Henry appears to have a good chance of not living as long as the average person with cystic fibrosis. However his mother says he takes good care of himself, takes his medication, and does his treatments without complaining. After seeing Henry in the hospital, Annette and Joyce have the following conversation:

Annette: "Henry is sure optimistic about his future. He

doesn't look at the statistics and his condition. And his pulmonary functioning is really compromised."

Joyce: "True."

Annette: "Well he's not facing facts."

Joyce: "So?"

Annette: "So how do we give him a wake up call about his condition?"

Joyce: "Why should we say anything?"

Annette: "Well deep down inside he may be hurting."

Joyce: "We gave him openings to express some inner doubts, and he didn't take us up on them. He is taking good care of himself. So be careful you don't advocate something to meet your own needs, not Henry's."

Denial is tough enough to handle when parents and other adults recognize it in children, but how can denial be handled when the adult is in denial, too? When dealing with life-threatening medical issues, this is an important thought to ponder. We may send our child unhealthy messages as a result of our denial about our own issues. *An awareness of our own denial, by definition, can only occur with outside input*, therefore it becomes essential, though difficult, to listen to medical professionals or the thoughtful responses of those we love. *When an "outsider" — family, friend, or loved one — confronts us on our denial, it almost always sounds to us like unmerited criticism!* Although we may not recognize denial in ourselves, we generally recognize it in others, which could be a "big hint" about where our own issues may lie. Thus, overweight parents are often overconcerned with what their children eat. A following section on obesity, illustrates a mother facing her own denial, thus helping her daughter face hers.

Chronic Illness Blurs Wants and Needs

Katie laughs and says with an almost embarrassed pride, "I played the sick roll to the hilt. I could get out of things I didn't want to do. I could get away with things at home and school because I was the sick child. I admit it!" Because chronically ill children can so easily drift into feeling "unfair-ed upon" by life, some become entitled and demanding, developing and exploiting placating parents who, as their child becomes more demanding, have increasing difficulty separating "wants" from "needs." Entitled people, children or adults, have a tendency to control others through what they define as their "needs."

Abe

Abe, a child diagnosed with CF at birth, controlled his family with outbursts and demands. It started when he was nine months old as he kept them up at night with his wails. Instead of letting him learn to comfort himself, his parents decreased his ability to sooth himself by taking turns playing nightly "officer of the deck" to attend to his upset. This escalated into bringing him milk to help him get to sleep. And that escalated into many entitlement issues, so that by the time Abe was eight he was literally telling his parents, "You need to pick me up at...; You need to help me with...; You should talk to my teacher about..." Abe's mother attended a Love and Logic Class, and the lessons she learned there helped her turn the ship around. One day when Abe told his mother what she *needed* to fix him for dinner, she responded matter-of-factly and without sarcasm:

"Small and about-to-be-unhappy child, I *need* to do nothing. The real question is whether I want to. And, not to rain on your parade, but the way you are talking to me has drained my energy. Rather than fix dinner, I think I'll relax right now to get my energy back."

Of course this massive change in his mom, who was now taking care of her own real needs, rather than responding to Abe's wants (which he defined as his needs), was a shock to Abe's entire system. He soon exploded into a howl of rage. But his mom stuck to her guns, saying simply, "I have more bad news. My energy is being even more sucked out of me. But I'm sure you can make it up to me later. Try not to worry about it!"

When chronic illness is present, preverbal children may have more reason than the average infant or toddler for crying; they may have physical pain. For instance, when the average one-year-old has a temper tantrum, it is handled matter-of-factly and a parent does not reinforce the demands of a tantrum by holding or comforting the child. But if a child is having pain in their gut because of trauma, infection, or illness, then holding and comforting is essential. It is in these situations that the line between demands and needs may become blurred. Parents must attempt to satisfy needs while never giving into baseless demands. Lisa Greene shares this experience:

Jacob

When Jacob (with CF) was a baby and cried constantly because of pain in his tummy, there were many long nights and days we held him. Of course as he grew older he became more and more demanding. But once he could talk and express his needs and/or demands, it became much easier to tell the difference between wants and needs and separate his pain and his demands. He went through a horrific period of tantrums between two and three because he was spoiled. But we worked that through with Love and

Logic tools, and he is now a sweet, responsible little boy.

Looking back on it, I'm satisfied with the way we handled it, although I know he was held and comforted far more than would have been healthy for a typical child. I am glad we erred on the side of love and nurturing when he was so young because now I know how critically important it is to meet those basic needs of youngsters under two.

As we have discussed, it is always best to err on the side of giving love and comfort with a preverbal child when we're unsure whether or not the child is expressing a need or a demand.

Setting firm limits, teaching children manners, limiting overindulgence of material things, helping kids earn some of the things they want, and teaching children to have a respectful attitude all help to stop entitlement in its tracks.

Where Is the Line Between "Can't" and "Won't"?

Separating "can'ts" and "won'ts" is often a problem when dealing with children with special healthcare needs. How does a parent discern whether or not their children are really capable of doing something when they say they "can't" or "won't"? The line becomes very blurry, especially when dealing with medical treatments or procedures. For example: Dad tells Cynthia to go ahead and start her breathing treatments while he makes a phone call. It's a task she has done several times with no problem, and she responds with, "I can't." What is she *really* saying? And, should a parent "push" a resisting child to do a task when it is known the child is capable of doing it?

There are four possibilities when children underperform in any area. The children say:

1. They "can't" when they really won't.

2. They "can't" when they really can't.
3. They "won't" when they really can't.
4. They "won't" when they really won't.

Occasionally, there are little overachievers who say they can, when they really can't. And, as long as it doesn't cause a problem, one can't help but admire the tenacity of a "can-do" attitude. And often these children keep at it until they can do it!

When discussing underperformance, these four possibilities are simply subsets of two basic alternatives. The child is either capable of the task or isn't.

When children say they "can't" when they really won't, or say they "won't" when they really won't, they are capable of completing the task but, for some reason, choose not to. So when Cynthia says, "Daddy, I can't do my breathing treatment," it could be Cynthia really just wants her dad's attention. He is often away from home, and if he were not helping her with her breathing treatment, he'd be in the home office not relating to her at all. If Cynthia simply said, "I don't want to," her dad would admonish her and she'd still be by herself. But when she says, "I can't," her dad stops what he is doing and helps her. Cynthia has figured out how to "use" her situation to get the attention she wants from her dad. When Cynthia is with her mom, she has no problems at all doing her breathing treatments without assistance. In fact, she is generally proud to do it herself. Thus it is that sometimes children have chronic "problems" with one parent and do the same job without trouble with the other; children may hassle their moms for help with a treatment while she is on the phone, but never, ever try that with dad. Children may have trouble with their homework at home but can easily solve the same problems at school.

When children say, "I can't" when they really can't or "I won't" when they really are unable to, they are not capable of completing the task. Children unable to complete a task will sometimes say, "I won't" when it is difficult to admit to themselves or others they don't understand or are incapable of the task. The "I won't" is a face-saving issue, exemplified by a little kindergarten boy, less neurologically mature than his female classmates, who says, "Art's for girls!!" When children don't understand or feel unable to complete a task, their response and ultimate outcome depends on how the adult handles the situation. Let's look at an example of how one dad helps his son through "I can't":

Teddy

Teddy received second-degree burns over much of his right arm while playing with gasoline he found in his dad's boathouse. Changing the dressing was a painful and exacting process. Dad asked Teddy if he would help him change the dressing and heard, "Dad, I can't." Dad responded by saying, "Well, let's see if that's true. We'll work on it together."

He showed Teddy how to carefully unwrap the ace and gauze beneath. Teddy's dad explained that the procedure hurt because the bugs were trying to hold on to his skin and would not let go because they hated sunlight. The more it hurt, the more bugs were being killed by light. Dad showed Teddy how to carefully apply the hydrogen peroxide to the edges of the burn, and when it fizzed and bubbled he noted with glee, "The bad bugs are being eaten alive!" Finally, when smearing on the antibiotic, "All the bugs that could possibly be left alive are being smothered under a layer of goop that kills 'em deader than a doornail!"

The Love and Logic steps for helping children with self-care tasks (or almost any task) are as follows:

1. Keep expectations high. Assume a child can do the task, and

be mildly surprised but interested if he or she can't, rather than the other way around.

2. If the child has problems with a task, teach the specifics step by step. Explain each step in detail and make the steps fun. Generally assume a struggling child needs an enjoyable teaching and clarification session, not lowered expectations.

3. Make sure the child has the skills to do the task.

4. Adjust an expectation downward only when it is obvious (after having fun teaching) the child is too immature or unable to learn the task. The way in which lowered expectations are presented may impact your child's self-image. Don't say, while showing disappointment or frustration, "Well, since you can't do that, let's try..." It is more effective to say, without frustration and perhaps with a bit of happy anticipation, something along the lines of, "Hey, wait a minute, I have a better idea. Let's try something that might make both of us happier..."

Let's look at parenting challenges around self-care. When children are forced or even encouraged to "try" a task in which the *child himself* is not invested, then almost always a bad attitude develops around completing that particular task. The bad attitude feeds the problem, which then contributes to even more difficulty with task completion, which continues to feed the bad attitude. Parents then understandably may say, "You'd be able to do it if you had a better attitude." On the other hand, if a child keeps trying a task where he or she can become invested in progress, success almost always results.

When a child has a real or perceived disability, the line between the can'ts and the won'ts becomes much less distinct. In fact, the line becomes an extended gray area.

When a child's "can'ts" are frequently validated, an infantile or whiney immaturity develops. The child shows less and less responsibility, and quality of life lessens for both child and caretaker.

Separating Can't from Won't

Separating the can'ts from the won'ts is an essential skill when working with children who experience medical challenges. To separate can't from won't, ask yourself whether the child performs better for others. In a home atmosphere of overconcern and obvious fear for the child's safety or health, some children become overdependent and appear less able. They say, "Mom, I can't do it." Parents may find it very revealing and informative to find how well the child did when sent to summer camp or on an overnighter. The child should ideally do as well for parents as he or she does for a camp counselor. For some children it is the other way around. They do great with their parents, but pull the "I can't do this" on school personnel. The point is, if they can do it for one person consistently, they can do it for all folks consistently.

Ask yourself whether the child responds quickly to tasks easily within the range of his or her ability. A child may be able to do a task but be resistant and say, "I can't" because he/she is:

- ♥ Sick, hungry, tired, frustrated, etc.
- ♥ Resistant to the task
- ♥ Resistant to the person
- ♥ Resistant in general, as a "mode of operation"

One easy way to help separate your child's "can'ts from the won'ts" is to determine if your child has a problem responding quickly to a request that is clearly within the range of his or her ability. For instance, when Willie's mother makes a simple request for her son to bring her a drink of water and he whines and complains, it doesn't take a diagnostic wizard to understand that Willie says, "I can't" when he really won't and simply doesn't want to. So, when he whines and complains, "I can't figure out how to put my (respiratory) tubing together!" that is also likely to be a hidden "won't."

It is also important to consider whether the child has problems with related tasks. Children may have problems in one area and no problems in another. For instance, Charles may be able to spell well and excel in many areas but have trouble with math. His problems may lead him to have attitude problems with math and while that may be blamed for his poor performance, the real reasons are his learning problems with numbers. He may outgrow these without any remedial classes at all! Dyslexia and problems with a sense of direction may be related.

Children who say, "I can't," when in fact they can, are *passive-resistant*. When dealing with such a child, it is generally not helpful to respond with such pronouncements as, "Oh, yes you can!" Such responses usually end in an argument. It is better to simply respond, "Oh, I'm sorry you are having that problem," and allow the child to cope with the consequences of not completing the task. This avoids the can't/won't hassle, and the parent does not respond in a critical manner that leads to a resentful child. Responding with, "Oh I'm sorry you are having that problem" may work with homework and finding shoes but be quite inappropriate for dealing with a child's life-and-death issues, such as monitoring glucose levels. However, when parents encourage the right response on non-medical issues like homework and chores, it is much more likely that essential medical tasks will be completed without passive resistant-responses.

When children say, "I can't" but are able to do the job, they may have a variety of motivations: outright control, a bid for attention, or a need for affection. If it is the latter, parents do best by simply encouraging straight communication: "Honey, if you ask me for a big hug and I give it to you, do you think that will help you to get your breathing treatments done now?"

Chronic Illness and the Burden of Responsibility

Throughout this book we have emphasized the importance of developing responsible children by using high expectations, choices, and the acceptance of consequences. But there is a wise saying that maintains it is always possible to have too much of a good thing. Overly responsible people can feel accountable for downturns, bad news, and worsening medical problems that are absolutely not under their control and certainly not the result of poor self-care decisions. If adults can take on too much responsibility for issues outside their control, it is understandable some children may do the same. Even with good self-care decisions, they may still develop infections or lose vision after responding responsibly to a parent who has noted, "If you carefully monitor your blood sugar levels, it will help your vision."

Jacob

Jacob, a very responsible seven-year-old with CF, has recurrent nasal infections. He faithfully washes his nasal passages daily and uses the prescribed nasal spray, but upon developing nasal polyps (again!), he breaks his mom's heart by inquiring with a quivering voice, "Mom, is this happening because I haven't taken good enough care of my nose?"

With many chronic illnesses, the situation does sometimes inexorably worsen, and in such cases the children have to be helped to walk the difficult, lonely, tumultuous, and highly personal line between feeling hopeless and giving up, and feeling overly responsible and guilty. The common refrain, "What did I do to deserve this?" must not become laced with needless self-incrimination.

Depending upon the situation, parents often respond to overly responsible children with reassuring variations along the lines of, "Your paper is just fine, you don't have to have a perfect paper"; or, "Honey it's not your fault those polyps developed"; or, "That sore could have happened no matter how carefully you avoided pressure over that bone."

Such responses are not always helpful for two reasons. Saying,

"You did well enough, you don't have to be perfect," comes through as criticism to perfectionistic children and they often rebel against the comment. Most children interpret such statements as validating some shortcoming and then often try even harder to reach perfection. On the other hand, when a parent says, "That problem could have happened no matter how well you cared for yourself," the statement opens the door that leads to a path of feeling futile and hopeless. This might also lead to a relaxing of self-care, "Why bother with nasal washes every day if I'm going to get polyps anyway?"

So what is a parent to do?

Listen with empathy to the child. Give caring responses without overreassurance. If parents don't become overly reassuring or take control by giving their own ideas, children often pull themselves out of the situation, "Well, even if it isn't perfect, it's probably good enough." Or "Well, if I hadn't taken such good care of my skin, it could have been a lot worse."

If the responsible child doesn't take that route, the parent can focus on the importance of self-care, regardless of a worsening situation, with an arm around the shoulder, a kiss on the cheek, and a truthful, enabling statement. Such statements delivered lovingly with a bit of humor, a smile, and a twinkle in the eye can take the edge off the situation and lighten the child's burden.

Jacob

"Jacob, one thing's for sure. If you hadn't taken such good care of your nose, those nasal polyps would be like baseballs! They are pretty small. Maybe you should give yourself some credit there."

Sometimes parents can rely on setting a healthy model for their overly perfectionist or self-critical children by lovingly commenting, "I'm sorry you feel so upset about that. Personally, I'm glad I don't do that or I could end up feeling upset all the time. But of course, dear, everyone is different." It might be noted some parents of overly responsible or perfectionist children have trouble making such a simple statement because they unconsciously recognize it just isn't true of them! For some people, using some of these Love and Logic techniques, though effective, can be like swimming upstream. When one has trouble with her/his own face, it's hard to change the one in the mirror! Some children are a chip off the old block!

Overreassurance

Generally, when we see a frightened and needy child, we also see a child who needs reassurance. However, we also commonly see a child who has had reams of reassurance. In fact, if the reassurance was effective, why does the child continue to need it? The proper amount of reassurance can be a very good thing, but (like all good things) when used in excess, it becomes a bad thing. Needing re-assurance is the opposite of being self-assured. Generally, reassur-ance does not build coping skills or resilience. It may make an individual feel better temporarily, but like a hit of heroin, it always seems to need to be repeated, often in larger doses or more fre-quently, if the benefit is to continue. Parents can use empathy, encouragement, and descriptive praise instead of reassurance. If reassuring comments, used infrequently, generally elicit a "Thanks, Mom" response, and the child is more relaxed, then reassurance may be just the ticket. But if the reassurance leads only to more worried questions, increased concern, and continued whining or negativism, then wise parents don't lock into a response that obvi-ously isn't working. Let's not turn the key harder when the car won't start on a cold day!

Overprotection and the Spiral of Hostile Dependency

Throughout this book, we emphasize the parenting tools and tech-niques that are most likely to result in children who, despite their illness, are most likely to be self-sufficient, loving, respectful, and responsive. Dealing with significant medical issues and illnesses in childhood can throw a monkey wrench into the usual parenting process. Parents of chronically ill children are understandably more protective, concerned, watchful, and involved in their children's affairs than parents of healthy children. This heightened involvement, which often shows up as overindulgence, can result in children who, as adults, will have difficulty dealing with the normal demands of adulthood.

This is because chronically ill children easily fall into a *hostile-dependent* lifestyle, which means feeling helpless or cheated and always demanding more while expecting others to give it to them, rather than accepting the responsibility of taking care of their own wants and needs. They can become angry, bitter, and blaming. It is so common that it might almost be considered "normal" for kids with serious health issues. But, happily, with the right techniques it is less likely to occur. Let's look closely at this cycle, which is illustrated in figure 8.1:

1. The child is ill.
2. The parents understandably become involved in care.
3. The child silently shifts more "units of concern" to the parents and feels less responsibility when things go wrong.
4. The child becomes resistant, demanding, blaming, and often hostile-dependent — especially when things get difficult or don't "go the child's way."
5. The parents feel guilty and withdraw or become angry.
6. Guilt causes parents to excuse unacceptable behavior.
7. The child's self-image decreases, leading to poorer self-care.
8. Poorer self-care causes a deterioration of health, which causes the parents to react even more... Spinning the spiral of unhappiness as the cycle continues.

Most readers know of families that have raised children who have trouble with emancipation. This can be a particular problem with

Figure 8.1 **Cycle of Overprotection**

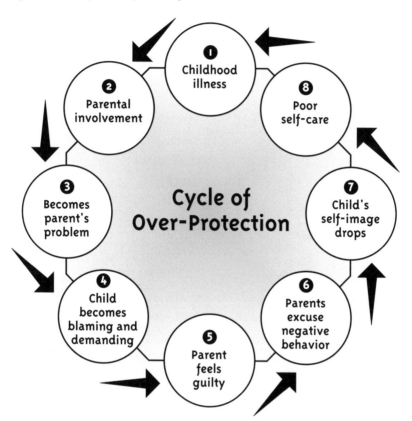

ill children who have been raised by moms and dads using ineffective parenting skills, such as overprotection or overindulgence. The following story is all too typical and clarifies how this can happen. We hope it will provide parents with a clear road map of a trip best avoided.

Bonnie

Bonnie S's story is a sad one, particularly because it has an unnecessarily unhappy ending. Things started out sunny. Bonnie was a beautiful five-year-old blonde, who had developed normally. Then she started stumbling. Her parents first attributed this to "growth problems," but when the stumbling was accompanied by headaches, nausea, and vomiting, her parents took her to the doctor. It was the first of many visits to healthcare professionals. After that first visit to a pediatrician, a subsequent MRI revealed a posterior medulloblastoma. The pediatric oncologist referred Bonnie for surgery, followed by radiation and chemotherapy. Things were never the same again for Bonnie.

At 32, Bonnie is unable to get her poorly functioning life together. She drifts through various living situations: sometimes she stays with girlfriends; sometimes she stays alone; more often she's with some guy who takes advantage of her for a year or so, then leaves. She holds jobs, perhaps for as long as a year, before being fired for being late, insubordinate, or disrespectful. She is estranged from an older sister and younger brother, both of whom will have absolutely nothing to do with her.

Perhaps it wouldn't be so sad if all this was the result of a compromised neurological system ravaged by tumor, surgery, radiation, and toxic drugs. Then, somehow, Bonnie's nearly wasted life would make sense, but that's not the case. Bonnie is psychologically, not physically, crippled.

During Bonnie's fifth year of life, the family's life was turned upside down with visits to the hospital and follow-up physician visits. For a year and a half, Bonnie's eventual recovery was uncertain. During the following years, Bonnie's folks turned what should have been simply a demanding and controlling phase of life into a life script. Their parental responses of continually excusing their daughter's immature and demanding behavior validated her attitude of entitlement, feelings of victimization, and her habit of blaming others for all the unhappy things in her life. In the years that followed, Bonnie's parents feared losing their daughter to a recurrence of tumor (that never occurred) and turned Bonnie into the witch-princess of the home. Whatever Bonnie wanted, Bonnie got. She antagonized her older sister, Rachael, who was admonished by her parents to put up with her antics and simply cope with her unremitting nastiness. Her younger brother, Bud, remembers Bonnie only as "the older sister from hell."

Perhaps these siblings could have recovered from the resentment of their childhood if Bonnie had grown up, but, sadly, she never did. In Bud's words, "She has continued to suck my parents dry. They took out a second mortgage on their home because Bonnie wastes her money on pedicures and DVDs instead of paying rent."

Somehow, Bonnie's parents have never been able to disentangle themselves from making Bonnie the center of their energy and attention. Now they are between a rock and a hard place, having created a demanding, hostile-dependent child who they fear could become a street person if they do not accede to her continuing demands on their resources and energy. Bonnie resentfully accepts their gifts ("it's not enough"), which have considerably drained the family estate, with nary a "thank you."

So how do well-meaning parents avoid raising hostile-dependent children? The answer is, develop responsible ones with the parenting tools and techniques given throughout this book. Teach your children respect and manners, model gratitude, and expect your special child to contribute to the family unit by performing appropriate chores.[19] *Responsible, respectful, grateful, contributing children can't be hostile-dependent.* They accept personal accountability for the quality of their own lives, hold others in high esteem, and are thankful for the blessings they have. Cicero said long ago: "Gratitude is not only the greatest of virtues, but the parent of all the others."[20]

Chapter 8 Key Concepts

1. The presence of an ill child amplifies the feelings, emotions, and resolutions common to general parenting. The guilt parents feel when children don't do well is intensified around healthcare issues. The irrational side of human nature, wishing to have some control over unpredictable life, leads to a search for controllable reasons for events: "What did I do to deserve this?" or "How could I have prevented this?" or even, "Why is God punishing us?" Parental guilt leads to a tacit acceptance and almost an "approving understanding" of misbehavior. Parents who radiate guilt inevitably raise blaming children!

2. One good option for coping with guilt is to determine if there are definite changes that could be made now to rectify or correct the situation. If not, then simple acceptance of the situation and moving on to issues that can be modified is the only healthy course. When blaming or resentful children bring up parental mistakes, real or imagined, it is best not to respond with excessive apologies but instead with the simple and sincere response, "I'm sorry you feel that way and I hope you get over it, for your own sake."

3. Denial is often present whenever there is a chronic problem that requires time and energy to control. In some cases where

no action will alleviate the situation, denial may be healthy and protective.

4. Parents may be in denial of their own issues, while focusing on those of their children. Hitting denial head-on by urging or insisting people see things differently often falls on deaf ears. It is better to set the good example and confine remarks to a softer, "I guess, dear, I see things differently." This chapter gives examples of dealing with denial.

5. Chronic Illness blurs the line between wants and needs:
   • Chronically ill children can easily drift into feelings of being "unfair-ed upon" by life, resulting in an entitled and demanding personality if their demands are met by parents who, because of guilt, denial, or "feeling sorry for" placate the demands.
   • When infants cry because of pain or illness or the discomfort of treatment, they need an overabundance of comfort and holding. Although this may result in a demanding toddler, that is an easier problem to rectify than a child who is diffi-cult to handle because of a lack of response to chronic pain in infancy.

6. Chronic illness blurs the line between "can't" and "won't":
   • Whenever a disability is present it gives the child a credible reason for underperforming. Some children take advantage of this by responding with an avalanche of "I can'ts," and other children excel and work particularly hard to overcome their challenges.

7. Separating the "can'ts from the "won'ts" may be clarified by determining:
   • Does the child perform better for others?

- Does the child respond quickly to tasks easily within the range of his or her ability?
- Does the child have problems with related tasks?

8. Overly responsible people can feel accountable for downturns, bad news, and worsening medical problems that are absolutely not under their control and certainly not the result of poor self-care decisions. Depending upon the situation, parents often respond to overly responsible children with reassuring variations along the lines of, "Honey it's not your fault those polyps developed." Such responses are not always helpful for the reasons outlined in the chapter. Instead, listen with empathy to the child and give caring without overreassurance.

9. Overreassurance: The proper amount of reassurance is helpful, but like all good things, when used in excess, it becomes harmful. Needing reassurance is the opposite of being self-assured. Empathy, encouragement, and descriptive praise can be used instead of reassurance.

10. The Spiral of Hostile-Dependency: This chapter diagrams the cycle of hostile-dependency. Chronically ill children easily fall into a hostile-dependent lifestyle, which means feeling helpless or cheated and always demanding more, while *expecting others to give* it to them rather than accepting the responsibility for taking care of their own wants and needs. Bitterness and blaming are so common they might almost be considered "normal" for children with health isues. Responsible children can't be hostile-dependent. Love and Logic tools and techniques given throughout this book are effective for raising children who beat this vicious cycle.

Chapter 9

"It's Not Fair!" Handling Sibling Relationships

Family faces are magic mirrors
looking at people who belong to us;
we see the past, present and future.
—Gail Lumet Buckley

Sibling issues can cause parents nearly as much aggravation and grief as dealing with the ill child's concerns. Certainly, siblings who don't get along or who are having problems handling the family's challenges add to the general chaos, stress, and frustration level around the home.

The power of modeling and example cannot be underestimated when discussing sibling issues. Children learn how to negotiate their differences by observing and copying the adults in their lives. Parents who manage conflict well with each other and their children are more likely to have kids who work things out with others in a healthy manner. If a parent uses ranting, raving, and venting as the "conflict-resolution tools of choice" then you can be sure their children will use those same methods when resolving conflict with each other. Parents who are calm and respectful when working through differences will be modeling self-control in the midst of conflict.

Most parents of ill children worry that siblings may feel resentful or left out. The reality is: siblings of kids with chronic illnesses often *really do* get short shrift. Depending upon a child's illness, parents may spend an inordinate amount of time on healthcare issues. Sometimes parents feel guilty about this and the resulting lack of time and energy they have for the other children. Such guilt is dangerous. Often, when parents feel guilty and they're short of time, they fill the gap with material gifts and overindulgence. This can sometimes lead to entitled and demanding children. Paradoxically, gifts often don't help and neither does excusing the insolent behavior of demanding children who understandably feel left out.

Chad

Chad's brother, Stephen, had cystic fibrosis. Chad grew up in the shadow of an illness that finally took his brother's life. The boys' parents, of course, focused much of their time and energy on caring for Stephen, especially near the end of his life, when Chad was a teenager. Chad was often overindulged with material things and his parents made excuses for his snippy, resentful behavior: "How can we blame him for being mad? Look at what he is dealing with." A sullen and shy child, he did not initiate much conversation with his parents on the matter; he just chugged along, generally blaming others for all his unhappiness.

As an adult he is still angry with his parents for his "lousy childhood." He rarely sees his parents, preferring not to have much of a relationship with them, except when he needs something. He has problems with relationships, and these problems have resulted in a failed marriage and job losses. He blames his parents for his failures. His parents sadly commented, "We didn't just lose one son to cystic fibrosis; we lost two. We wish we had done things differently with Chad. It breaks our hearts to see what he has become."

These dear parents realize now, through counseling, how they could have handled Chad differently. They also accept that they were doing their very best at the time. They have asked us to help others learn from their mistakes. Let's learn from an intimate, transcribed conversation between a different mother and her child. A little bit of background is given first:

Paul

Paul was four years old when his younger brother, Dale, then two, was diagnosed with cancer. During the following year, the Ronald McDonald House became the parents' second home. There were innumerable trips to the hospital, many invasive diagnostic tests, and, finally, brain surgery. During this roller-coaster year, Paul spent a great deal of time with his grandparents.

When Dale's mom, Nancy, brought him home from the hospital, wearing his little French beret perched jauntily atop his shaved and scarred head, she would look into his brave little face with eyes brimming with love and tears. Feelings of gratitude and concern stabbed deep into her heart as she imagined how empty life would be without him.

Dale was home from the hospital for a week before

Paul joined the family after living with his grandparents. Paul had always been a pretty quiet, stoic little kid. But shortly after coming home he became loud and disruptive. At dinnertime the second week after homecoming, Paul was obnoxiously playing with his food when a slippery beet flipped from his plate and hit Dale on the cheek. Dale's cheek was splattered with bright red beet juice, which dripped down below his innocent, big blue eyes. He turned to his mother and said calmly, "Mama, please make him stop." Seeing the red liquid splattered across Dale's face, Nancy lost it completely. She screamed at Paul, "Why are you always such a problem! Can't you settle down?!! Get up to your room now!" Later that night Nancy's husband, Robert, put his arms around his wife and said, "You were a little rough on the kid, don't you think, honey?" Nancy burst into sobs. She tried to justify her behavior while Robert simply held her, but her words sounded hollow even to herself. That sleepless night, Nancy resolved to speak to Paul. But more importantly, she resolved to do it right!

Let's eavesdrop here on a beautiful conversation and resolution:

"Honey, do you have a minute to talk with me about last night?"

Paul (resentfully), "I guess."

"Come on over here and sit with me on the couch." Nancy tries to put her arm around Paul, but he is stiff and rigid. "What are your thoughts about last night?" Note that Nancy did not start right out with an apology. She gave her son a chance to focus on his behavior, not hers, and happily he did!

"I got too mad, I guess."

"I think we all do at times. What do you think is going on?"

(Snippy, with anger) "I didn't mean for my beet to hit him in the face. I'm sorry! Okay?!"

Nancy ignores the sassy answer, "I am sure you didn't honey, but I'm not just talking about the beet. You don't seem very happy these days." Wise mom! She focuses here on his feelings, not his tacky behavior.

"What?"

"I think you know what I'm talking about, Paul. You just don't seem like the old happy kid I used to know."

"It's just not fair!"

"What's not fair?"

"I don't know, just everything!"

"Tell me more."

"I hate Dale."

Nancy neatly avoids saying, "You don't mean that" or "That's not a nice thing to say." Instead she says: "Really. Tell me about that, Paul."

Paul starts crying angrily: "He gets everything. You guys spend all your time with him. You love him more than you love me! I hate him!"

Nancy responds gently, "This whole year with Dale's cancer has been pretty hard on you, hasn't it?" Imagine how easily Nancy could have said what a hard year Dale had experienced! Or the whole family had experienced! But she continues to focus on Paul and empathize with his feelings.

"Yeah."

"I'm sure it has, honey. I'm sorry. You've been pretty left out, haven't you?" Nancy reaches out to Paul and he snuggles into her, suddenly racked by sobs. She holds him for 30 seconds saying nothing at all. "How do you feel about hating Dale?"

"I wish I didn't."

"I know that. You know, it is always hard on an older kid when a younger one comes along and is the baby of the family. Lots of kids have trouble handling that. But, when the younger one has cancer, he takes even more of our time. You get a triple dose to deal with, don'tcha? A lot of kids would have trouble handling that. However, Paul, you have always been a tough and wonderful kid. I am so appreciative of the help and understanding you do show."

"Thanks, Mom," Paul responds, still sobbing.

"I've always thought that if anyone could handle a tough situation, Paul, it would be you. I think, in the long run, you're going to be stronger than most kids because of all you have gone through. And I think you'll be more understanding and loving than a lot of others, too. That's what I think. What do you think?"

"Maybe."

Nancy and Paul sit on the sofa for another four or five minutes, just holding each other. They explore ideas about how Paul's parents can spend some time alone with him.

"Thanks for talking with me, Paul."

"I love you, Mom."

"I love you too, Paul."

Why did this conversation work so well? Let's look at the seven steps in successful communication and problem solving:

1. Nancy thought about how she wanted to approach Paul and practiced the conversation in her head.
2. Nancy waited until both of them were in a good mood.

3. Nancy gained Paul's respect by requesting, not demanding, to talk with him. She didn't just lay it on him, she obtained an agreement to discuss this issue. This is called obtaining contract for the conversation.

4. She explored his point of view. She explored his anger and his blaming of her without becoming defensive. (Gold star! This is difficult!)

5. She shared her thoughts and observations gently, with love.

6. She expressed high expectations and gave her son the "can do" message.

7. She ended the conversation with a hug.

Coping with a Sibling's Feelings and Behavior

Let's take a look at some of the ways a parent can help the "healthy child" cope with their feelings around their sibling's health issues.

Focus on Feelings

The real solution is to simply take the time to sit down and explore the child's feelings. Parents are sometimes reluctant to talk about issues when there is no obvious good solution and it is almost impossible or difficult to solve the problem. Surprisingly, simply listening and exploring feelings actually solves many problems. Remember, most therapists help a great deal and they spend a lot of time just listening and exploring feelings! Don't be overly apologetic or defensive about the time and energy you need to spend on the ill child. Such defensiveness can feed the validity of the resentful responses of some controlling children. There is all the difference in the world between a parent who whines defensively saying, "You have to understand how much time I need to spend on Stephen. I want to spend more time with you, but I just can't right now," vs. the parent who, with compassionate understanding, says, "I'm sure you do feel left out, honey. It is hard when Stephen is taking so much of my time. I appreciate your understanding. Thanks for talking this over with me." Such a parent vibrates an expectation that the child can handle the situation, and most children meet parents' expectations.

Facts are something most children will accept if they are given with understanding and empathy. Siblings do need to get their feelings off their chests. They need to be able to express the anger and resentment they sometimes feel. They need to know their parents understand they've had a difficult time, too. If it is too difficult to have these discussions without becoming defensive or overly apologetic, allowing the children to speak to a therapist or relative about the situation can be helpful.

If a sibling chronically and constantly whines and complains, a parent giving explanations that the child already knows and has already discussed simply feeds the problem. It validates the whine. On the other hand, giving empathy and high expectations works better: "Honey, I'm sure you are upset. We've already talked about that and I know you can handle it." If the fussing continues on, then the following comment, gently delivered, can be used: "Further discussion, dear, is draining my energy. So will you please take it somewhere else? Thanks."

Make Time

If parents make it a priority, it is often possible, even in very difficult times, to spend some time alone with the healthy child. It may be simply taking him or her to breakfast or dinner at a fast-food restaurant while a babysitter or spouse watches the ill child. It's not a matter of how much you spend, or that you are simply going for fast food. Most children really appreciate the effort and time, knowing it is valuable to you. Time alone, even in bits and pieces, can bring magical results.

Let Them Help

Involving the healthy children in the care of the ill child can help foster a spirit of family cohesion and cooperation. We are not suggesting you assign medical tasks to siblings, but when there is an offer to help, instead of responding with, "That's okay, I'll handle it," let them help. Young children, especially, always want to "help." Encouraging that helpful attitude and involvement in appropriate ways can help them feel included and important. This will also foster the bond between the children as we model appreciation and thankfulness for their helpful, loving spirit.

Finally, siblings can benefit greatly from sibling support groups, camps, and workshops. The Sibling Support Project (www.siblingsupport.org) provides valuable information and resources for siblings affected by special health, developmental, or mental health concerns of a brother or sister. One child's health issues are truly a family affair.

Chapter 9 Key Concepts

1. Sibling issues can cause parents nearly as much aggravation and grief as dealing with their ill child.

2. The power of modeling and example cannot be overestimated when dealing with sibling issues. Children learn how to negotiate their differences by observing and copying the adults in their lives.

3. Siblings of ill children may feel resentful or left out. This may be a reality, causing parents who feel guilty about time constraints to fill the gap with material gifts and overindulgence, often leading to entitled and demanding children. Paradoxically, gifts and excusing insolent behavior of demanding children does not help, and the children continue to feel resentful and left out. Healthy parental expectations of respectful and acceptable behavior must be upheld, even when the going gets

tough. Take the time to sit down and explore the child's feelings, following the communication model taught in this chapter. Time alone, even if it is short, is helpful in dealing with healthy siblings and involves them in the care of the ill child in an appropriate way. This helps foster a spirit of family cohesion and cooperation, without robbing the brothers or sisters of a healthy childhood of their own.

Chapter 10

Unique Situations: Developmental Disabilities and Eating Disorders

Have courage for the great sorrows
of life and patience for the small ones;
and when you have laboriously
accomplished your daily task,
go to sleep in peace. God is awake.
—Victor Hugo (1802-1885)

Medical Issues and Developmental Disabilities

Some parents don't parent "just" children. Instead, they live with *personal growth systems* that are presented to them in different versions and models. Some of the growth systems are called Down Kids; some are called Kids with Klinefelter's Syndrome; some are known as Kids with Asperger Syndrome; some are autistic. Bundled together they may be known as Developmentally Disabled Children, Developmentally Delayed Children, Challenged Children, or Special Needs Children. These mobile and surprisingly unique personal growth systems are present in many homes. In the United States there are 350,000 children with Down syndrome alone.

Whatever the "flavor" of the child's developmental problems, they give parents and siblings the opportunity to:

- ♥ Become citizens with a social consciousness and an increased awareness of, and sensitivity toward, the needs of others.
- ♥ Learn to be people who enjoy random hugs and affection.
- ♥ Help everyone in the community rejoice in diversity, appreciate the uniqueness of others, and respect their strengths rather than focus on their deficits: "Nothing's wrong with Jeff. That's just him."
- ♥ Encourage every individual to reach his or her own level of competence and potential.
- ♥ Expect others to be genuine and honest when expressing themselves.
- ♥ Come to love crazy dancing and off-key singing to almost any music.
- ♥ Know the value of organization, structure, rituals, and predictability in life.
- ♥ Know that any passing stranger could be an instant friend.
- ♥ Come to accept, if not enjoy, repetitive phrases and monosyllables.
- ♥ Understand the importance of smelling the flowers, catching butterflies, and chasing ducks.
- ♥ Learn patience and remain optimistic and positive in the midst of coping with problem behavior.

Medical problems are often present in Developmentally Disabled Children. This includes eye, ear, bone, cardiac, and GI problems.

Sleep apnea and celiac disease are common. In fact, whenever there is a change in behavior or a new behavioral problem crops up, medical problems must first be ruled out.

Patience is a key concept when working with a Developmentally Disabled Child who must learn to care for himself. They need to be taught self-care issues in smaller steps with more patience and must be cued with organizational assistance, clues, and reminders. Changes in routine are very difficult for most Developmentally Disabled Children. The authors know of one child so threatened by changes in routine that she can scarcely leave the town in which she lives without great trauma, which severely restricts the movement of the parents. Wise parents have tight structures and schedules that are adhered to precisely in order to avoid power struggles and reactions that may be difficult to manage.

Learning from negative consequences may be less effective with Developmentally Disabled Children for a number of reasons:

- ♥ They are more likely to be hurt, offended, or pained by the consequence rather than learn from it.
- ♥ Cause-and-effect thinking, essential for learning from consequences, may not be as developed due to neurological differences in the brain.
- ♥ Impulsiveness may override long-term memory and the ability for self-control.

In place of learning from logical consequences, whether natural or imposed, parents of Developmentally Disabled Children often correctly focus almost exclusively on the child's strengths and congratulate correct behavior. Parents of most children can take good behavior, wise decisions, and thoughtful responses somewhat for granted, and they may, understandably, even ignore appropriate choices. This is not recommended for any child, but most children don't need inordinate amounts of positive reinforcement for wise decisions and everyday self-care issues. Developmentally Disabled

Children may. Focusing on strengths and a job well done are essential. These children like plenty of praise. When a child has thought disorders or is more severely compromised, success is much more likely when a parent says, "That makes me so happy," rather than, "How did you figure out how to do that?" This is the exact opposite of how a parent would encourage a child with fully functioning cognitive abilities as discussed in Chapter 5.

The intervention techniques may not be that different with Developmentally Delayed Children, but the timing changes. For instance, temper tantrums, common in young toddlers, may not occur in a child with Down syndrome until three or four years of age, and the phases may last a bit longer. The behavior itself is really no different, and neither are the techniques parents use to intervene. *The most important point: relate to the developmental age, not the chronological age.* Becoming well versed in good parenting techniques used for the early childhood years will serve you well; keeping in mind some techniques that are appropriate for a four year old may not be effective for an eleven year old who is developmentally age four.

Throughout this work we have cautioned against *showing* frustration about a child's poor healthcare (or other) choices. This is particularly true of Developmentally Disabled Children whose feelings are easily hurt, who can hold grudges, and are likely to be more obstinate. Using empathy and one-liners is a good way for parents to handle the frustration they inevitably feel but shouldn't show.

Giving a child choices is always important but only *when the child is able to make good choices, willingly choose from the choices given, or learn from the consequences of poor choices.* Let's look at an example. A parent might say, "Rob, would you like to take the green pill or the red pill first?" This would be a useful question for many younger children but a Developmentally Disabled Child might just repeat "no.. no... no" in a sing-song. At such a point, rather than fall into a control battle that could be won only with a hassle, it might be more prudent, efficient, and effective just to break the medicine capsule and dump the contents into the soup. More than ever, parents need to ask themselves before getting into a control battle, "Is this one I can easily win, or if we hassle it through, will the learning last?"

Robert

Robert, a child with Down syndrome, was prescribed medication both for a cardiac problem and asthma. The school was to administer both at noon. However, while not completely negativistic, Robert was not enthusiastic about reporting to the nurse's office for his meds — sometimes he didn't even show up. He was consistently slow, and upon arrival was inevitably low-grade uncooperative. This surprised Rob's parents, who, at home, found him to be compliant and responsive in taking his medication. Two simple changes turned things around at school.

Trista, Rob's mother explains in her own words:

Trista

I found that the school expected Rob to walk down to the nurse's station by himself. Certainly he is capable of that, but he wanted to be with the other kids. And, particularly, I think he wanted to be around Susan because he would sing-song her name at home. So I suggested Susan walk Rob to the nurse's station. Susan was more than willing to do that. She's the type of kid who likes to be helpful and that's probably what appealed to Rob. So, no matter how fast she walked, Rob stayed right on her heels! They were both happy about that. Then I found out the nurse wasn't always there on time or she would be seeing another kid. And Rob, like a lot of these kids, insists on taking his medication *on time*. Structure and predictability are God's writ for these kids! For Rob, that meant *the* time to take his meds was not 12:02 and not 10 minutes early. It had to be 12:00 or nothing. That's when the hands of his watch were together, and that's that! I think his demands to take his medication at 12:00 probably irritated the nurse because he is good at being insistent about things like that. She evidently told Rob his meds "didn't have to be taken on the dot of noon." We told her that, for Rob, it *does* need to be right on the dot. Thankfully, she was willing to work with us on this, and now life is much easier for us all (including the poor nurse!).

Wise parents are quick to learn that a child who is lazy, messy, and obstinate about treatments can be entertaining and fun at the same time. A routine bordering on ritual may be helpful when it comes to treatments, dental visits, and physician's appointments. This routine might include:

- ♥ Singing a special song in preparation.
- ♥ Making sure the favorite stuffed animal is ready to go.
- ♥ Exclamations of joy, punctuated with a hug when the self-care job is well done.
- ♥ Arranging the timetable to be consistent with the job expected.

The transition to adulthood is perhaps the major issue when parenting Developmentally Disabled Children and is beyond the scope of this work. However, the website maintained by the National Association for Down syndrome (www.nads.org) contains a discussion forum and allows families to discuss issues and receive valuable support on many relevant matters. A variety of good reference material is available to help parents navigate the educational system as well.[21] When raising Developmentally Disabled Children, wise parents get involved with community agencies and learn about the many special programs available for assistance and support. Cooperative planning and interagency collaboration are helpful and necessary parental partners.

In summary, we advise the parents of children with special needs to read the tools and techniques explained throughout this book and adjust them as appropriate for the child's developmental age. Recognize that to build self-confidence in individuals with disabilities it is essential expectations remain high. These children must not be viewed as helpless and must be encouraged to become as self-sufficient and independent as possible. Each child is very different, so the climb may be completed on different mountaintops, but the climb itself doesn't vary. Every parent's goal must be to develop his or her child's maximum potential for accepting responsibility for self-care, with the hope of raising a respectful, responsible citizen, regardless of the eventual employment or living environment. When parents emphasize enjoyment of their child's competency and strengths and practice the tools in this book, while encouraging their children to experience success, then self-esteem and higher functioning are the usual results.

Eating Disorders

Bulimia and Anorexia

Anorexia and bulimia are life-threatening eating disorders, which generally occur in the adolescent or young adulthood years. Anorexia reportedly affects 2.5 million Americans.[22] Anorexics lose weight by starving themselves; bulimics binge on food and then purge. Both may lose weight to the point of emaciation, taxing their hearts, and die of malnutrition and/or cardiac complications. Eating disorders have historically been considered "a girl problem" but are now also being diagnosed more frequently in adolescent boys.

"Eating disorders have been increasing among boys at an alarming pace," says Leigh Cohn, co-author of *Making Weight: Men's Conflicts with Food, Weight, Shape & Appearance*. He points to the two most recent studies, which show the rate among young men is at least three times what had been considered as the status quo, or up to 2 percent of young men. (By comparison, the rate among young women is about 4.5 percent.)[23]

Significantly, too, nine- and ten-year-olds are being diagnosed with anorexia, and residential facilities now specialize in treating these younger children. At the time of this writing there is no explanation for the declining age of onset. Once thought to be a problem affecting mainly Caucasian adolescents, real ethnic diversity is blooming, with black, Asian and Hispanic children being treated for anorexia.

The cause of these disorders in any one child is unclear, because multiple factors appear to play a role. Genetic factors, family interaction patterns, and the individual's own character and personality have all been implicated. The Internet has literally hundreds, if not thousands, of pages devoted to this subject, its possible origins and the difficulties of treatment. To summarize the problem in a single sentence, it appears that *the illness is a response to coping with stress in genetically predisposed children who are filled with denial about their feelings and weight*. There! Quick, short, concise, and anything but simple.

This single sentence has many implications for parents and parenting. Let us examine each of the possible contributing factors individually, and provide parenting responses that might be helpful in combating eating disorders.[24]

The Genetic Factor in Eating Disorders

Eating disorders, like many other behavioral illnesses, appear to run in families and have a genetic predisposition. A few of the others are drug abuse, alcoholism, anxiety, depression, and obsessive-compulsive disorder. With eating disorders, genetic factors have been found in at least one study to account for 56 percent of the risk factors,[25] and girls with a mother or sister with a history of anorexia nervosa are 12 times more likely than the average woman to develop anorexia themselves and four times more likely to develop bulimia.[26] Not only does the illness itself run in families but the predisposing temperament seems to as well.

The one good thing about illnesses that run in families is the fact that children can be prepared to recognize warning factors prior to the onset of the problem. Understanding a problem, and properly preparing for it, may allow some to avoid many disasters or at least soften their effects. When children are forewarned, they are forearmed. This forewarning is best carried out in a heart-to-heart discussion about possible future problems. A loving parent, relative, or counselor initiates the dialogue before the child is an adolescent, in an informative, non-hand-wringing and factual manner that indicates a hopeful outlook for a healthy future as is shown in Chapter 7.

Discussions about anorexia and bulimia must take place with a loving, nonaffected adult, as those with the disease are generally filled with denial. Naturally, the give-and-take of this type of conversation is longer and more of a dialogue than the following short example, but we know our readers will get the drift:

> "Darling, in our family, both your aunt and your sister have had an eating disorder. Anorexia is a problem because those who have it can't see it. Slowly, women become more and more concerned about how they look and how much they weigh. They become way, way too worried about being fat. The problem sort of sneaks up on some girls and the more weight they lose, the more they can't see it, until, eventually, some

die. It would be so sad if something like that happened to you. But I don't think that's very likely because for one, you know about it and you have always been good at avoiding big problems and figuring things out. Secondly, when you are mad or upset, you always talk about it. Sometimes, honey, the problem happens when people have the same thought or idea over and over, and they can't get it out of their minds. Or they feel they're not good enough, or something like that, but don't talk about it with someone. In that case, the problem can just get worse and worse. But I think you will probably always be good at talking about your feelings. At least I hope so for your sake! Do you think you will always feel good about talking to me (or someone) about how you are feeling as you go through your teen years?"

Children are almost always helped by a loving discussion about possible future problems when given a hopeful expectation by a calm and factual adult who models the ability to cope with tough times. Parents sometimes worry that such talks may be "borrowing trouble." But, like talking with teens about suicide, a factual discussion about possible future problems makes avoiding potential disasters more likely. Naturally, such talks assume:

- ♥ A loving parent/child relationship.
- ♥ Parents who can be factual and warm, not worried and over-concerned, and who do not take on responsibility for the problem.
- ♥ Parents who are able to be involved and work with counseling which is almost always required and often more effective with family involvement.

Anorexia and Bulimia as a Way of Coping with Stress

Food and emotions are closely linked. In fact, food, love, affection, disappointment, and loss have always been linguistically connected. When folks say, "I feel empty" or "You fill me up" or "When you do that, I just want to throw up" or "Sweetie, I love you" or "You are the apple of my eye" or "I'm starved for affection," they are not talking about food! They are talking about their emotions and using food as a metaphor.

Over- and undereating change brain chemicals that affect anxiety and depression. They are both often unhappy and ineffective ways of coping with stress. An authority on anorexia recently noted that a child's inherent vulnerabilities "load the gun," and environmental stresses "pull the trigger."[27] So, assuming "inherent vulnerabilities" are unchangeable, how can we avoid "pulling the trigger"? It is a complex issue well beyond the scope of this work, but we can say that Love and Logic techniques excel at raising children who effectively learn to cope with stress in healthy ways. They gain wisdom through experiencing the consequences of their decisions. Such children, having been allowed to cause themselves both good and bad times, are much less likely to deny the results of poor choices and are far more likely to realistically plan ahead. These are great immunizations against the use of food as a dysfunctional coping response because:

- ♥ The experience of coping and overcoming difficulties with good problem-solving skills leads to the ability to confront feelings and issues in a healthy manner, rather than displacing them with changes in food intake.

- ♥ The child's history of successfully coping with painful outcomes of poor choices makes denial much less likely.

Psychological and Possible Chemical Factors in Eating Disorders

Two personality factors have often been reported to be present in eating disorders: perfectionism and high, unrealistic expectations of self. Even when anorexic adults have achieved success, deep down they report feeling insecure and inadequate. There is a tendency to see things only in extremes without shades of gray.

- ♥ "I'm good or I'm bad."
- ♥ "I'm pretty or I'm ugly."
- ♥ "I'm successful or a complete failure."
- ♥ "I'm perfect or defective."
- ♥ "I'm fat or I'm thin."

During the elementary school years, Consultant Parents discourage this type of thinking in the two ways we discussed previously in this book.

- ♥ Parents don't overreassure their children. Overreassurance by definition takes the child's negative concept or behavior very seriously. When a child habitually says, "I'm no good" and the parent habitually responds, "Yes you are!" it actually validates the child's negative thinking.[28] And it may lead to the "either/or" black-and-white thinking of individuals who don't recognize gray. Responding with, "Gee, honey, I see it differently, but tell me how you are no good," allows for less manipulation, more acceptance of responsibility, and a child's far more accurate self-examination.
- ♥ Consultant parents use encouragement rather than praise because encouragement increases children's self-awareness and gives them experience in viewing themselves, their responses, and their creations realistically, rather than simply trying to please an authority figure.[29] As we discussed in Chapter 5, saying, "How did you decide to do it that way?" will generally be more productive than the simple praise, "Good job!"

In addition to psychological factors, there may be chemical factors at play in eating disorders. Recent research has shown the level of serotonin activity in the brains of anorexics is abnormally high, and this may relate to feelings of anxiety and obsessional thinking — classic traits of anorexia. Therefore, it is speculated starvation may prevent the absorption of the building blocks that produce serotonin which might then act as a chemical brake on negative feelings.[30]

The Role of the Family

There are a number of family factors that have been indicated and are thought to play a role in eating disorders. Remember, this is only speculation! As we noted, genetic factors and personality patterns themselves seem to play the most important roles in the genesis of eating disorders. As we delve into these interaction factors, it is safe to say that while healthy parenting patterns certainly will not ever cause or aggravate the problem, they may not be able to alleviate the problem either. Loving, effective parents are known to have had children suffering depression, suicide, and eating disorders. So, as we delve into family and societal factors, we do so with the foundational belief that parenting styles should never be used as an excuse for a child's poor choices. Parents do the best they can, under the circumstances they experience, to raise their children with the love they are able to show.

The problem in examining family patterns lies with the fact that all sorts of dysfunctional patterns have been reported. These form a long list:

- ♥ Smothering and overprotective families
- ♥ Controlling and critical parents
- ♥ A chronic feeling of being abandoned and misunderstood
- ♥ Having parents or a family that overemphasize appearance
- ♥ Having rigid parents who don't model good conflict resolution skills

The list of unhealthy family patterns goes on and on. The effect of unintentional, yet unhealthy, parental responses cannot be ignored. Again, good parenting techniques do not guarantee success, but at least they are unlikely to contribute to the problem. So rather than focusing on what is speculatively wrong, it is more effective to focus on raising kids who are most likely to make healthy choices and who are respectful, responsible, and pleasant to be around. Whether or not an eating disorder is present, or may be present in the future, it will never hurt for parents to show healthy responses and good parenting techniques.

Healthy Parenting Responses

Before we go into the specifics of healthy parenting responses to a child's eating disorder, we want to make it absolutely clear this material is not intended to replace professional medical and mental health support. *When anorexia or bulimia is present, professional intervention is an absolute necessity.* Medication, counseling, and hospitalization have all proved helpful in individual situations. Changing the family dynamics, even for the better, in the midst of a life-threatening situation should be supervised by professionals who know the specifics of your situation.

Eating disorders, like any other chronic illness, require the family and parents' intimate involvement in the child's recovery process. *Parental responses may play an important role in the child's responses to their disease.* It is neither healthy nor helpful for parents to accept the responsibility (or "take the blame") for a child's misbehavior or poor living choices, even when the choice is not to eat, conscious or not. Love and Logic teaches parents to put the responsibility for poor choices directly upon the person who makes them. *This does not mean parents are uninvolved in their children's problems* but it does mean parents make it clear to the child, in the loving way taught throughout this book, that the child has the primary responsibility for resolving the problem with the adults' loving support, but not rescue.[31] With this approach, children are much less likely to avoid responsibility by thinking, "I don't need to worry about this problem because Mom and Dad worry for me," or shift the blame to the parents by saying, "This is all your fault."

No matter how parents handle the situation within their family, it is essential to discuss any approach thoroughly with your mental health professional before discussing these issues with a severely ill child. Further, the use of newer medications has proved very helpful in cases of bulimia.

Bulimia is embarrassing for most young ladies to talk about. Thus, talking to family members about the problem may be difficult in many families. Talking to others who have had the disease and overcome it may prove helpful, as is counseling.

It may be that the best, or perhaps the only, thing a parent can do is to react in such a way that does not exacerbate or escalate the child's life-threatening situation. Remember, parents ultimately have control over the actions of only one person: themselves.[32] Engaging in control battles and power struggles with your anorexic teenager over food issues will rarely improve the situation; and, in some cases, exceedingly inappropriate parental responses may have a negative impact. Dealing with a child's life-threatening denial takes finesse.[33] Reacting by showing frustration, anger, and hand-wringing or blaming the child or society is never as effective as responding with sorrow, curiosity, and interest in a child's poor choices and difficult situations.

Modeling can be a useful and important component in the process of a child's recovery from an eating disorder. A parent's own obsession about physical appearance or athletic prowess will send an unstated message that speaks louder than words to a child who may be already hypersensitive to body image and parental approval. Wise parents model cheerful acceptance of one's own physical imperfections and demonstrate a healthy balance around health issues, such as exercise and eating properly. An upcoming section on obesity demonstrates how one mother helped her daughter deal with her body weight issues by adopting a healthy outlook and lifestyle for herself.

Societal Influences

Finally, there are possible societal factors that influence eating disorders. Big drinks and big burgers have enticed the population into a diabetic frenzy. While most of the population is downright overweight, the females that populate the media (those who model prettiness and good looks) are generally thin to the point of appearing anorexic themselves. Talk about image confusion!

On the "male side" of the issue, we have this: "Studies also demonstrate that cultural and media pressures on men for the 'ideal body' are on the rise. This increased focus on body shape, size, and physical appearance will likely contribute to increased numbers of eating disorder in males. Research indicates eating disorders in males are clinically similar to eating disorders in females (Schneider & Argas, 1987). Studies also demonstrate that certain athletic activities appear to put males at risk for developing eating disorders. Body builders, wrestlers, dancers, swimmers, runners, rowers, gymnasts, and jockeys are prone to eating disorders due to the weight restrictions necessitated by their sports (Andersen, Bartlett, Morgan & Rowena, 1995)." [34]

With so much emphasis in our culture on athletic performance and good looks, it is not too surprising that some predisposed children take things too far. And, although on the surface it seems reasonable enough to blame society for the self-destructive choices of an individual, this is ultimately self-defeating when dealing with individual situations. Blaming society or others simply removes individual responsibility and accountability and actually increases the likelihood of the negative behavior, as we'll see in the next section on obesity.

When all is said and done, nobody, at this point, can say with any certainty the exact cause of an eating disorder in any one particular child, but we can say with absolute certainty that all the speculation, studies, reports, and conjecture in the literature do not implicate the family interaction patterns advocated by Love and Logic. It would appear the personality of the anorexic person is not that of children who have grown up in a home advocating honest acceptance of personal responsibility; where children are lovingly supported by parents who view mistakes as learning experiences and where children are encouraged to cope.

Childhood Obesity

The Epidemic Problem Facing Today's Youth

For years America and other developed countries have been in chronic denial around childhood obesity. Overweight children behind and in front of the world's fast-food counters, sipping their "super-sized soda pops" have become the accepted norm. The alarming statistics, the reasons, and issues surrounding the epidemic of obesity can be found on the Internet and in the news. The statistics clarify a typical pattern that contributes to the obesity problem as it exists in many homes around the globe. Because of these similarities, rather than write in generalities, we will use an individual child. Her specifics can be applied, almost verbatim, in a context that will be relevant for most parents coping with this problem.

When I (Dr. Cline) first met Maria she was a sweet, soft-spoken, generally sensitive, and quiet child of 11. She said that deep down inside she felt like "Ms. Cellophane," the Amos character in the musical *Chicago*, and was convinced most of the other kids looked right through her. In her quiet, shy way she did her best to fit in, but it was particularly difficult because she had a childhood problem that has become an epidemic. Maria was fat. Because she was so typical of the problem, and because her solution was so complete and gratifying, we will tell her story here.

The obesity epidemic presently threatens the health of millions of children and future adults across America and in many developed nations. Maria was at increased risk of developing type 2 diabetes and heart disease. For every extra pound she put on, her body was forced to build an extra mile of unnecessary capillary scaffolding for her 11-year-old heart to shove blood through year after life-shortening year.[35]

Naturally, Maria's single mom, Elaina, was very concerned about her daughter's weight problem. But she was in a predicament herself, because she was also overweight. In fact, statistics show the propensity for being overweight runs through families like an avenging angel of isolation and early death.[36]

Elaina, like many parents, would express her concern for her daughter's obesity by attempting to control what Maria ate, and while attempting to not be overcontrolling, she would sweetly nag Maria. "You don't need two helpings of potatoes, Maria." And Maria would look back at her mother with her soft, liquid brown eyes saying with quiet accusation, "Who are you to talk?" In fact, when her mother would bring up her weight, Maria either fell silent, acted as if it was no problem at all, or became low-grade snippy. Maria's most workable response was her retort that "lots of kids are fat" and she hung out at school with a group of chubby girls who formed their own club of mutual isolation from other kids.

If obesity is a difficult issue for adults, it is doubly difficult for children, particularly when they are surrounded by overweight role-models talking the talk, but certainly not walking the walk.

Contributing Factors for Obesity

Of course, in addition to being surrounded by poor modeling at home, Maria's obesity was compounded by a number of other common factors that bedevil Americans and many people in leading Western nations.

First, like many others, Maria spent hours in front of the computer screen sending instant messages to vaguely known friends. In this environment, her weight, unseen, was a nonissue. She bravely shared with me examples of her messages to her "e-friends" and it was apparent Maria had a keen sense of humor and high intelligence that lay buried undiscovered by those who didn't see the real her beneath the extra rolls of fat. In those e-messages, both her hidden strengths and her hopes shone through clearly.

Secondly, Maria then watched about two hours of TV a day, snacking between meals while watching her favorite programs. Spending several hours a day in front of "a screen," Maria is, almost unfortunately, a statistically average American kid.[37]

Finally, Maria was surrounded by carbohydrates. In the cafeteria at school, vending machines were crammed with high-carb delights. The school menu itself had more than its share of carbohydrates. Across the street from the school, the fast-food restaurant offered to "super size" the hamburgers and French fries. The drinks that were labeled "large" 15 years ago were now "small," and large drinks made of liquid sugar came in nearly bucket-sized containers, proudly proclaiming "big gulp."

So that was Maria's life; a fairly typical one for obese children. She lived in a technologically magical world swamped by nutritiously poor but tantalizing foods, and she was surrounded by poor modeling at home. This world encouraged lethargy, and the problems engendered by this lethargy were aggravated by the nagging of Maria's mom.

No wonder America, indeed the world, is packed with overweight children!

Necessary Ingredients for Overcoming Addictions

Like most overweight children, way down deep inside, Maria felt hopeless about gaining control of her problem; a hopelessness that remained unexpressed and seldom overtly recognized. Lifestyles are addictive, even when they are self-destructive, and overeating is a

tough addiction to overcome. To overcome addictions, which are always a chronic problem, one must have:
- ♥ Motivation or desire to change
- ♥ An action plan
- ♥ Commitment
- ♥ Support

The first essential requirement for overcoming addiction is a strong desire to change. This desire must burn like a flare if the problem is to be overcome. Unfortunately, rather than a flare that might light the path of possible changes in her life, Maria, like her obese mother, felt only the distant glow of a buried ember, a glow of ever-present, but seldom-expressed subterranean desire.

Naturally, without the motivation there was no action plan, commitment, or support as each must lead to the other.

Necessary Steps to Deal with Childhood Obesity

Latency age children take their cues about values, belief systems, and lifestyle from the adults in their environment. (See Chapter 6 to see how children change as they approach the teen years.)

It was Elaina, Maria's mother, who had to take the initial steps to fan the ember of desire into the flame of plan and commitment.

Elaina's life as a single mother was busy and finances were very tight, but she made the difficult decision to seek therapy because she knew somehow life could be better for them both. After talking with Elaina, it was apparent to me she didn't need therapy at all. But, like so many parents who grew up without good modeling, she simply needed some training about the attitudes, tools, and techniques of effective parenting.

Rather than having Elaina spend her hard-earned money on expensive and unnecessary therapy, I recommended she take a parenting class and consider working with a parent coach instead.

In the class, Elaina realized that with Maria she had focused on all of the externals that led to her obesity problem. She had blamed the school menu, she had decried the vending machines and the fast-food restaurant menus, and she had even blamed the Internet! Elaina had never realized that by focusing on all the external reasons for Maria's weight problems, she had excused Maria from taking responsibility for her own body. Without realizing the implications, Elaina had conveyed to her daughter, "With all the problems in society no wonder you have problems with weight."

By taking responsibility for the problem away from Maria and laying it, instead, at the feet of society, Elaina gave her daughter an "easy-out" and a scapegoat on which to blame her weight problems. This is a common mistake made by many parents.

Elaina recognized the importance of concentrating on *Maria's choices, not society, the school, or other externals that had so easily been the focus of her ire, and perhaps had even been gratifying to blame.* The instructor drove home the Es and Cs of Love and Logic. The concepts of Example, Experience, Empathy, Expectations, and Encouragement, as well as Choices, Consequences, and Curiosity burned into Elaina's consciousness like the light of a new day! Realizing how lacking these had been in her home, the new ideas made her feel uncomfortable but at the same time infused her with hope for change.

- ♥ Example, Experience, Empathy, Expectations and Encouragement lock in respect for adults and help the child make changes by hurting from the inside out.
- ♥ Choices and Consequences must be owned by the child.
- ♥ Curiosity and Interest: No one listens to what we say until we first listen to what they say. Listening with curiosity and interest always trumps worry and concern.

Parents who deal successfully with their child's obesity must follow the path Elaina blazed in her home. Let's look at the essential steps.

Motivating a Child for Health

Motivation has to come from inside! How often is that simple fact forgotten or ignored as parents push, shove, implore, and demand change from their children? Motivation comes when parents set the model, while encouraging and exciting the child about making attainable changes.

When parents are their child's confidant and encourager, they must set the example. An individual buried in his or her own problems can't expect the respect necessary to encourage another to take a difficult path that they, themselves, have been unwilling to tread. Fortunately, Elaina recognized two very important things:

1. She needed to change her parenting techniques, and
2. She, herself, needed a makeover to set an exciting new example.

Elaina began by seeing a nutritionist, who helped her with a food and eating plan and who was willing to follow through with her. Then, after practicing what she needed to say both with her parenting coach and in the mirror at home, she asked Maria when would be a good time to have an important talk.

At the appointed time, she had the following conversation with Maria: "Honey, I am so glad you agreed to have this conversation with me. I've been troubled by something about myself for a long time. I just never felt I could do anything about it. I find that many people, when they see me in the store, look away. Sometimes people ignore me. I know that's because I am just plain fat. And lots of the time I feel outright ugly. I never said that about myself, but it's true! I've never done anything about it because I thought it would be too hard. But now, I think I can do something about it."

"Let me show you something I am really excited about. It is a new scale! See, it shows how much I weigh in red letters, and I can hardly wait to see those numbers go down. I am sure they will! You see, Maria, this is the plan I have developed *for myself*. I am so excited! I can hardly wait to try it..."

At that point, Elaina described the nutritional plan she had developed with her "new friend," the nutritionist.

Without overdoing it, Elaina was very clear she was tired of being overweight and felt she would have a much better chance to live longer, make more friends, be prettier, and have a more fulfilling life if she let out the beautiful person she had hidden inside of herself. Her enthusiasm was infectious.

Elaina had become the example. Then, she enabled her daughter to become a willing, even excited, partner in the quest "for a new me" by enlisting her help.

Elaina said to Maria, "This would be a lot easier for me, sweetheart, if you could help me graph my weight loss and encourage me to take walks every day. I think my main problem, Maria, is that I simply don't like to exercise. But I think if I had your company, I would be encouraged to walk around the block a couple of times every day. So, I am hoping you will walk with me, because there is no one I would rather be with than you!"

Then Elaina discussed now much easier it would be for her if Maria were willing to eat the same food and in the same proportions. She emphasized again what a blessing it would be for her to walk this new path with her daughter's help. In fact, maybe they could help each other!

At this point Maria asked her mother if she could have her own graph and put it up beside her mother's. Elaina said that would be okay, as long as they didn't get into some kind of contest. "After all," Elaina noted, "I have a lot more weight to lose!" She hoped to lose two or three pounds for every one pound Maria lost. And, with humor, she also jokingly hoped Maria wouldn't foul things up for her by losing weight too fast!

The path Elaina and Maria took together was not easy, but they walked the walk together and became closer. As an added visual incentive, Maria (we told you she was a bright child) bought a bag of clay. For every pound of weight she and her mother lost, she fashioned an ugly little troll and watched it grow pound by pound. "I want to see what I'm leaving behind!" she said.

In summary:
- ♥ Parents must model healthy responses in their own lives.
- ♥ The child must come to be dissatisfied with his or her present state of health or lack of good self-care.
- ♥ The child must be helped to develop a plan in which he or she can be capable, take ownership, and measure progress.
- ♥ An adult must provide support and lovingly hold the child accountable but not take on the burden of responsibility for the problem themselves.

Chapter 10 Key Concepts

1. Parents of Developmentally Disabled Children must have patience above all else as they learn a different way of being. Structure and routine are necessary to avoid control battles. For Developmentally Disabled Children, consequences are often not as effective as positive reinforcement and praise. Parents must relate to the developmental age, not the chronological age of the child. Using empathy, one-liners, and choices can be effective. Community support is essential. As always, expectations should remain reasonably high and your child should be encouraged to become as self-sufficient and independent as possible, while keeping in mind individual differences and capabilities.

2. Eating Disorders: The causes of eating disorders are unclear. It is safe to say these life-threatening illnesses are likely a response to coping with stress in genetically predisposed, and often insecure, children who are filled with denial about their

feelings and weight. This chapter covers parental responses to all these possible causes.

3. Chronic obesity is a condition around which denial is often present. Overweight children and their overweight parents are often in an unhealthy, synergistic dance that will both shorten and decrease the quality of their lives. This chapter provides an example of a successful response to childhood obesity and application of the steps necessary to motivate a child for health:
   - Parents must model healthy responses in their own lives.
   - The child must come to be dissatisfied with his or her present state of health or lack of good self-care.
   - The child must be helped to develop a plan in which he or she can be capable, take ownership, and measure progress.
   - An adult must provide support and lovingly hold the child accountable but not take on the burden of responsibility for the problem themselves.

Chapter 11

Caution: Medical Challenges Affect Marriage and Family Relationships

Turn your wounds into wisdom.
—Oprah Winfrey

Children are certainly shaped by their families, but special children can shape families as well. Families faced with chronic illnesses and medical issues deal not just with the medical challenges but also with the mix of feelings that swirl around personality patterns, coping mechanisms, and difficult times that test a person's resources. Chronically ill children can rule family and marriage/couple responses.

Difficult Situations Strain Coping Skills

Right off the top, in every situation, national,

regional, or within a family, *the more difficult and dangerous the situation, the more likely it is that strong feelings throw clear thinking right out the window*. An understandable but troubling swamp of feelings often bubbles up in families with children who suffer from chronic illnesses. These intense feelings are present in every serious situation where dark results are possible or probable. If a negative outcome is inevitable, people often just give up, and there is actually less psychic and interpersonal turmoil. People make their peace and reach acceptance. However, in situations where there is a possibility of success, or the probability of prolonging life, the interpersonal turmoil can become intense because the stakes are perceived as higher. It is in this realm that parenting skills can make the difference between life and death.

Intense emotions and intense situations frequently lead to mistakes! Parents who insist their children eat healthy foods often develop children who are extremely picky eaters. Pastors are known for raising children who go through their teen years as rebellious nonbelievers. There are plenty of mental health professionals who have raised children with severe behavior problems. The solution to this problem is to set loving but firm limits, exercise parental control over emotions, use empathy before consequences, and share control and problem solving. When parents have a good toolbox of effective parenting responses they are less likely to overreact to difficult situations and make mistakes. In addition, a good support system is essential.

Difficult Situations Are Ripe for Triangulation

What is triangulation? It takes place when two or more people have a problem and one vents or expresses dissatisfaction or blame (usually in a frustrated manner) to a person not directly involved with the problem. Triangulation takes place when a person attempts to gain sympathy, control, or manipulate difficult situations. Really, it is a type of purposeful transfer of misinformation in order to promote discord. It might be seen as a form of manipulative gossip.

People normally differ on how situations should be handled. When the situation is complex or difficult, those differences can result in mutually destructive communication patterns, blame, accusations, and recriminations. We have seen this happen over and over again in our nation when the government responds to emergency situations and citizens complain loudly to the media that the help wasn't extensive or fast enough. Often, those who have been helped the most are the ones who complain the loudest. This triangulation also frequently happens after divorce and is present as couples attempt to cope with a multitude of severe threats to health, financial stability, and relational well-being.

Let's look at an example of a common triangulation situation. We will follow George and Cyndy as we discuss communication skills.

George & Cyndy

George is uninvolved in helping with his son's extensive treatment regimen, which he leaves completely to his wife, Cyndy. Cyndy expresses considerable frustration to her mother-in-law rather than addressing the issue directly with her husband.

Sometimes, the whole family is involved in this communication style, which is ultimately unhealthy and often damaging. When a family member experiences frustration with the actions of another, the most effective response is to deal directly and assertively with the "offending party." Talking the situation over with a counselor may be helpful. Adult communication tools are covered in the next section of this chapter.

When a third party becomes involved and attempts to fix the situation, it frequently causes damage to all of the relationships. This often ends with the third party lamely expressing, "I was only trying to help." The third party can best help by empathizing with the venting person's frustration without validating the actual complaint and remembering there are always two sides to every story. Encourage the person doing the venting to talk about the issue directly with the offending person. Don't get involved unless it affects you directly or there is a threat to someone's safety.

Chronic Stress and Self-Destructive Choices

A couple facing severe and chronic stress may make destructive choices in their attempt to cope. When a child has a significant medical condition, it forces the couple to relate primarily around problem solving, crisis, and survival. Life with the spouse/significant other becomes focused on constant, unremitting mutual responses to stressful situations. Life becomes simply surviving from one crisis to another. The human need for respite and a break from the stress leads to the understandable response, "I just want to get away from it all." The relief of an outside relationship, which focuses mostly on pleasure, can be overwhelmingly appealing and lead to an affair. Turning to drugs, alcohol, workaholism, materialism, gambling, and other addictions can all be an attempt to escape from the unrelenting stress of constantly dealing with life-and-death issues. This is well expressed in the old Kenny Rogers song:

"You picked a fine time to leave me Lucille,
With four hungry children and crops in the field."

In Chapter 1, we have discussed ways to mitigate these challenges. We also discuss these issues on the DVD version of this program in the section on marriage. The next section will also give you some tools to handle communication.

Communication and Problem-Solving Tools for Adult Relationships

Good communication tools are essential when discussing emotionally charged issues under highly stressful conditions. We have written at length about good communication skills between adults and children. Here we address the adult-to-adult issues that may be pertinent for families dealing with chronically ill children. Why is this relevant in a book on parenting? Because, the way parents handle conflict with each other (and other adults) sets the model for the way their children will handle conflict, both in childhood and adulthood. The probability of effective parenting increases when partners get along reasonably well and know how to handle their differences in a healthy manner.

Love and Logic is really a leadership program packaged as a parenting program. One of the great hallmarks of a true leader is the ability to communicate well and resolve problems/differences with others. Let's face it, when people interact with each other at any level, whether as spouses, co-workers, parents, church members, or classmates, there will be conflict. It's how we handle that conflict that determines how our relationships thrive. When dealing with chronic illness in the family, there is more opportunity for conflict due to the high stakes and high stress of the situation. There is also more opportunity to demonstrate true leadership.

Basic skills and ground rules are helpful when dealing with conflict-ridden issues. Using them will keep a possibly simple problem from escalating and increase the odds you will actually solve the problem! These tools were taken from Foster and Hermie Cline's book, *Marriage Love and Logic*.[38]

Tool 1: Are We Going to Vent or Problem Solve?

Sometimes a person just wants to let off steam, rather than actually solve a problem. This is okay on rare occasions, but it could be an indication of anger problems if it happens regularly. Chronic anger has many causes, including pain, illness (physical and/or mental), genetics, childhood issues, and constant, unrelenting stress. If chronic anger is an issue, it is probably a good idea to seek therapy to find ways to resolve it because it is difficult to solve relational problems rationally when anger gets in the way. Chronic anger can be very destructive to spouses and children and is often a problem when dealing with chronic illnesses. Problem solving occurs when partners:

- ♥ Are not angry
- ♥ Are willing to look at the situation in a non-emotional and thoughtful manner
- ♥ Know you both have the time to solve the problem
- ♥ Can look thoughtfully at each other's issues

The secret of problem solving lies in using the right tools when it's appropriate to do so. Each partner should ask self-examining questions such as: "What am I doing to contribute to the problem?" and "What can I do that would make the problem easier for you to handle or help you with it?"

Problem solving does not take place by looking only at the other person's problem and deciding what *they* need to do about it. Partners need to look at the ways they are individually contributing to the problem and how they might correct it. For instance, when couples triangulate, they make the initial problem even worse. The problem itself does not get resolved and venting/tattling/ triangulation creates even more hurt feelings and anger, which makes it even harder to effectively solve the problem. To revisit one scenario:

George & Cyndy

George is uninvolved in helping with his son's extensive treatment regimen, which he leaves completely to his wife, Cyndy. Cyndy expresses considerable frustration to her mother-in-law rather than addressing the issue directly with her husband.

In the example, Cyndy vents to her mother-in-law about George not helping take care of their son. George's mother gets angry with her son for not pitching in and chastises him. Now George is upset with his wife for "embarrassing him again" in front of his mom (this is most likely a recurring pattern). George is hurt and angry and probably even more resistant to helping his wife, which causes her to complain even more. This cycle of anger and hurt never resolves the original problem.

Tool 2: Don't Generalize

Generalizing is saying things like: "You *always...*" or "You *never...*" When we say things like this, even if they are not true, they can shape our partner's self-image, and he or she can become more that way. It also triggers defensive mechanisms, such as "I do not always...!", and can evoke flight or fight, rather than a loving desire to effectively solve the problem.

Tool 3: Stick to the Topic

There are often underlying issues that come up when attempting to problem solve — especially if using good problem-solving tools are not part of your past experiences both as a child and an adult. It is important not to "dredge" or bring up other issues when trying to resolve a particular challenge. Stick to one issue, resolve it, and then work on the next.

Tool 4: Stop Name Calling

Need we explain further? This gets no one anywhere and simply breeds anger and resentment. In moments of anger, we've all done it. "You're selfish!" or "You're a jerk!" can be equally hurtful. The words "I'm sorry" can go a long way here. Name-calling is an invitation to fight.

Tool 5: Use Terms of Endearment and Stay within "Touching Distance"

Loved ones need to know they are loved even in the midst of a fight. It is nice to say, "Sweetheart, the thing that makes me angry right now is ..." Don't yell from across the room; be close enough to touch lovingly.

Tool 6: Discussion by Appointment

Couples will sometimes try to solve a problem at the wrong time. Timing can be everything! The following times are not good to bring up an emotionally charged issue:

- ♥ Just before leaving for work
- ♥ While someone is cooking
- ♥ While someone is concentrating on an important task
- ♥ When someone is tired and/or hungry
- ♥ When a woman is possibly dealing with Premenstrual Syndrome (Men, don't underestimate the "power of PMS" to infect a sweet demeanor with turmoil; do both of you a favor, know her cycle and give her an extra dose of grace at this time. Of course, Lisa contributed this important fifth point!)

Arguments are more likely to take place when a person is tired, physically ill, or hungry. Low blood sugar and/or fatigue, like alcohol or drugs, inhibits and distorts thinking and heightens one's tendency towards emotional responses. One client said in therapy, "Once we decided not to fight when either of us was tired, we found we had nothing to fight about! What a difference that one rule made!"

A by-product of dealing with chronic illness and the resulting stress is fatigue. Taking care of kids with special needs takes a lot of emotional and physical effort. As we discussed in Chapter 1, it is important for parents to take good care of themselves, which includes respecting refuel time. When partners in a relationship have long, hard days, they should trade off taking care of the kids and handling other menial chores around the house to give their significant other refueling time. Refueling may involve taking a cat-nap, sitting with a newspaper for fifteen minutes, playing checkers with Junior, taking a bubble bath, or getting something to eat. The purpose is to refresh so each partner is alert and attentive to the couple's situation at hand.

Set an appointment to discuss issues calmly. If possible, get a babysitter and enjoy each other; then discuss the issue with the tools that are yet to come.

Tool 7: Don't Assume Negative Motivation

The fact is, in a lasting relationship, couples will commit acts *that* hurt the other. But healthy people seldom commit such acts *to* hurt the other. When we accuse our partner of "Doing _____ just to hurt me," or say, "You are trying to upset me," we are making statements that are generally not true of healthy people. Such accusations, per-haps tried out to incite guilt, may become self-fulfilling prophecies. They almost always bring defensive responses and increased dis-tancing; they also make resolution much more difficult. The correct response is, "When you do this, it upsets me. I hope you take that into consideration." Such a statement does not imply negative moti-vation and assumes that in our love relationships, another's feelings are important.

George & Cyndy

In our ongoing example Cyndy says, "You're doing this just to make me mad!" And George responds defensively with, "No, I am not! I don't *need* to do any-

thing to make *you* mad. You're always mad anyways!"
And the fight rages on.

Now let's have George and Cyndy model this correctly.

George & Cyndy

Cyndy says: "Honey, are you doing this just to make
me mad?" and George responds, wearily with, "No,
sweetheart. I am not. I am just so tired and stressed
out at the end of the day from work, and the sight of
Billy's blood freaks me out so much I have a hard time
dealing with it then."

Now, this is something that can be worked through! Perhaps
George can take the morning or weekend shift to relieve Cyndy,
and she can give him a bit of down time in the evening to recover
from his stressful day.

Tool 8: Stay in the Here and Now

When problem solving, it is helpful to stay in the "present tense" by
saying things like:
- ♥ "Do you feel like I am listening to you right now?"
- ♥ "Let me repeat what you're saying to see if I understand your
  point of view."
- ♥ "Is there something I could say right now that would help you
  feel better?"
- ♥ "What exactly do you need from me right now?"

Make sure the questions are answerable, and answerable in the here
and now. Avoid questions that are actually accusations hiding within questions, such as:
- ♥ "Why do you try to upset me all the time?"
- ♥ "What do I have to do to make you love me?"

♥ "Why don't you ever tell the truth?"

When an unanswerable question comes at you, your best response is to ask, "Is there an answer now that could help the situation?" In this way, a receptive partner will see that an unanswerable question may be the heart of the problem.

Staying in the present helps you stick to the topic, helps avoid "You always" or "You never" statements, and keeps the "problem" at a more manageable, bite-sized level.

Tool 9: Limit Discussion Time

One-hour of thoughtful discussion time is enough! Therapists generally limit their therapeutic hour to 50 minutes because most resolvable issues can be handled within this time frame. Longer discussions simply allow more time for the Deadly Ds of discussions: *Dredge, Digress, Divert, Defend, Deny,* and *Defeat.* If a discussion is taking more than 50 minutes, it is best to take a break, give the issue thought, and return to the discussion in 24 hours.

Tool 10: Use "I Messages"

Just like using enforceable statements with our kids, "I Messages" are an important tool for adult communications as well. An I Message is about the speaker. It never puts a burden on the partner. I Messages work almost all the time for almost everyone.

They are assertive statements about where we stand. They are never aggressive demands as to how another person ought to think, act, or respond.

We leave nothing for others to argue about when we use an I Message. After its use, a conflict-habituated response from a partner could only be, "Don't you use that psycho-babble on me!" The receiving partner can only fight about the fact that the I Message was used. Every I Message has three parts:

1. "I feel _____

2. when someone (don't use the word *you*, use *someone*) _____
3. because then I feel (become, think, experience) _____."

Notice that this sentence does not use the accusatory "you," nor does it tell your partner what to do. I Messages assume your partner cares and has a solution to offer.

When beginning to use I Messages, they may sound phony, especially when partners have been experiencing more "thrilling" disagreements using accusations and demands. It may be almost boring to say, "Honey, I have a hard time really listening when someone sounds so angry with me." But you know what? It works! With practice and in due time, the use of this beneficial phrasing will become natural. Couples who employ it find the I Message opens new vistas for expressing loving opinions and requests, without resulting in battles for control. Let's look at our favorite couple, George and Cyndy, as they use I Messages:

George & Cyndy

Cyndy: "George, honey (as she touches his hand gently and makes eye contact with him), I feel overwhelmed and very alone when I don't get help with Billy's treatments, because then I think I have to handle this all by myself and it's scary as well as very tiring."

Tool 11: Contract for Your Partner's Help in Your Way

Some spouses are forever trying to help change their partner's ways. It doesn't work to say things like, "Your problem is..." or "What you ought to do is..." Usually such statements are poorly received, ending in resentment and frustration. Let your partner decide how he or she would like you to be of help with an issue he/she recognizes and wants to change.

George & Cyndy

George, recognizing the need for a change in his approach to helping with Billy's treatments, tells Cyndy, "Honey, if I am starting to slip in helping you with Billy's treatments, it would be just great if you let me know you need a break and ask for my help." Notice he doesn't add, "instead of nagging at me, yelling at me, or complaining to my mother." That would not be helpful to the long-term success of their marriage.

Tool 12: Choose the Right Timing

Never try to solve a chronic problem while it's occurring. When George is tired and cranky from a long day at work, and Cyndy is resentful at his lack of help as she hooks up Billy's IV lines, this is not the time to say, "George, let's discuss your unhelpful attitude."

One good thing about a chronic problem is the fact that we can count on it to always recur! We can wait for the perfect time to discuss and solve the problem, when both individuals are in a good mood. It's just not productive to talk to a person about their drinking when they are drunk!

In responding to children, it is sometimes important to act immediately (like pulling a small child out of the street). But even then, unless there is a threat to life and limb, it's best to try to solve the problem when it's not occurring. It's perfectly fine to "delay the consequences." Likewise, in adult relationships, doing something is sometimes different from solving the issue. For instance, Bob may not wait for Tracy (who is habitually late) and be late himself getting to church again. He may decide to take their new car and let her drive herself in the old pickup. However, later, they will want to problem-solve the issue for the future.

Tool 13: Be Attentive to Your Partner's Actual Words

Loving, lasting relationships are not built on your interpretations of your spouse's body language and facial gestures. Cyndy says to George, "I need your help tonight with Billy's IV," and George responds (angrily) with, "Fine! Whatever you say, dear!" But, his facial expressions, tone of voice, and body language all undoubtedly show his annoyance. If Cyndy has been really listening to George's words only, she would say, "Thank you" right then, and go off to start her bubble bath. But, instead, she reacts to what she sees in his expressions. She says, "You sure don't sound like it's okay with you." And, although she is right, her words open the door for George's insecure, reactive side to blossom anew. Since this is an old issue, and there is no "new information" it would be better for Cyndy to reinforce George's healthy side by saying a simple, "Thank you."

We all have trouble controlling our tone of voice and facial expressions at times. We may look angry when we don't want to convey angry feelings. Although we cannot always control our tone of voice, we *can* be responsible for what we say. Colleen noted, "When John says in an angry way, 'Colleen, I'm not trying to make you mad,' I believe him now. It has made our life so much simpler. I used to say, 'You sound like you are trying to make me mad.' And then we'd go at it! Listening more closely to his actual words has really helped to resolve this issue!"

Tool 14: Turn Accusations and Statements into Questions

Almost all accusations, demands, and statements are more effectively expressed as questions. Encouraging your spouse to answer a question that is asked in a loving and nonaccusatory way empowers him or her to come up with a solution. For instance:

- ♥ "You were so embarrassing at the party" might be more effectively expressed: "Do you have any concerns about your behavior at the party last night?"
- ♥ "That shirt's too dirty to wear" might be more effectively

expressed, "Does that shirt look too dirty to you?" If the spouse says no, you can always still make your statement, "Well, honey, it looks dirty to me." You haven't lost anything by asking first and letting your spouse come to the conclusion you've already figured out.

- ♥ "Now don't be late" can be more effectively expressed: "Do you think I can count on you being on time?"
- ♥ Instead of, "Your manners are atrocious in public!" you might ask: "Honey, do you ever worry about how you appear in public?"

Loving couples ought to be able to make statements and just be direct. They don't always need to dance around with questions. But questions, at times, can have more finesse. And if there are control issues in the marriage, passive-rebellion and argument are more easily avoided. Most effective counseling works through the use of questions. Try it, practice it, you may like it.

Tool 15: Your Way Isn't the Only Way

Many marriages end up on the rocks because the partners don't celebrate or appreciate their differences in handling the heavy emotional challenges that medical issues bring. Don't assume "your way" of handling a problem is the only "right" way.

Travis and Suzanne

Travis and Suzanne's baby girl was born with a very severe form of muscular dystrophy which took little Bella's life at nine months of age. They weathered the trauma of her illness fairly well but upon her death, things began to fall apart. Suzanne was very emotional and reached out to others for support, crying often and expressing her pain to Travis and those close to her. Travis, on the other hand, was very stoic. He did not express much emotion, and instead buried himself in his work. Suzanne began to feel that Travis did not care and didn't love her and Bella; she accused him of such. Travis began to feel depressed every time he was around his wife's constant emoting, coupled with her blame that he either didn't feel the loss as deeply or wasn't dealing with it. He responded with, "You just need to get over it and move on." The more he distanced himself from Suzanne's pain and blame, the harder she pushed him to show a "meaningful" (as defined by her) emotional reaction. Travis eventually had an affair and subsequently married a co-worker, leaving his wife of fifteen years and their other young daughter.

So what went wrong? Each felt that the way they were handling the emotional fallout was the "only right way" and did not recognize the differences in personality styles or give their spouse the space to handle the emotional devastation in their own way. Travis deeply loved Bella and his wife at one time; he was devastated by his daughter's death and his wife's despair. He simply didn't express it the same way as Suzanne. And Suzanne, feeling very deeply and equally devastated, was certainly within her "right" to express her feelings and seek support from others.

When dealing with such heavy issues and intensely emotional times, recognize personality differences. Some people, like Travis, are task-driven, and others, like Suzanne, are people-driven. Some people are fast-paced, others are slow-paced. We often marry our opposite personality style in an unconscious attempt to "complete" ourselves and balance out our weaknesses. Unfortunately, the very traits that attract us to our spouse in the beginning often become the very ones we try to change or condemn after the honeymoon is over. We begin to assume that because they don't react the same way we do, they don't care. This is a dangerous assumption and can become a self-fulfilling prophecy.

There are many good books available on personality typing, which include DISC Personality Profiling and Meyer's Briggs Personality Types. The book mentioned previously, *Different Children, Different Needs*, by Charles F. Boyd is an excellent resource for understanding personality typing. Counseling is also helpful in understanding and dealing with personality differences.

Tool 16: Check How You Feel about the Resolution

It may be a good idea to close discussions by checking mutual perceptions:

- ♥ "I feel good about this conversation, how about you?"
- ♥ "Thanks for being so understanding."
- ♥ "How do you think we did on really listening to each other this time?"

Mutual Couple Support

As the months and years pass and parents deal with chronically ill children, support is essential. Although support from friends, peers, and professionals is necessary, lucky are those whose primary support comes from within a committed, loving relationship. These lucky ones learn to cope successfully and thoughtfully with the bumps and bruises, joys and tears that are inevitably present. The following excerpt gives hope to all couples who work through and appreciate their differences. Often, the traits which lead us to fall in love and be intrigued with each other are the very same ones that later become the focus of disappointment and incrimination.

This is an excerpt from Lisa's marriage metaphor, *Living on Faith, Hope and Love*:

Lisa and Carl

I have been the explorer, the initiator, and the dreamer.

Carl is the dependable, steady, and predictable one. I carry us along on a wave of adventure, ideas, and new experiences, while he provides the stability and practicality that makes sure we don't get swept away by a tidal wave! Together, we make a great team. One without the other would either be too impulsive or too staid. And yet, in the blurred vision of these many differences, we have at times lost sight of each other. The differences through the years have become less a cause for celebration and cooperation and more of a reason for dissent and dissatisfaction

Here we are, ten years and two beautiful, special children later, on a very different kind of journey and adventure. And, like that first trip to Europe as newlyweds, there are many wonderful moments and some sad and difficult ones. Like that first trip, we are still learning to navigate our differences, gain from each other's strengths, and trying to laugh a bit along the way. We just seem to have a few more bricks tucked away into our backpacks. It is an ongoing, purposeful, and painful process, this "becoming soul mates." It sure doesn't "just happen" and we are not there quite yet.

Helen Keller said, "Character cannot be developed in ease and quiet. Only through experience of trial and suffering can the soul be strengthened, ambition inspired, and success achieved."

Maybe it's also true that it is only through trial and suffering that a soul mate relationship can be achieved. It is when times are tough and the journey hard that the character of the travelers is not only revealed but molded; molded not only by the circumstances but by each other. Right now, we are in the process of molding each other and persevering through the many trials of having two kids with cystic fibrosis. I'm hopeful and curious about our journey which is not yet done. With a very high divorce rate among families living with chronic illnesses, the odds are against us. And yet, we are hopeful. We just keep living on faith, hope, and love.

Our wise friend Foster said it so well: "No one has the opportunity to help us grow and change like our life partners. When folks become soul mates, couples individually grow impacting each other on the side of the angels. You and Carl have been placed together as life partners in quite an amazing theater of opportunity. So, the journey is yours, in his company. Much of your journey, of course, must be that individual trek. But, along stretches of it, your holding hands, and lifting each other up is, if not essential, most joyful and helpful. Ultimately, if you are truly lucky, you will both have the other in a form that you each helped create."

I hope we will, someday, have each other in a form we both helped create and that we will each continue to appreciate whom the other has become. We are well on our way down that road with faith, hope, and love as our trusted guides. And, the greatest of these, is love.

Hebrews 11:1 says: "Faith is being sure of what we hope for and certain of what we do not see." I have faith that someday, we will be not just fellow travelers, but soul mates.

Chapter 11 Key Concepts

1. A child's medical conditions may compound the difficulties parents face in their communication with each other. Misunderstandings can more frequently occur around tough issues

and uncertain outcomes, which are both often present in homes with ill children. Because emotions and intense situations frequently lead to mistakes, good communication tools and techniques are essential. Ill children, perhaps more than average children, have situations where parents can be manipulated and triangulated around differences in coping decisions.

2. Couples facing the chronic stress of raising chronically ill children may make destructive choices in an attempt to cope. Turning to drugs, alcohol, affairs, workaholism, materialism, gambling, and other addictions can all be an attempt to escape from the unrelenting stress of constantly dealing with life-and-death issues.

3. Specific tools and techniques are essential for clear communication when adults are dealing with chronic illness in the family. Sixteen basic communications skills and ground rules are helpful when dealing with conflict-ridden issues.
   - Tool 1: Are we going to vent or problem solve?
   - Tool 2: Don't generalize.
   - Tool 3: Stick to the topic.
   - Tool 4: Stop name calling.
   - Tool 5: Use terms of endearment and stay within "touching distance."
   - Tool 6: Discussion by appointment.
   - Tool 7: Don't assume negative motivation.
   - Tool 8: Stay in the here and now.
   - Tool 9: Limit discussion time.
   - Tool 10: Use "I Messages."
   - Tool 11: Contract for your partner's help in your own way.
   - Tool 12: Choose the right timing.
   - Tool 13: Be attentive to your partner's actual words.
   - Tool 14: Turn accusations and statements into questions.

- Tool 15: Your way isn't the only way.
- Tool 16: Check how you feel about the resolution.

Chapter 12

The Final Word

The price of greatness is
responsibility.
—Winston Churchill (1874–1965)

There is a danger in writing about dealing with chronic illnesses and other medical issues. For, although we are focusing on parenting issues around illness per se, the illness is not the important thing. The important thing is the child. Keep in mind we are dealing with a child, not an illness. No matter what the illness, we are dealing with an aware and sensitive being who needs to build character, be related to as an important person, and develop self-respect and respect for others. This may sound obvious, but it's not.

We have seen many parents relate to the illness and not the child. They allow the child to be disrespectful, annoying, discourteous, spoiled, or difficult and excuse it all because of the illness. It is not uncommon to see illness and obnoxious behavior all wrapped together in the same little body. It is as if the parents say to themselves, "I feel so sorry for him, I just can't bring myself to do anything that might upset him." A variation of this with "normal" children is the maternal response, "He's a sensitive child," which is used to excuse poor coping behavior when someone jokes around with the child.

We have emphasized that this program is built on the Love and Logic foundations that all kids need all the time. We cripple our children greatly by not treating them as nearly as possible like "normal" kids. And, as normal kids, they will have normal problems. Materials available from Love and Logic (1-800-338-4065 or www.loveandlogic.com) cover almost all of the parenting issues that deal with topics beyond the scope of this work.

Finally, when we discuss and deal successfully with difficult life-and-death issues with our children, it presents us with a unique opportunity to encourage the development of coping skills and character. Coping with adversity lays the foundation for almost all true greatness. We have found this to be particularly true of the children and parents we have met while creating this program. Everyone is afforded the opportunity to show love and demonstrate good character when facing adversity. Because of the opportunity their illnesses have afforded them, we have met children and parents who set the model for greatness. True greatness is within everyone's grasp, and probably the greatest people are the unsung and unrecognized souls who go about the world enriching the lives of others, never coming close to making it into the pages of a book.

We thank the many truly great children and adults you have met within the pages of this book. They cope every day with the nuances and intricacies of difficult self-care routines and set a great example of handling life's challenges with grace and hope. We trust they have inspired and touched you, as they have us, as you continue to Be a Great Parent When Every Moment Matters.

Bonus Section

Quick Tips
In Their Own Words: Inspiring Stories
Remembering Heroes
Helpful Resources
A Note to Medical & Mental Health Professionals

Section 1

Love and Logic
Quick Tips

Love and Logic®
INSTITUTE, Inc.

Copy the quick tips on the following pages and post them where you'll often see them. You'll have the right words handy at just the right moment. Permission is granted to photocopy Love and Logic Quick Tips© for personal use only.

The Love and Logic Institute, Inc.
2207 Jackson St., Suite 102
Golden, Colorado 80401-2300
Phone: 800-588-5644
Fax: 800-455-7557
www.loveandlogic.com

Love and Logic *Quick Tips*

Love and Logic Starts with a Hug

Love

It takes a great deal of love to...

- Find the positives in our kids when they act poorly
- Hug them before we ask them about their homework
- Set limits without anger, lectures, or threats
- Hold them accountable for their poor decisions by providing empathy first and consequences second

Logic

When we give this special kind of love, a wise type of logic grows in our children's minds: "When I make poor decisions, it makes my life pretty sad. I wonder how my next decision will affect my life?"

Visit www.loveandlogic.com or call 800-338-4064

Love and Logic *Quick Tips*

The Rules of Love and Logic

Rule 1

Adults set firm limits in loving ways without anger, lecture, or threats.

Rule 2

When a child causes a problem, the adult hands it back in loving ways:

1. The adult lovingly holds the child accountable for his/her problems in a way that does not make a problem for others.
2. Children are offered choices with limits.
3. Adults use enforceable statements.
4. Adults provide delayed/ extended consequences.
5. The adult's empathy is "locked in" before consequences are delivered.

Visit www.loveandlogic.com or call 800-338-4064

Quick Tips

How to Neutralize Arguments

Step 1: Go brain dead.

Step 2: Softly repeat a one-liner

- "I know."
- "What do you think?"
- "How sad."
- "I bet it feels that way."
- "Nice try."
- "I love you too much to argue."
- "Probably so."
- "What did I say?"

Keys to neutralize arguing

- No sarcasm or frustration shown; only empathy, understanding, and compassion.
- Speak slowly with a low voice.
- Watch body language, tone of voice, and facial expressions.
- Pick your favorite one-liner. Then practice it, perfect it, and stick with it!

Quick Tips

Empathy Is the Most Important Skill

Love and Logic Empathetic Statements

- "This is so sad..."
- "Oh no, honey..."
- "Oh, man..."
- "Oh, that's too bad..."
- "What a bummer..."
- "This is hard..."

Tips to Ensure Success

- Use empathy *before* delivering consequences.
- Show genuine understanding; no sarcasm or frustration.
- Watch body language, tone of voice, and facial expressions.
- Keep your empathetic statement short, sweet, simple, and repetitive.

Benefits of Empathy and Consequences

- The adult remains the "good guy."
- The child is in the thinking state rather than the defensive mode.
- Children learn self-control.
- Every time we use empathy, we teach it!

Love and Logic®
INSTITUTE, INC.

Quick Tips

Enforceable Statements

When we set Love and Logic limits by saying what we will do or what we will allow:

- We avoid looking like a fool when we can't get our kids to do what we say.
- We share some control with our children. As a result, they are much less likely to resist in order to regain control.
- We avoid getting sucked into trying to control something we really can't.

Examples of Love and Logic Enforceable Statements:

- "I'll give you ___ when ___."
- "I'll be happy to ___ when ___."
- "Feel free to ___ when ___."
- "I'll be glad to ___ when ___."
- "You're welcome to ___ when ___."

Visit www.loveandlogic.com or call 800-338-4064

The Love and Logic Institute, Inc. 2207 Jackson St. Suite 102 Golden, Colorado 80401-2300 Fax: 800-455-7557
© 2007, Love and Logic Institute. Permission to copy Love and Logic Quick Tips is granted for personal use only.

Love and Logic®
INSTITUTE, INC.

Quick Tips

The Magic of Choices

Use phrases such as:

- "Would you rather ___ or ___?"
- "Would it be best for you to ___ or ___?"
- "You can either ___ or ___."
- "Feel free to ___ or ___."
- "Are you going to ___ or ___?"
- "Will you be ___ or ___?"
- "Do you plan to ___ or ___?"

Love and Logic guidelines for choices:

- Make lots of deposits when things are going well.
- For each choice, give two options you like.
- Give choices *before* resistance, not after.
- Give your child 10 seconds to decide.
- Use care not to disguise choices as threats.
- When things aren't going well, make a withdrawal.

Visit www.loveandlogic.com or call 800-338-4064

The Love and Logic Institute, Inc. 2207 Jackson St. Suite 102 Golden, Colorado 80401-2300 Fax: 800-455-7557
© 2007, Love and Logic Institute. Permission to copy Love and Logic Quick Tips is granted for personal use only.

Quick Tips

How to Guide a Child to Solve the Problem

Step 1: Express curiosity, interest, and empathy: "Ooh, I bet that hurt!"

Step 2: Send the Power Message: "What do you think you'll do?"

Step 3: Offer choices: "Would you like to hear what other kids have tried?"

Step 4: Have the child state the consequences.

Step 5: Lovingly give permission for the child to either solve or not solve the problem: "Good luck with that, sweetheart. Let me know how it goes."

Quick Tips

The Energy Drain

Step 1: Deliver a strong dose of sincere empathy. "Oh, this is so sad."

Step 2: Notify the child that their misbehavior has drained your energy. "When you _____, it drains energy right out of me."

Step 3: Ask how he or she plans to replace the energy. "How are you planning to put that energy back?"

Step 4: If you hear, "I don't know," offer some payback options. "Some kids decide to do Mom's chores. How would that work?" Hiring babysitters or paying for a nice cup of coffee are other energy replacement options. Be creative and have fun!

Step 5: If the child completes the chores or replaces the energy, thank them and don't lecture.

Step 6: If the child refuses or forgets, don't warn or remind. Actions speak louder than words!

Step 7: As a last resort, go on strike or sell a toy to pay for the drain. "What a bummer. I don't have the energy to take you to Silly Willie's Fun Park this weekend."

Step 8: Frequently reward good behavior with a *reverse energy drain*. "Wow, you kids behaved so nicely today at the grocery store, I have lots of extra energy! Let's go see a movie tonight."

In Their Own Words: Inspiring Stories about Coping with Chronic Medical Conditions

It's only when we truly know and understand
that we have a limited time on earth —
and that we have no way of knowing when our
time is up — that we will begin to live each day
to the fullest, as if it was the only one we had.
—Elisabeth Kübler-Ross (1926-2004)

Welcome To Holland

by Emily Perl Kingsley
Copyright (c) 1987 by Emily Perl Kingsley. All rights reserved. Reprinted with permission.

I am often asked to describe the experience of raising a child with a disability — to try to help people who have not shared that unique experience to understand it, to imagine how it would feel. It's like this...

When you're going to have a baby, it's like planning a fabulous vacation trip — to Italy. You buy a bunch of guide books and make your wonderful plans. The Coliseum. The Michelangelo David. The gondolas in Venice. You may learn some handy phrases in Italian. It's all very exciting.

After months of eager anticipation, the day finally arrives. You pack your bags and off you go. Several hours later, the plane lands. The stewardess comes in and says, "Welcome to Holland."

"Holland?!?" you say. "What do you mean Holland?? I signed up for Italy! I'm supposed to be in Italy. All my life I've dreamed of going to Italy."

But there's been a change in the flight plan. They've landed in Holland and there you must stay.

The important thing is that they haven't taken you to a horrible, disgusting, filthy place, full of pestilence, famine, and disease. It's just a different place.

So you must go out and buy new guide books. And you must learn a whole new language. And you will meet a whole new group of people you would never have met.

It's just a *different* place. It's slower-paced than Italy, less flashy than Italy. But after you've been there for a while and you catch your breath, you look around.... and you begin to notice Holland has windmills.... and Holland has tulips. Holland even has Rembrandts.

But everyone you know is busy coming and going from Italy... and they're all bragging about what a wonderful time they had there. And for the rest of your life, you will say, "Yes, that's where I was supposed to go. That's what I had planned."

And the pain of that will never, ever, ever, ever go away... because the loss of that dream is a very, very significant loss.

But... if you spend your life mourning the fact that you didn't get to Italy, you may never be free to enjoy the very special, the very lovely things... about Holland.

Band-Aides and Blackboards

Ms. Fleitas wrote this as an introduction to her award-winning Band-Aides and Blackboards website. Some of the stories you have read in this book were reprinted from this website, with the author's permission.

Thanks for visiting "Band-Aides and Blackboards." The intention of the site is to sensitize people to what it's like to grow up with a medical problem. Too often, youngsters so affected must cope with stigma as well as with their medical conditions. Teasing often accompanies this stigma and adds a layer of pain to their childhood experience. Unnecessary pain. Pain that isolates. Pain that affects not only the children who look or act or even just feel different, but all of the children in the classroom.

For the past few years, I have been the student, and children have been my teachers. They have taught me what it's like for them to live in bodies that don't always behave, and what it's like for them to be growing up in a world that is too frequently insensitive to their needs. They have spoken about a wide range of dilemmas. For some children, the dilemma is the ambivalence of enjoying extra privileges, yet hating the reason they're offered. For others it's the shame associated with medical diagnoses and a need that grows from that shame to keep hidden what is not directly observable. For many it's the ache to be popular and the belief that popularity is purchased with the coins of conformity. When that conformity forces children to ignore their need for medication and treatment, and when it demands of them a secrecy that consumes energy as it isolates, the price is very high.

The children who write to me, talk to me, and tell me their stories are children who are bothered to some degree by the social dimensions of their medical conditions. Many prefer not to think about their differences. And not to talk about them, either.

Acknowledging them seems to tattoo the reality of the disease, condition, illness, medical problem... you name it, on their identity. What they call it, then, becomes extremely important to them, with certain words having more power to isolate than others. As one child assured me, "I have this condition called diabetes. It's not a disease, because you can't catch it." And from a young man recalling his early school experiences with muscular dystrophy, "What I have is neither a chronic illness nor a disease. It's just a condition that seemed to affect others more than it did me, though I was teased unmercifully for my differences."

The most important thing I've learned from my conversations with children has been that they are first of all children, with the same needs, joys, hurts and misconceptions all children share. Their chronic illnesses or other medical conditions are part of them, but do not define them. I hope they will learn as they grow that they can be proud of who they are, and that what's going on with their health is a part of that pride, not something to be ashamed of.

I've tried to help children tell their stories in the hopes that through the narratives, others will have an opportunity to "walk in their footsteps" for a short time and will, in the process, begin to understand.

Please visit Joan's website at
www.lehman.cuny.edu/faculty/jfleitas/bandaides

Say Yes to Life! Stories of Living with Cystic Fibrosis

One of the big questions I asked when our newborn son was first diagnosed with cystic fibrosis was: "Will my child still be able to enjoy life? And, will I?" I have gathered some writings I believe will help answer these questions. These responses testify to the ability of each one of us to face life-and-death issues and still live each day to the full. Thank you to these writers who have so graciously opened up their hearts to encourage others. —*Lisa*

Kathleen's Story

Am I glad to be alive despite my CF? Well, it depends on what time of the day you ask me this question. When it's early in the morning before class and I'm up at an unseemly hour breathing disgusting medicine and being shaken by an uncomfortable VEST, my answer might not be an altogether hopeful one. If you ask me on a Great Strides day when my friends and family are gathered around me and I just can't stop smiling because I know I'm loved, my answer might be an altogether different one.

I was diagnosed late in my life, when I was nine years old. I don't know what my parents would have done had they known earlier than that, and frankly, I don't want to know. I always knew there was something wrong with me, and when I would tell someone I felt sick or had a cough (which was a good once a week) they would shrug it off as me complaining. You could say my diagnosis was the biggest "I TOLD you so" ever. But despite having my CF, I have gone on hikes every year with my family at Christmas, played soccer, tennis, basketball, track and field, and softball, cheered on my brothers at their sports events, cried over a boy (or two, or three...) maintained an A-average in school, gotten in fights with my parents, almost lost my best friend because of my own selfishness, been envious of other people's families for having relationships that mine don't, cried at my older brother's graduation speech, cried when my other older brother went away to college, accidentally laughed at one of my dad's stupidly funny jokes, and had a mama who will always take care of me no matter what. I have screamed at the ones I love, had my first kiss, taken dance classes, been lonely, helped out in my community, become a clichéd aspiring actress, written and performed my own play, made a wish with the Make-A-Wish Foundation, raised around $30,000 for cystic fibrosis (with a LOT of help from my friends), recently gotten out of my first two-week tune-up in the hospital because I stopped taking my medications, dared my disease to kill me so I wouldn't have to do it myself, dared my disease to let me live so I could beat it, looked up to, and learned from, every teacher I've ever had, always striven to make a difference, and loved God and my family and my friends with more passion and care than I could ever tell you — and I turn 16 next week. I'm proud of the life I lead. I'm proud of who I am. I love myself, I love my life, and I love the people in it. CF has taught me to live like this. The people in my life have inspired me to remember there is something worth living for. I wouldn't be the person I am today without cystic fibrosis, and for that I am thankful.

And you asked me, am I glad to be alive despite my CF? But my question to you is, would I be glad to be alive without it?

—*Kathleen Burke, June 2006, teen with CF*

April's Story

You can never predict what type of child will be born to you. What color hair, eyes, or skin tone will they have? Will they be shy or outgoing? Will they be athletic, artistic, a genius, or all of these things? A child is a wonderful gift... a surprise. Most parents don't automatically wonder, "Will my child be born healthy?" It is usually assumed that this will be the case. But when it is not, when our gift is an amazing child with a chronic illness, our job as parents is still the same. Give them the best and happiest life possible.

I have two children with cystic fibrosis. Yes, the disease can sound scary and overwhelming at first, but it can be a very manageable disease. The disease affects different people in different ways, so there is no guarantee that other children will have the same experiences as mine have. But in our family my kids are very healthy and live their lives like any other child their age. The difference is, they take enzymes before they eat or drink to help digest their food. They also do various treatments in the morning and evening to keep their lungs healthy and clear. Basically we take more time out of our day than the average family does to make sure our kids are keeping their bodies healthy and strong. We take more time to help them feel comfortable with the differences that may set them apart from their peers. They look the same as other children. They play and learn, laugh and love like other children. We teach them the same values and lessons we would teach other children. And we love them unconditionally as we would any child who came to us. Do I wish they were disease-free and had an easier path ahead of them? Of course. Would I trade this challenge? Never. My children have taken my life down one of those "paths less traveled." And yes, that has made all the difference.

—April Lloyd, April 2006, CF parent

Ana's Story

My twin and I were born in an era where prenatal diagnosis of CF was not available. My parents, though shocked at the news of the diagnosis of their twin daughters at three days of age, put their best foot forward to raise us as normally as possible and to do everything they could to help us reach our fullest potential. Though CF had a much grimmer prognosis in the early 70s compared to now, my parents took the news as a way to find strength within, to be closer as a family, and to live each day to the fullest. Multiple hospitalizations, daily medical treatments, and doctors' visits characterized our childhood. But so did chores, swim teams, girl scouts, sibling rivalry, camping trips, and homework. I do believe in the words of Emily Perl Kingsley in "Welcome to Holland," that our family's journey was rerouted to another world, but a journey more beautiful and exciting, despite the many bumps in the road.

I believe that because of my experiences with CF I am more compassionate, human, real, spiritual, accepting, and honest than the average person. Today, at 34, I reflect on the disbelief that my twin and I have surpassed the age my mother was when she was told of our diagnosis.

Because of my CF I have received many gifts: resilience, closeness with loved ones, the amazing people one meets in the CF community, and the maturity and depth that living with a chronic and life-threatening disease can bring. Despite living with progressive lung disease that ultimately required me to have a lung transplant at the age of 28, I have nonetheless learned, loved, seen, heard, eaten, walked, talked, touched, thanked, hoped, and dreamed in my lifetime. And I have no regrets.

—*Ana Stenzel, May 2006, adult with CF*

Kim's Story

My name is Kim and I have two sons. John is almost 2 without CF and Christopher is 7 months with CF. We also knew Christopher had CF prior to his birth. I am so glad we found out for sure because we've been able to give him the best care from day one. He had meconium ileus and had to have surgery at 2 days old. We've had a pretty rough time for his 7 months of life, but we as a family have changed for the better because of it. We've learned to take one day at a time and to enjoy every minute of it. Christopher is such a joy, and his big brother just loves him.

Christopher's CF requires a lot of management but it is becoming more and more the way of our lives. He laughs and smiles and barrel-rolls across the floor all the time. He also likes to watch baseball, which I encourage. Staying fit and exercising will be important in Christopher's life, and we make that a family thing. Christopher isn't the only one with C; it's a family disease, and we all do whatever we can to involve John in his treatments and live our lives the best we know how. Hope this helps. CF isn't a death sentence, it's something God has put in our lives and feels we can handle. And we are handling it day by day. There are times when I feel I've had enough, but it passes. And Christopher is just Christopher, our little soldier, the bravest little boy I know.

—*Kim Elliott, April 2006, CF parent*

Laurisa's Story

Reflecting upon my 40 years of life, I would say yes, a child who is dealing with a serious illness can still enjoy life. Living with a chronic lung disease has had its challenges. I'd be the first to tell you that there have been difficult moments, but I also believe that dealing with the disease and all that it entails has made me a better person: a person with an underlying hope; a person of greater understanding; a person with the ability to extend compassion towards others for the difficulties they are facing. It has also afforded me the opportunity to create a lasting bond of friendship with others, whom I otherwise might not have been given the privilege of meeting and/or sharing our life stories. Cystic fibrosis (CF) has caused many of us to grow up quickly. We realized at an early age that we had to take control of and do our best to keep ahead of our varying schedule of airway clearance, chest pt (physiotherapy), dietary needs, and numerous medications; to bear those responsibilities because if we ignored the symptoms for any length of time, it then became detrimental to our health and survival.

Comparing my childhood to now, I have found CF has invaded many facets of my life. I am not able to prance through a field of mustard seed flowers as quickly as I used to or participate in a full nine-inning game of softball (snagging the line drive at third base). Now, I have to take more precautions so I don't catch a cold because it could be damaging to my lungs.

With any disease, an individual can choose to adapt to his or her specific needs and challenges or choose to avoid them. Eventually all are forced to face their disease and by God's grace can remain in the fight, facing each challenge and knowing there is a purpose in each one. I am grateful for the circle of family, friends, and CF cohorts

who have supported all of my efforts. In all that life brings our way, not only can the challenge be for our betterment, but we discover there is no greater joy than doing our part to fulfill God's purposes.
—*Laurisa F. Thurner, August 2006, adult with CF*

Lisa's Story

Motherhood is never easy. Being the mother of two children with CF brings special mothering challenges. There are some days when the pain of the reality of life with CF is hard to face, and there are days when the joy of life clearly shows on my face. There was a time, in the beginning, when I just didn't think I could handle it. I have since realized that I *can* handle it if I choose to. I could so easily wander down the road of angst and despair and just stay there, but I choose instead to take the high road — to count my blessings and remain grounded in hope-filled reality. This is not easy for me; it takes real, conscious effort and loving support, but, in doing so, I have found my life has changed immeasurably for the better.

I dearly love our precious children and treasure each opportunity to enjoy them as I watch their little personalities unfold like flowers, appreciate their love of life and their delight in all things new. I continue to marvel at their ability to cope well with the challenges of their illness with acceptance, curiosity, optimism, and a simple, innocent trust in the goodness of life. They have been, and will always be, my mentors.

Through this experience called motherhood, I have soared to the heights of joy and plunged to the depths of despair, and couldn't appreciate the one without the other. It is in having been to the depths that I can appreciate the gift of life God has so graciously bestowed upon us and not take a single second of it for granted. It has been during the most difficult times that my faith has deepened, my hope renewed, and my character shaped and molded. I am grateful for the life we share together and intend to live every moment to the fullest in the good times and the bad.

—*Lisa C. Greene, August 2006, CF parent*

Michele's Story

Am I glad to be alive despite having CF? I wake up miserable and grumpy in the morning until I finish my lengthy self-care routine. But after I take care of myself, I feel better and life doesn't look so grim. I had to nearly die to get a diagnosis late in life at 36 and am still recovering from not having the proper medical care for so long. So at times I "hate my life" because I do suffer physically. But it passes. There is light at the end of the tunnel and the future looks pretty bright to me these days.

But would I take away my CF if I could? No, I would not. Nor would I take away my oldest child's CF, and I know he feels the same. I believe we are souls on a spiritual journey in the physical world and that our life circumstances grow out of some soul need or "goal." If a soul wants to learn things like patience or compassion, having serious medical problems or raising a special needs child will teach you such lessons very well. I feel that people in the CF community are, generally speaking, more patient, compassionate, forgiving, and kind than people I meet in "normal" settings. I cannot bring myself to regret that people with such qualities exist in the world and I feel certain that these qualities arise from what we have suffered.

I do not see CF as a disease but as a "genetic variation" and I do not think the things we are told about will necessarily happen as it "progresses." I think that if you accept the conventional views of CF then you tend to make such things a self-fulfilling prophecy. I have lived too long without a label to be capable of accepting what I am told to believe about CF when it flies in the face of everything I know to be true based on my own personal experiences.

—*Doreen Michele Traylor, January 2007,*
adult with cystic fibrosis and mother of a teenager with CF

Carroll's Story

Many people with cystic fibrosis are teachers for the rest of us; my stepson and his community are that for me. They show us how to be fully present, how to face chronic illness with courage, how to seize adventure and make the most of each day. The heartache and struggle of living with this disease is offset by an appreciation for life; they do not take the little things for granted. I feel honored to be a part of the CF community and determined to be a part of improving the quality of health for those with CF. I am grateful for these teachers among us.

—*Carroll Jenkins, June 2006, CF parent and
Executive Director of Cystic Fibrosis Resources, Inc. (CFRI)*

Finding Nemo, Finding a Hero:
Parenting Kids with Chronic Illnesses

by Lisa C. Greene
Copyright (c) 2004 by Lisa C. Greene. All rights reserved.
Reprinted with permission from the author.

Ask me about any adult movie (i.e.: Have you seen *blank* movie?) and my response is likely to be No. Ask me about any kid movie and I could tell you about the characters, plot, and punch-line all in one breath. That's how it is when you live with a six-year-old and a four-year-old.

So, it shouldn't be too surprising when I tell you it was in the children's movie *Finding Nemo* that I saw a great metaphor of what it is like to live with kids with chronic illnesses. You see, both of our children have cystic fibrosis so I do know what it's like. And, like the clown fish dad on Nemo (named Marlin) I have journeyed from the place of overprotective and "worried about everything" parent to "still worried about everything but handling it a lot better" parent. This is largely due to my parenting training with Love and Logic.

I suppose there is always room for improvement in most things in life, especially parenting. The problem with parenting is that we may not realize how much improvement we really need until it's too late (i.e. my teenagers become hellions, and I wonder what happened). The problem with parenting kids with chronic illnesses is that "too late" doesn't mean just a dented car or some experimentation with booze or sex — it can mean the difference between life and death.

The struggle to resist one's overriding and all-powerful parental impulses to rescue, hover, and (over) protect a beloved child is played out only too well in *Finding Nemo*, just as it is in the homes of millions of families across America and the rest of the world. Sadly, the triumph of overcoming those impulses and the achievement of healthy acceptance is not experienced nearly enough. The paradox is, it is in letting go of the intense need for control and protection that actually gives the child (and those around him or her) the freedom to become a hero and unlock the greatness of spirit inherent within the soul of one who has learned to cope well with suffering. Just like Nemo!

We begin Nemo's story with a happy little fish couple embarking on one of life's greatest adventures — sharing their love and multiplying it by bearing a child or, as in the case of Nemo, bearing thousands of fish eggs! After a disastrous start, where the mommy fish and all the eggs but one are devoured by a big, hungry fish the real story begins with Nemo and his dad "picking up the pieces" of the initial trauma. To make it all the more poignant, Nemo is born with a deformed, or "lucky," fin. So, here we have initial trauma and physical disability — a perfect recipe to create an overprotective, hovering parent, oozing with overconcern for his son's welfare and condition. He limits, rescues, protects, and controls Nemo; his expectations of Nemo's ability are low (due to his disability), and he does not trust Nemo. Furthermore, Dad has very little sense of humor. He is somber, worried, and agitated about every detail in

Nemo's fishy little life. In fact, Dad's life completely revolves around Nemo's life. Sound familiar?

The big event in Nemo's life is his decision to rebel against his father's controlling, overprotective nature. No big surprise, there. Nemo has no choice but to exert his independence in a way that is contrary to his dad's wishes because Nemo has never had the freedom to make his own choices. What else is an overprotected, over-controlled clownfish to do? So, he touches the "butt" (boat) in defiance of his dad's commands just to prove to dad, friends, and himself that he can do it. And, in doing so (if you haven't seen the movie), he gets swept up by a scuba diver and appears destined to become part of a fish collection in a dental aquarium.

How many kids with chronic illnesses have no choice but to rebel against parental authority by refusing to comply with medical requirements? If a child is not "allowed" to make the choice for death, then they cannot make the choice for life. Parents need to allow their children the possibility of making the "wrong" decision in order to give them the opportunity (and desire) to make the right decision. It is best to allow those decisions (or choices) to take place in small, non-life-threatening ways, so that the control over the child's body is shared over the years, over time. For example, a parent might say, "Would you like to do your breathing treatment before or after your homework?" or "Would you like your insulin shot in five minutes or ten minutes?" or "Would you like to take your pills with juice or milk?" A lifetime of small choices creates a "savings account" of shared control that can be "cashed in" when it's time for the big decisions of life — such as whether or not to live.

The movie follows two tracks at this point — the story of the dad's search-and-rescue operation for his son, and the story of Nemo's journey of rescuing himself. The movie becomes the story of a parent struggling to let go, of learning to trust and accept, thereby enabling the child to become more than either had ever dreamed possible.

As Nemo starts to "make his own way" around the aquarium, he gets stuck in a filter. I think it is his life's first defining moment. Immediately, the other fish around him leap to rescue him and pull him out. But Gil, the seasoned old master of the aquarium, stops them and forces Nemo to rescue himself. Listen to this: Nemo (in panic), "Can you help me?" Gil (calmly and kindly), "No, you got yourself in there; you can get yourself out." No rescue, no overprotection. Gil proceeds to tell him how to do it, gives him encouragement and high expectations, and Nemo gets unstuck all by himself. And Nemo is proud. He can do it! Effective parents (Consultant Parents) do not hover, rescue, and protect like Helicopter Parents. They help the child identify the problem, provide empathy and support, set appropriately high expectations, ask good questions, and encourage the child to find his or her own solutions to the problems at hand. They say, "You got yourself in there; you can get yourself out, and I love you, no matter what."

Meanwhile, Dad is learning a few things about himself, too. As he searches the ocean for his son, many fellow fish and assorted sea life help him, but one in particular, Dory, joins him on his journey. Dory is a great example of loving support. She is steadfast, loyal, concerned, helpful, reflective, and, best of all, she has a great sense of humor. She is downright funny. And, she trusts. A few words are needed here about a sense of humor. When you have a child with a chronic illness, a sense of humor is sometimes elusive. What is funny about medical treatments, financial burdens, and seeing a child suffer physically and/or emotionally? But, as we find and develop that sense of humor (and it does take time and practice) we can overcome the adversity and focus on life's blessings rather than its curses. This lightens the heart and lessens the burden. Humor just makes life more fun for everyone around us. Poor Marlin has no sense of humor in the beginning, but, after letting go and accepting his son (at the end of the movie), his humor flourishes and it becomes clear he enjoys life as he reveals his true nature as a clown fish. But it took a journey with many trials to bring him there. Humor on the outside is a reflection of joy on the inside. Sometimes, we have to fake it till we make it. But, that's okay, too. Humor on the outside can bring joy to the inside.

Dory knows how to have fun in the face of adversity; to look on the bright side of life; to trust in the moment. When Dory and Marlin get caught inside the whale, Marlin gets very angry. He blames others (including Dory) for his dire circumstances. Then he hits a wall of despair. He is so wrapped up in his own plight that he fails to see the love around him, the beauty of God's creation, and the humor of the moment (stuck inside the belly of a whale that Dory actually talks to in whale-ese). He sees only his single-minded quest — to rescue his son — and its impending failure (in his eyes). Listen to the exchange between Marlin and Dory, which marks the beginning of his acceptance of the situation in which he finds himself. Marlin: "I promised him I would never let anything happen to him." Dory: "That's a funny thing to promise. Well, you can't never let anything happen to him — then nothing would ever happen to him. Not much fun for little Nemo." Parents who overprotect and rescue their kids erode their opportunities for life, experience, and growth. They also erode the child's chance to become a hero.

The climax of the movie brings us to the reuniting of father and son. Note: Dad did not rescue his son. With the help of friends, Nemo finds his own way out of the aquarium and back into the ocean. When first reunited, Dad immediately adopts his old attitude of protection and control, but Nemo's persevering and compassionate spirit will not allow his father to stop him from rescuing the many fish caught in the gill net, which is about to be hauled to the surface of the water. Nemo has had a taste of freedom from his father's well-meaning tyranny. Now he has the opportunity to become a hero — not only in his own eyes but in the eyes of the underwater world in which he lives. His dad has no choice but to let him go and to trust. With this freedom, Nemo is able to release the hero that had been bottled up inside his soul by his father's control, overprotection, and rescue. And, in releasing that hero by courageously rising to the occasion, Nemo changes the lives of those around him.

I think that deep down inside the soul of every child who suffers from a chronic illness is that same hero just bursting to come out. As parents we can encourage our children to become that hero, to face life courageously and joyfully in the face of adversity and suffering. By doing this, we also become heroes — both to our children and to others around us. In modeling this, we teach our children how to release the hero within them. It is not an easy journey, but a worthwhile one. Just ask Nemo. And, his dad.

Section 3

Remembering Heroes

Matthew & Gregory Bailey

We dedicate this program to all those who live with cystic fibrosis, as well as those who have surrendered to it. We especially remember Matthew and Gregory Bailey, brothers who were born with CF. In one of many moments of grief following the diagnosis of both children, their mother, Jeannine, had a flash of insight that all she needed to do was to love Matt and Greg. Loving them meant many things, which had to be discerned along the way, but this guiding philosophy has sustained Jeannine and her husband Ron through the years. Even though the final consequences of the disease were devastating, and the physical care required was an overwhelming routine, love generated joy as well as strength, endurance, and courage for this family. Matthew died at the age of 23, and Gregory at the age of 17. Ron and Jeannine continue to seek ways of sharing love, which sustains them in the absence of their beloved children.

Matt was born November 2, 1969, and died October 2, 1993.
Greg was born April 7, 1961, and died August 28, 1978.

Elizabeth Nash

We remember the perseverance, sense of purpose, and inspiration of Elizabeth Nash, who dedicated herself to the fight against CF. Liz was a scientist, accomplished musician, expert skier, enthusiastic sports fan, and sprint tri-athlete, who happened to have cystic fibrosis. That's the way she saw life, the way she lived it, and why she is such an inspiration.

When Liz was diagnosed in 1973, her parents were told not to expect her to graduate from high school. She did much more than that. Liz earned a PhD in molecular genetics and went on to become a research scientist in CF. She did an internship at Johns Hopkins University and post-doctoral work at the University of California, San Francisco. She volunteered as a mentor to teens with

CF, who struggled with thoughts about their future and medical compliance. When she could no longer work full-time as a bench scientist, Liz continued her fight as chair of the Research Advisory Committee of Cystic Fibrosis Research, Inc (CFRI). When Liz died at nearly 33, CFRI honored her by renaming their post-doctoral research funding as the Elizabeth Nash Memorial Fellowship Program.

Liz was optimistic, enthusiastic, and passionate about her life's work and interests. She shunned the limitations imposed by CF. As captain of her college ski team, she refused to give up the sport when oxygen became necessary. She simply skied with a backpack filled with portable oxygen tanks. As an inspiring individual, Liz was selected to carry the 2002 Olympic Torch through Union Square in San Francisco. Liz's family established a foundation to honor her spirit and to continue her lifelong fight against cystic fibrosis: The Elizabeth Nash Foundation (www.elizabethnashfoundation.org)

Liz was born March 5, 1970, and died February 22, 2003.

Section 4

Helpful Resources

There are painters who transform the sun
into a yellow spot, but there are others who,
with the help of their art and intelligence,
transform a yellow spot into the sun.
—Pablo Picasso (1881–1973)

Suggested Reading List
Books about Children with Health Issues and Special Needs

Changed by a Child: Companion Notes for Parents of a Child With a Disability; Barbara Gill, 1998, ISBN: 385482434

Chronic Kids, Constant Hope: Help and Encouragement for Parents of Children with Chronic Conditions; Elizabeth Hoekstra and Mary Bradford, 2000, ISBN: 1581341849 (Contains religious content)

Coping with Your Child's Chronic Illness; Alesia T. Singer, 1999, ISBN: 1885003145

From the Heart: On Being the Mother of a Child with Special Needs; Martha Grady, Jayne D. March (editor), 1995, ISBN: 933149794

Healing After Loss: Daily Meditations for Working Through Grief; Martha Whitmore Hickman, 1994, ISBN: 380773384

Married with Special Needs Children: A Couple's Guide to Keeping Connected; Laura E. Marshak and Fran P. Prezant, 2007, ISBN-10: 1890627100 and ISBN-13: 978-1890627102

Special Kids Need Special Parents: A Resource for Parents of Children with Special Needs; Judith Loseff Lavin, 2001, ISBN: 425176622 (Contains some religious content)

You Will Dream New Dreams: Inspiring Personal Stories by Parents of Children with Disabilities; Stanley D. Klein, Ph.D. and Kim Schive, 2001, ISBN: 1575665603

Young People and Chronic Illness: True Stories, Help and Hope; Kelly Huegel and Elizabeth Verdick (editor), ISBN: 1575420414

Books for General Parenting Education

Different Children, Different Needs: Understanding the Unique Personality of Your Child; Charles F. Boyd, 1994, ISBN: 1576737500 (Contains religious content)

The Five Love Languages of Children; Gary Chapman and Ross Campbell, M.D., 1997, ISBN: 1881273652 (Contains religious content)

From Innocence to Entitlement: A Love and Logic Cure for the Tragedy of Entitlement; Jim Fay and Dawn Billings, 2005, ISBN: 1930429746

Help Kids Cope With Stress and Trauma; Caron Goode Ed.D., Tom Goode ND, David Russell, SFO, Ph.D., ND, 2006, ISBN-10: 142430024x and ISBN-13: 978-1424300242

Love and Logic Magic for Early Childhood: Practical Parenting from Birth to Six Years; Jim Fay and Charles Fay, Ph.D., 2000, ISBN: 1930429002

Love and Logic Magic When Kids Leave You Speechless; Jim Fay and Charles Fay, Ph.D., 2000, ISBN: 1930429045

Parenting Well in a Media Age: Keeping Our Kids Human; Gloria DeGaetano, 2004, ISBN: 1932181121

Parenting With Love and Logic: Teaching Children Responsibility (Updated and Expanded Edition); Foster W. Cline M.D. and Jim Fay, 2006, ISBN-10: 1576839540 and ISBN-13: 978-1576839546 (Contains some religious content)

Parenting Teens With Love and Logic: Preparing Adolescents for Responsible Adulthood (Updated and Expanded Edition); Foster W. Cline M.D. and Jim Fay, 2006, ISBN-10: 1576839303 and ISBN-13: 978-1576839300 (Contains some religious content)

Words Will Never Hurt Me: Helping Kids Handle Teasing, Bullying and Putdowns; Sally Northway Ogden; 2001, ISBN: 1586190318

Internet Resources

NOTE: The website information provided here is simply as a courtesy and may change without notice. We have not screened these references based on any standards of finances, morality, religion, politics, etc. We are making no assertions or recommendations of the quality of these organizations. In fact, just because we have listed a company doesn't mean we endorse them and vice-versa. If you are considering donations, please be sure to do your own research. The Better Business Bureau Wise Giving Guide is a great place to start at www.give.org.

Helpful Websites — General

www.ParentingChildrenWithHealthIssues.com
This is our website which will provide ongoing support for these teachings including Q & A, free articles, etc.

www.loveandlogic.com
Love and Logic educator and parenting resources

www.bravekids.org
This website includes thousands of resource references, including disease-specific links, and is the source of some of the books in the suggested reading list. Be sure to visit this one.

www.aap.org
The American Academy of Pediatrics

www.lehman.cuny.edu/faculty/jfleitas/bandaides
The Band-Aids and Blackboards website is for teachers and families of children with medical issues. Features articles, stories, etc.

www.caringbridge.com
> Caring Bridge offers free websites so that families and friends can easily communicate information about a child's medical condition.

www.fda.gov/cder/drug/
> The US Food and Drug Administration provides excellent information about prescription drugs.

www.cdc.gov/ncidod/diseases/
> The National Center for Infectious Diseases. This is a great, unbiased resource for many diseases.

www.nlm.nih.gov/
> National Institutes of Health (NIH) National Library of Medicine. This is also another great, unbiased resource for diseases, including genetic and noninfectious diseases.

www.quotationspage.com
> Resource for the quotations we used

Helpful Websites for Specific Medical Conditions

AIDS: **www.pedaids.org**
> Elizabeth Glaser Pediatric Aids Foundation

Allergies and Asthma: **www.aafa.org** and **www.aaaai.org**

Cancer: **www.cancer.org**
> The American Cancer Society

Cerebral Palsy: **www.ucp.org**
> United Cerebral Palsy

Cystic Fibrosis: **www.cff.org, www.cfri.org** and **www.esiason.org**

Diabetes: **www.jdrf.org**
  Juvenile Diabetes Research Foundation
and **www.diabetes.org**
  American Diabetes Association

Disabilities: **www.easterseals.com**
  Helping People with Disabilities

Down Syndrome: **www.ndss.org**
  National Down Syndrome Society

Dwarfism: **www.lpaonline.org**
  Little People of America

Eating Disorders: **www.edap.org**
  National Eating Disorders Association

Epilepsy: **www.epilepsyfoundation.org**
  Epilepsy Foundation

Hemophilia: **www.hemophilia.org**
  National Hemophilia Foundation

Leukemia: **www.leukemia.org**
  The Leukemia and Lymphoma Society

Muscular Dystrophy: **www.mdausa.org**
  Muscular Dystrophy Association

Obesity: **www.obesity.org**
  American Obesity Association

Premature Births, Birth Defects and Low Birth-weight:
www.marchofdimes.com

Sickle Cell Anemia: **www.ascaa.org**
American Sickle Cell Anemia Association

Skin Diseases: **www.aad.org**
American Academy of Dermatology

A Note to Medical and Mental Health Professionals

This book is a part of a comprehensive program which includes written, audio, and video formats. There is a similar curriculum directed to medical and mental health professionals and other providers who work with the families of kids with chronic illnesses. Information and website support for these programs is available at: www.ParentingChildrenWithHealthIssues.com.

The information in our programs will help you be effective with children who are often understandably resistant to time-consuming self-care protocols. Parents need your input to help them cope with chronic illnesses and handling the frustration that occurs when their children show poor self care. The children, in their resistance, can become passively noncompliant or overtly rebellious. Our materials and workshops provide professionals with tools and techniques built on a useful conceptual framework to address these issues. This framework provides a foundation that will best ensure that professionals are able to quickly assess family dynamics and have available a tool bag of precise responses to provide guidance and relief to both parents and children.

All parents face child-raising challenges. Certainly when the average child is sick with a "short-term" illness, it increases family tension and may impact family dynamics. However, the average family, unlike those dealing with chronic illnesses, is not faced with coping day in and day out with the difficulty of staving off death that continually lurks around a child's poor self-care or resistance to medical treatment. Parents with chronically ill children need parenting strategies specifically designed to help them effectively cope with the unique challenges they face. This program will teach those strategies, tools, and techniques in an uncomplicated manner.

As professionals we wish to effectively help families confront the common but often misunderstood dynamics that swirl about in the home of a child with inordinate medical needs. These issues, with your help, can lead to admirable character growth rather than a child with immature character traits that are demonstrated in noncompliant, passive resistant, and/or hostile dependent responses.

Let us help you encourage families when:
- ♥ Parents are unable to encourage their children to accept reasonable healthcare expectations.
- ♥ Parents express frustration and anger rather than sorrow when children show irresponsible or self-destructive responses.
- ♥ Parents confuse praise and encouragement.
- ♥ Parents have trouble showing disapproval with acceptance.

♥ Parents consciously or unconsciously feel guilty about their child's condition and commonly:
  • Excuse irresponsible behavior
  • Accept disrespect
  • Make excuses for poor decisions
  • Encourage immature development

Dr. Cline and other trained professionals are available for presentations to medical providers, mental health professionals, and anyone else that provides support to families who deal with pediatric health issues. The multimedia presentations and workshops are designed to give healthcare professionals effective, immediately applicable tools and techniques for use when consulting with families facing extraordinary medical challenges. Video and audio examples provide useful and easily understandable examples that can be put to use the next day. We will provide you with practical information to use in helping parents to create happy home atmospheres where children are respectful, responsible, and medically compliant. For more information, please contact us at www.ParentingChildrenWithHealthIssues.com.

Appendices

Endnotes
Index
Other Resources by Foster Cline, MD
Website Info

Endnotes

1. The terms *chronic illnesses*, *medical conditions*, *medical issues*, and *special healthcare needs* are used interchangeably as we refer to *all* kids who need ongoing medical treatments of any kind. Most of the information in this book is also applicable to children who require medical attention for a finite period of time, like recovering from an accident.

2. See www.LoveandLogic.com and www.ParentingChildren-WithHealthIssues.com for more information.

3. Some of these paragraphs are paraphrased from *Early Childhood Parenting Made Fun! Creating Happy Families and Responsible Kids from Birth to Six* by Jim Fay and Dr. Charles Fay. Information about this multimedia parent training program is available at www.LoveandLogic.com.

4. Quoted from the book *Love and Logic Magic for Early Childhood: Practical Parenting from Birth to Six Years* by Jim Fay and Dr. Charles Fay (Golden, CO: The Love and Logic Press, 2000).

5. Charles F. Boyd, *Different Children, Different Needs: Understanding the Unique Personality of Your Child* (Sisters, OR: Multnomah Publishers, Inc., 1994).

6. Parts of this section were quoted from Love and Logic's multimedia parent training program *Becoming a Love and Logic Parent*. Love and Logic offers much information on parenting styles. Jim Fay has an excellent audio tape titled, "Helicopters, Drill Sergeants and Consultants: Parenting Styles and the Messages They Send." The DVD version of *Parenting Children with Health Issues* includes role plays demonstrating these styles as they apply to chest physical therapy for a child with CF.

7. The award-winning Band-Aides and Blackboards website at www.lehman.cuny.edu/faculty/jfleitas/bandaides provides great information about these issues from the child's perspective.

8. The passage of the Individuals with Disabilities Education Act (IDEA 97) created provisions to give parents of children with special needs the legal means to ensure their children's needs are met at school. Individualized education plans (IEPs) and 504 plans are two options to carefully investigate as your child nears the school-age years.

9. Sally Northway Ogden has authored a very helpful book called *Words Will Never Hurt Me: Helping Kids Handle Teasing, Bullying and Putdowns*, which is available through www.loveandlogic.com.

10. Wonderful examples abound. Erik Weihenmayer is a universal inspiration, being the first blind person to scale Mt. Everest. His A&E original movie, *Touch the Top of the World*, outlines his phenomenal journey. The Juvenile Diabetes Research Founda-

tion (www.jdrf.org) has many inspirational stories and information for children with the disease.

11. Lucile Packard Children's Hospital at Stanford University publishes a helpful booklet titled, "A Transition Guide: For Patients and Families Moving from the Pediatric to the Adult Care Team." See www.lpch.org for information.

12. There is a picture of Matt and Greg in the Remembering Heroes section of this book. An interview with Jeannine and Ron Bailey can be seen on the DVD version of *Parenting Children with Health Issues*.

13. Chapter 8 includes a detailed discussion about entitlement and hostile-dependency.

14. The Remembering Heroes section of this book includes a picture of Elizabeth Nash holding the Olympic torch. See www.elizabethnashfoundation.org for more information.

15. See www.esiason.org and www.jerrycahill.com for more information.

16. Excerpted from the article "Love and Logic Is Cheaper than Family Therapy" by Lisa C. Greene, which is available at www.ParentingChildrenWithHealthIssues.com.

17. Myra Bluebond-Langner addresses these issues in her book *The Private Worlds of Dying Children* (Princeton: Princeton University Press, 1978); quotes from pages 234-235.

18. Elisabeth Kubler-Ross, M.D., *On Death and Dying* (New York: Touchstone, 1969).

19. This is expertly discussed in *From Innocence to Entitlement: A Love and Logic Cure for the Tragedy of Entitlement* by Jim Fay and Dawn Billings; available at www.loveandlogic.com.

20. "Marcus Tullius Cicero (106 BC- 43 BC) was an orator, statesman, political theorist, and philosopher of Ancient Rome. He is considered by some to be the greatest orator and speech-and prose-writer in history." This information was quoted from www.wikipedia.com and Cicero's quote came from www.quotationspage.com.

21. For a good source of information about education for special needs kids, see *Getting Special Needs Kids Ready for the Real World* by David Funk; available at www.loveandlogic.com

22. Peg Tyre, "Fighting Anorexia: No One to Blame," *Newseek*, December 5, 2005. p. 53.

23 Quoted from *Making Weight: Men's Conflicts with Food, Weight, Shape & Appearance* by Andersen, Cohn, and Holbrook (Carlsbad, CA: Gurze Books, 2000).

24. In individual cases, there can be other contributing factors to eating disorders, such as sexual abuse, but here we focus on the most common and generally accepted causes.

25. Cynthia M. Bulik, et al., "Prevalence, Heritability, and Prospective Risk Factors for Anorexia Nervosa," *Archives of General Psychiatry* (2006): 63:305-312.

26. *Eating Disorders Review*, Nov/Dec 2002.

27. Cynthia Bulik, University of North Carolina at Chapel Hill,

quoted in "Fighting Anorexia: No One to Blame" by Peg Tyre, *Newsweek*, December 5, 2005, p. 53.

28. See a discussion on overreassurance in Chapter 8.

29. See a discussion of praise vs. encouragement in Chapter 5.

30. Research of Dr. Walter Kaye University of Pittsburgh, reported in "Fighting Anorexia: No One to Blame" by Peg Tyre, *Newsweek*, December 5, 2005, p. 53.

31. This is demonstrated with the interaction between Laura Scott Ferris and her mother at the end of Chapter 4.

32. When your child is under 18, forced hospitalizations and feedings may be necessary to save his or her life. Certainly, such decisions must be made, and handling this unfortunate experience with loving sorrow over the child's sad decision not to get well is more helpful than responding with anger, blame, and hand-wringing.

33. See the discussion in Chapter 8 about denial and illness, which includes a helpful example.

34. Quoted from www.edreferral.com. Resources: J. A. Schneider and W. S. Agras, "Bulimia in males: A matched comparison with females," *International Journal of Eating Disorders* (6): 235-242; and R. E. Andersen, et al., "Weight loss, psychological and nutritional patterns in competitive male body builders," *International Journal of Eating Disorders* (18): 49-57.

35. On the Internet, authorities differ on the estimates of how many miles of blood vessels are contained in each pound of

fat. In the body as a whole, blood vessels, if placed end to end, are reported to stretch four times around the earth or 100,000 miles! A pound of fat is thought to contain at least one mile of blood vessels, but it may be much more.

36. "If one parent is obese, there is a 50 percent chance that the children will also be obese. However, when both parents are obese, the children have an 80 percent chance of being obese." Obtained from "Obesity in Children and Teens," *American Academy of Child & Adolescent Psychiatry* 79 (January 2001).

37. "Children in the United States watch an average of three to four hours of television a day. By the time of high school graduation, they will have spent more time watching television than they have in the classroom." Obtained from "Children and Watching TV," *American Academy of Child & Adolescent Psychiatry*, 54 (revised February 2005).

38. *Love and Logic Marriage* by Foster W. Cline MD and Hermie Drill Cline; 2005. Available at www.loveandlogic.com or 800-338-4065.

Index

Page numbers followed by an *f* or *t* indicate figures and tables.

Books & More from
Foster Cline, MD

Visit your favorite retail bookseller or www.loveandlogic.com for other *Parenting Children with Health Issues* resources such as audio and video programming.

Books by Foster W. Cline, MD:

Parenting with Love and Logic by Foster W. Cline, MD and Jim Fay

Parenting Teens with Love and Logic by Foster W. Cline, MD and Jim Fay

Grandparenting with Love and Logic by Jim Fay and Foster W. Cline, MD

Pearls of Love and Logic for Parents and Teachers by Jim Fay and Foster W. Cline, MD

Discipline with Love and Logic Resource Guide by Jim Fay and Foster W. Cline, MD

10th Anniversary Journal Collection by Jim Fay and Foster W. Cline, MD

Meeting the Challenge: Using Love and Logic to Help Children Develop Attention & Behavior Skills (with Jim Fay and Bob Sornson, PhD)

Marriage Love and Logic by Foster W. Cline, MD and Hermie Drill-Cline

Can This Child Be Saved? Solutions for Adoptive and Foster Families by Foster W. Cline, MD and Cathy Helding

Uncontrollable Kids: From Heartbreak to Hope by Foster W. Cline, MD

Audio Resources by Foster W. Cline, MD:

Parenting with Love and Logic Audio Book by Foster W. Cline, MD and Jim Fay

Parenting Teens with Love and Logic Audio Book by Foster W. Cline, MD and Jim Fay

Trouble Free Teens- Smart Suggestions for Parenting Your Preteen by Jim Fay and Foster W. Cline, MD

Toddlers and Preschoolers: Love and Logic Parenting for Early Childhood by Jim Fay and Foster W. Cline, MD

Didn't I Tell You to Take Out the Trash? Techniques for Getting Kids to Do Chores Without Hassles by Jim Fay and Foster W. Cline, MD

Avoiding Power Struggles with Kids by Jim Fay and Foster W. Cline, MD

Winning the Homework Battle: Helping Children Discover and Celebrate Their Strengths by Jim Fay and Foster W. Cline, MD

Allowing Kids to Choose Success by Foster W. Cline, MD

Childhood Lying, Cheating and Stealing by Foster W. Cline, MD

Grief Trauma and Loss: Helping Children Cope by Foster W. Cline, MD

Secrets of Step Parenting by Jim Fay and Foster W. Cline, MD

DVDs by Foster W. Cline, MD:

Helping Kids Face Today's World by Foster W. Cline, MD

Parenting Doesn't Have to Be Rocket Science by Foster W. Cline, MD

Who Says Parenting Can't Be Fun? Jim Fay, Foster W. Cline, MD, and Betsy Geddes EdD

Parenting Children with Health Issues
Essential Tools, Tips & Tactics for Being a Great Parent when Every Moment Matters

DVD Series

The *Parenting Children with Health Issues* DVD series provides an in-depth look at Love and Logic tools as they apply to children with health issues. The programming includes presentations by Dr. Foster Cline as well as role plays and interviews with doctors, parents and children who cope with the daily challenges of living with chronic illness.

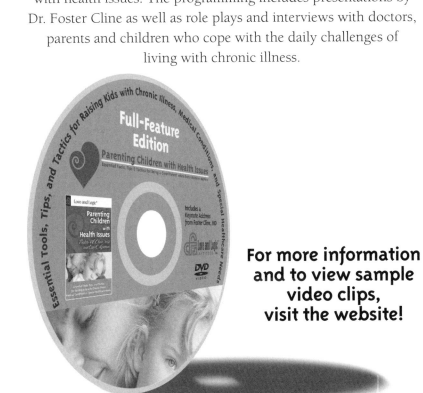

For more information and to view sample video clips, visit the website!

www.ParentingChildrenWithHealthIssues.com

Hey Parents & Professionals...

Visit the website for updated info from Dr. Foster Cline

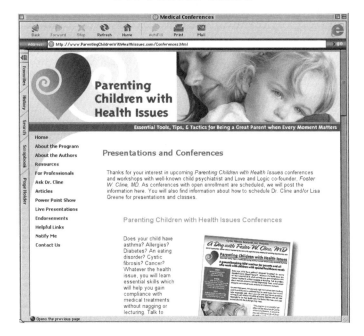

Learning new parenting techniques takes time and effort for every parent. This process can be even more difficult when dealing with a child's serious health issues. We want you to be successful. You may get stuck at times. We want to be there to help you.

This website provides you with an ongoing, updated resource. Relevant articles are posted. You can ask questions and get answers from the experts. You will find a community of others who struggle with similar parenting issues. And you will find opportunities to sharpen your new parenting skills.

Visit us online at
www.ParentingChildrenWithHealthIssues.com

Be a Great Parent When Every Moment Matters.

More Help from Love and Logic

Visit Love and Logic's website for help with "every day" parenting challenges

Kids can bring much joy, laughter and fulfillment into our lives. They can also be confusing, bewildering, and frustrating at times. Love and Logic will give you the tools to raise responsible, happy and well-adjusted kids.

💜 Listen or download free audios: *Funny Parenting Stories* and *Funny Stories from the Classroom*

💜 Download free articles for parents and educators

💜 Listen or download "The Love and Logic Show" with Dr. Charles Fay

💜 Join the Insider's Club and receive free online articles plus special promotions available only to members.

💜 View video clips of Jim Fay, Dr. Charles Fay and Foster Cline, MD

💜 Find a complete listing of products and upcoming conferences

www.LoveAndLogic.com